HOLY
TRINITY,
SUTTON
COLDFIELD

HOLY TRINITY, SUTTON COLDFIELD

THE STORY OF A
PARISH CHURCH
AND ITS PEOPLE,
1250–2020

EDITED BY
STELLA THEBRIDGE

The
History
Press

To the memory of the late Norman Evans, whom I sadly never met, and the late Margaret Gardner, who kindled my interest in the history of Holy Trinity Parish Church, with thanks for all their meticulous research and writing that paved the way for this book.

AMDG
Stella Thebridge

First published 2020

The History Press
97 St George's Place, Cheltenham,
Gloucestershire, GL50 3QB
www.thehistorypress.co.uk

© PCC Holy Trinity Sutton Coldfield, 2020

Text by Stella Thebridge except where stated as written by:
Elizabeth Allison
Marian Baxter
Carol Hoare
Sue Ingley

The right of Stella Thebridge to be identified as the Author of this work has been asserted in accordance with the Copyright, Designs and Patents Act 1988.

British Library Cataloguing in Publication Data.
A catalogue record for this book is available from the British Library.

ISBN 978 0 7509 9252 7

Typesetting and origination by The History Press
Printed in Turkey by Imak.

MIX
Paper from responsible sources
FSC
www.fsc.org
FSC® C013056

CONTENTS

Unless otherwise stated, the text has been written by the editor, Stella Thebridge

FOREWORD

When my friend, the late Norman Granville Evans, led a tour of Holy Trinity Church in 1980, he had to borrow a key from the churchwarden, the church being locked when not in use for services, for security reasons. The church was rather dimly lit in those days, but the main items of historical interest (which are described in this book) were pointed out and explained. Norman later began his investigation of the history of the church, using many primary sources as well as the published accounts, resulting in what I considered to be a definitive work.

How different now for a visitor to the church, welcomed by a steward to a brightly lit interior and free to wander round with the guidebook in hand. The church has been re-ordered since Norman died in 1992; the main features are spot-lit and the west window stained glass revealed. Historic items have been given more prominence, mostly thanks to the hard work of the heritage group under the leadership of the editor of this history.

In view of these changes, the present volume was begun, the various writers experiencing the satisfactions of making new discoveries about aspects of the past as well as the frustrations of having to give up a line of research through lack of evidence. Puzzles remain – for example three Sutton clergymen witnessed a charter dated c1200, so can we infer that there was a well-established church here before the conquest? Or, given that the mediaeval rectory was not located in Coleshill Street, as Norman Evans supposed, where was it?

The Church has had a central role to play throughout the history of the town, so this new history should find its way into every Sutton household, to be read with interest and enjoyment, and the many illustrations inspire you to visit the church to see for yourself.

Roger Lea
Chairman
Sutton Coldfield Local History Research Group

LIST OF WELL-WISHERS

The following list of names and organisations is linked to those who have purchased a copy of the book prior to publication and who have asked for their own name, and/ or that of a loved one who has passed away, to be recorded here. A cross (†) following a first or surname denotes a name given in memoriam.

Because in some instances individuals wished to be recorded alongside their loved ones, those whose names are given in memoriam are recorded with a cross following the first name. Where all the names recorded are in memoriam and from the same family, then the cross comes at the end of the surname.

The authors are very grateful to all who have shown their commitment to the book and to the church of Holy Trinity in this way, from the congregation, past and present, and the wider community.

Janet Al-Rubaie
The Ambler family
Tanya Arroba
The Baines and Beales families
Archives & Collections, Library of Birmingham
Michael† and Margaret Box
Andrew and Gillian Bullock
Judith and Michael Carr
Chris D Cherry† and Pam, Belinda and Fiona
David† and Vivien Chubb
Chris, Louise, Daniel, Lily and Charlotte Chubb
Ralph Harmar Collins†
Revd John and Gill Cooper
The Deanery CE Primary School
Brian and Mary Dixon
Ba, Denis, Lindsay and Ian Dodd† and Rosemary Young (née Dodd)
Robin Draper
Paul and Pat Duckers
Bob and Ros Dyke
Rahim, Gail, Deena and Tarik Elsharief
Val Ferneyhough
Paul John Fletcher†
David and Cicely† Gale
Clive, Margaret and Janet Gardner†
Robin† and Shelagh Gelling
Muriel Goldsby†

The Griffiths family
Donald E Grove†
Richard Halsey
Karen Hancox†
George and Marjorie Harvey†
Frank† and Wendy Hill and family
Terence Hoare
Benedict Hoare and family
Dr Daniel Hoare and family
Deborah Hodgson
Paul and Stella Holden†
Peter† and Nina Hollow
Rt Revd Anne Hollinghurst, Bishop of Aston
Gerald and Dodie† Hollyoak
Keith and Janet Jordan
Shaun† and Wendy Kent
Chris and Judy Kettel
Jack Larwood
Diane Littler
Ted and Rose Longman
Andrew MacFarlane
Pauline Manfield
Rt Hon Andrew and Dr Sharon Mitchell
Brenda Moore†
Robert Morffew and parents†
Russ Mulholland
Harold WS Osborne†
Kerry Osbourne
Viva Owen† and AGB Owen
Oliver and Elizabeth Pearcey

Elizabeth, Richard, James and Helen Petley
Bryant† Pickles
Marie and John Prestage†
Nick and Nicola Revell
Michael Richmond†
Sheila and Alan Roberts
Pat Round
Tony and Barbara Seal†
Jim† and Mary Simmons
John Slater†
Elsie Smith†
Mike and Steph Somers
Tony and Maureen Spinks
Staffordshire Libraries and Arts Service
Nigel† and Jane Steeley
Sutton Coldfield Library
Jenny Taylor
The Teece family†
Phil Thebridge
Brenda Thorogood
David and Diane Tipping
Barry and Sylvia Ulyatt
Judith Wareham
Warwickshire County Record Office
Warwickshire Libraries
Graham and Sarah West
Marjorie & Bertie Williams†
Kara Jayne Willis†
Revd Carole Young

INTRODUCTION

The re-ordering work of 2016–2018, which saw the transformation of the interior of Holy Trinity Parish Church, led to a renewed interest in the heritage of the church: its building and people.

The congregation wished to share the new comfort and accessibility of the building. There had always been a welcome for worship and occasional events within the church such as fairs and flower festivals, and from 2013 the new Friends of Holy Trinity organisation began its annual series of six ticketed events of concerts and theatre performances. However, the standard closure of the church outside of service or event times meant that the interior was rarely seen by the community.

Coupled with a wish to open the church more frequently was a will to draw together the many resources written about its long history.

GRADE I LISTING

On 18 October 1949, Holy Trinity, along with a number of other buildings of historical interest in Sutton Coldfield, became 'listed buildings'. This affords them legal protection from changes to the structure or features without special permission. Holy Trinity is Grade I listed, and, according to the website of listed buildings at www.britishlistedbuildings.co.uk, 'Grade I buildings are of exceptional interest, sometimes considered to be internationally important. Just 2.5% of listed buildings are Grade I.'

The entry for the listing gives specific features of interest as follows:

West tower late C15. Aisles circa 1533. Mid C16 north and south chapels. Nave with clerestory rebuilt circa 1760. C13 chancel, restored and altered by C E Bateman 1914, retains C15 arch and east window. North aisle doubled 1874-9. South porch early C16. South aisle gallery circa 1760. Earlier C17 ornate screens and panelling, re[m]oved 1864 from choir and organ casing at Worcester Cathedral, installed 1875. Interlaced aroaded [?eroded] circular Norman font, removed C19 from Church of St Lawrence, Over Winacre,

Nottinghamshire. Earlier C18 wrought iron porch gates, 1748, moved from round Bishop Vesey monument of circa 1555 with effigy. Pudsey monuments 1677 (with busts in aedicule), 1719. Finely carved Sacheverell wall monument 1715. Jesson monument with busts 1705. Holy Trinity Church and No 16 Coleshill Street form a group.

(See 'Grade I listing' under 'Websites' in References)

We can see some mistakes here, including the name of the village and county of the church from which the font ultimately found its way to Holy Trinity (it also did not come directly from the original church), and also the date of the woodwork from Worcester Cathedral, now discovered to be earlier. Here the north and south aisles are described as dating from 1533 and the chapels as mid-sixteenth century, and it is now thought the aisles are late-fifteenth century and the chapels part of Vesey's work in 1530 or so.

HISTORIES OF THE TOWN AND CHURCH

Much is already in print about the history of Sutton Coldfield. The town itself is in Domesday Book of 1086. Since then there have been numerous mentions, not least in the work of Dugdale (1656; 1730).

In the nineteenth century, a long-standing Rector, William Kirkpatrick Riland Bedford, wrote a concise volume which was published in 1891 and which the town corporation saw fit to reprint in 1968.

However, earlier writers had researched the subject and written works which have been used as sources ever since. One was Thomas Bonell who is thought to have written the unpublished *History of Sutton Coldfield by an impartial hand* (Bonell, 1762). Another is the acclaimed member of Holy Trinity congregation, Agnes Bracken, who wrote *The forest and chase of Sutton Coldfield*, published in 1860.

A third was Zachariah Twamley, whose unpublished history is in Sutton Coldfield Library and available on the website of the local history research group, having been transcribed and indexed by Janet Jordan. Twamley wrote of himself as author as follows:

With deference he submits to his fellow native parishioners and friends: a compendious account of the history of Sutton Coldfield, together with … dates of different occurrences. (Twamley, 1855)

Moving into the twentieth century, 1904 saw the publication of Midgley's *A short history of Sutton Coldfield Town and Chase*. Rectors at the church wrote or commissioned church guides of varying length throughout the twentieth century, and there was often a history of the church in town guides of the period. The church features in county histories such as W Hobart Bird's book about churches in Warwickshire (1940), Arthur Mee's book in the *King's England* county series (1947) and Pevsner's guide to the buildings of Warwickshire (1966).

The latter half of the century saw a great deal of work by local historians – Douglas V Jones, Marian Baxter and Roger Lea in particular – as well as evidence of a growing body of work by a number of other local history researchers as sources became more readily traceable, both in local archives and through the emergence of the internet.

NORMAN EVANS (1911-1992)

A key amateur historian writing about Holy Trinity was Norman Granville Evans, a native of Sutton Coldfield and a local dentist who was also an active member of the Sutton Coldfield Local History Research Group (see below).

In 1987 Evans produced 'An investigation of Holy Trinity Parish Church', a typescript of which a few copies were made and distributed to the church, the local library and one or two other individuals, but it was not generally for sale. The book was the result of an approach by the Rector in 1983, Alaric Rose, for a new guidebook. Evans found there was so much potential content that he embarked on this much fuller work.

Margaret Gardner, a worshipper at Holy Trinity and Parish Archivist at the time, then drew extensively on Evans' work (and with his permission) to compile that new church guidebook, which also incorporated a great deal of the history of the church and some good colour photographs. It also appeared in 1987 and was in use (with minor additions to take account of the building of the Trinity Centre in 1996) until the major re-ordering of the church interior in 2016.

Evans' book is a rich source for much of the information in this history. Sadly it appeared just before the explosion of the internet and massive changes in publishing methods. In order to create a work which could be reproduced on a duplicating machine, Evans drew and annotated many of his images from photographs, a true labour of love. Our book is able to incorporate a greater quantity of information about Holy Trinity, benefitting from the advantages of wider dissemination of research material via the internet to produce a text together with images in black and white and colour. As a published work, with complementary website, this, at last, makes the history accessible to a much wider audience, as Norman Evans would, we hope, have liked.

Sutton Coldfield Local History Research Group

The members of this long-standing group have been a major force for progress in both the research and writing of the history of the whole town, and their publications have included a large number of articles and booklets on areas which touch closely on the church as well. Many of these writings are listed in the references. The Parochial Church Council of Holy Trinity remains indebted to the many historians who have chosen to research aspects of the town's history, and its citizens owe a debt of gratitude to those who in most cases have done this entirely voluntarily from a desire to establish facts, to confirm the chronology of events and to disseminate information about the history of the town and church.

Why this Book?

In addition to the need to bring together the array of disparate writings about Holy Trinity, there have been other factors, notably the administrative changes, such as the move of the borough from the county of Warwickshire to Birmingham City Council within the new West Midlands authority in 1974. This diversified the retention of archives, with some remaining in the Warwickshire County Record Office in Warwick and newer items being deposited in Birmingham Central Archives, whose accommodation moved to the new Library of Birmingham in 2013. Early diocesan records are actually with the records of Lichfield Record Office in Staffordshire (now housed in Stafford), as Holy Trinity was, for the majority of its history, part of the Archdeaconry of Coventry in the extensive diocese of Lichfield and Coventry. Holy Trinity also has valuable silverware deposited at Birmingham Museum and Art Gallery. Sutton Coldfield Library has an excellent archive and local history section but has not escaped the austerity in local government of the twenty-first century, meaning that capacity to preserve and store materials is constrained.

All these factors have contributed to a feeling among the church congregation that a dedicated project was needed, to record in one place historical information about the church which is currently scattered, and to promote it to a wider public in person, in print and online.

HOLY TRINITY'S HERITAGE PROJECT

A bid to the Heritage Lottery Fund (Heritage Interpretation Fund) in 2016 was successful, and the publication of the history of the church was made possible as part of that grant. The project ran from 2017–2019 and secured the following:

- The creation of a new church website with a large section devoted to the history of the church.
- The establishment of a formal recruitment and training programme for volunteer stewards to enable the church to open during the week every week.
- The production of a new church guidebook.
- This full history of the church.

Artists were commissioned who worked with the local community to create a booklet reflecting on the church's relationship with the town and to produce some of the website content, notably films about the history of the town with a local school.

The fully illustrated church guidebook, published in December 2018, describes a tour of the church, pointing out the key features of the building and supporting historical information as required. It also provides a memento of the visit in a similar way to guidebooks of stately homes, cathedrals and other churches.

The website provides the history in a format that is easy to search, but also keeps the text to a minimum. It also, at last, provides a means for information to be updated as new discoveries about the history of the church are revealed.

This history book aims to provide fuller information for those who wish to know more about the long history of our building and its place in the community. It also pulls together the stories that make the history come alive: of parishioners, clergy and townspeople. In short, it attempts to distil the many sources into a coherent whole, while avoiding stating as facts any contentious areas of the history which may subsequently be clarified following future research.

The comprehensive list of sources in the references section of this volume makes clear what a task this is. We have sometimes referred to this as the definitive history, but it quite clearly will never be that. We hope that it remains the most comprehensive history to date in one volume and that it can be supplemented by new information on the website. If a new edition becomes inevitable, we will look to honour that on a future occasion!

Meanwhile, if the reader does find any errors or omissions, we would be most interested to receive them via email at: heritage@htsc.org.uk

FORMAT

Such a vast history needs breaking into manageable parts. This will enable readers to dip in and out as well as being able to read through the whole text if they prefer. For this reason we have chosen to recount first the history of the church building and the many alterations it has undergone, as well as changes to the hilltop location, now part of a designated conservation area in Sutton Coldfield, Church Hill. This chronological account describes the bigger structural changes, such as galleries and extensions, as well as giving information about refurbishments, decoration and larger-scale memorials and items of furniture. It also covers related building work in the town, e.g. rectories, graveyards and church halls.

Other chapters describe in more detail specific features of the church which are unique to the building and have been central to the heritage project of 2017–19. There is a chapter dedicated to events where the church and the royal town have worked together to commemorate great occasions or to raise funds. Several chapters tell the stories of people associated with the church, from the most well-known – Bishop John Vesey – through the long line of Rectors and other clergy to prominent and less well-known parishioners.

Some individual elements of the history, where there is a large amount of detail, will be published separately in the future, most particularly information on the people commemorated in the many memorials in the church and grounds. This is explained further in Chapter 8.

Our aim is to inform, be accurate and write in a way which helps our readers engage with the rich history of this church and its people. In turn, we hope there will be increased understanding by all age groups of both Holy Trinity Parish Church and the town of Sutton Coldfield with which it is so closely interwoven – understanding of the past, to inform us in the present and to secure the future of this place, so that there can continue to be a welcome for all, whether people come to worship, to walk around, or just to reflect within its space.

Stella Thebridge
Editor

ACKNOWLEDGEMENTS

The process of writing this book has relied on help from a number of people in different ways. I would like to convey my heartfelt thanks to the following:

- The group of writers who researched and wrote some of the sections of the book – Elizabeth Allison, Marian Baxter, Revd Carol Hoare and Sue Ingley.
- The commissioned artists on the heritage project, *Holy Trinity Parish Church: heritage at the heart of Sutton Coldfield (2017–19),* notably Louise Jackson, who took photographs, and Bob Moulder, who created four artists' impressions of Holy Trinity at different times in its history. All four of these pictures appear in this book. Mandy Ross and Pyn Stockman of Secret City Arts created high quality historical resources, including films and print materials, which continue to be of use for individuals and groups visiting the church.
- Esteemed local historians, especially Marian Baxter, who is also a contributor to the volume, and Roger Lea, who has been the main adviser on the heritage project and church publications and is the source of some of the most insightful and helpful writing about the church and town. We are privileged that he agreed to write the foreword to this volume.
- Other members of the Sutton Coldfield Local History Research Group, especially Janet and Keith Jordan, and those who worked on the memorial histories with Marian: Eileen Donohoe, Ann Geraghty, Janet Lillywhite and Don McCollam.
- Jon Bayliss, monuments researcher.
- Robin Draper, a local monuments historian and church tour guide.
- Andy Foster, a local historian and writer of guides to different areas of Birmingham and the surrounding area including Sutton Coldfield.
- Revd David Frost for information on John Vesey.
- The late Margaret Gardner, parishioner of Holy Trinity and designated church archivist from the 1980s until the turn of the century.
- Richard Halsey who decoded and translated Latin abbreviations.
- Dr Mike Hodder, archaeologist on the Birmingham Diocesan Advisory Committee.
- Dr Nicholas Riall, who first alerted us to the true and unique nature of our

woodwork acquired from Worcester Cathedral in the nineteenth century, and generously shared his research with us.

- Susie Walker, who trawled internet resources and came up with answers to many questions for all the writing team, helping us to round out many unfinished stories of people associated with the church.

- Tony Walker for sense-checking and style-editing of the text.

I am most indebted to the late Norman Granville Evans (1911-1992), whose painstaking research and scrutiny of original documents has enabled this book to be published where his own work was not. Not only did Norman study these documents and write about them, he transcribed large parts of some of them and, in addition to the main section of his work, he produced a 100-page appendix, covering numerous subjects in greater depth that were not strictly required for a church guidebook. However, for the purposes of this full history they have shown their worth repeatedly, enabling us to write with authority on matters as diverse as church tithes, faculties for new work in the building, marriages during the period of the Commonwealth, and the detail of changes in religious persuasion in England from the time of Henry VIII and the consequent changes to the liturgy at Holy Trinity. The more we read of Evans' work, the more we appreciate what he achieved without the benefit of the internet or modern reprographic methods. Hopefully we have been able to build on his work and to be as certain as we can that we have only deviated from his original information where we have established new facts reliably through the increased access to sources that the internet has brought us.

For images, I am extremely grateful to the staff at Sutton Coldfield Library, especially Abi and Emma, for their help in sourcing photographs in their keeping, as well as to Marian Baxter and Roger Lea.

As well as all those mentioned above, there have been others from the church congregation who have helped in a variety of ways as follows:

- Chris Chubb (photographs).

- Brian Dixon (primary sources).

- Ros Dyke (churchwarden).

- Colin Ingley (churchwarden).

- Nick Revell (chair of Friends of Holy Trinity).

- Revd John Routh (Rector).

- Kristina Routh (guidebook and website editing).

- Mike Somers (chair of the Re-ordering Campaign of 2016 and firm believer in the potential merits of a heritage project).

- Phil Thebridge (word-processing).

- Karen Wright (initial research).

- Revd Carole Young (church administrator).

- The team of 'heritage' stewards who have been supportive in so many ways.

- Many friends and family members who put up with my lack of hospitality over the last year or more.

The last and most important person to thank is Dave Thebridge, my husband, who weathered my regular slinking off to the computer to 'write a bit more' and furnished me not only with meals but also with many cups of tea and coffee along the way.

Stella Thebridge

CONTRIBUTORS

These are listed in the order that their contributions first appear.

STELLA THEBRIDGE

Stella is a lifelong Anglican who has been an active member of the congregation at Holy Trinity since moving to Sutton Coldfield with her husband in 1986. Their three children were all born and brought up in the parish, and the church has always been a major part of family life.

Stella's degree subjects at Sheffield University were German and Music, and she subsequently qualified as a librarian. Her work in a range of libraries has included six years as a researcher, and she has always loved writing and editing, including the magazines of three churches with which she has been associated (including Holy Trinity's).

Her interest in the history of Holy Trinity and the wider town has grown over the years, and, when the re-ordering project was completed, she found she had volunteered to co-ordinate the heritage project that followed. She has co-created the new church guidebook (with Kristina Routh) and also written and compiled the majority of the history content of the new church website. Despite the encroachment of the day job, she has loved every minute of it.

MARIAN BAXTER

Following qualification as a librarian, Marian worked in the Birmingham Local Studies and Archives Department for several years before moving to Sutton Coldfield Library as the Local Studies Librarian from 1979–2012. While at the library she was secretary to the Sutton Coldfield Local History Research Group for many years and is now vice chair. She helped set up the Friends of New Hall Mill and has been their secretary, then chair, for over twenty years. She also helped set up the New Hall Valley Country Park and is currently the vice chair of the Friends of New Hall Valley. She is also the current chair of the Friends of Sutton Park, and on the Sutton Park Advisory Committee. She continues to give talks on local history to community groups and has to date published some eight photographic books, four of which have been about Sutton Coldfield and Sutton Park.

SUE INGLEY

Sue was born and raised in Sutton Coldfield and first became acquainted with Holy Trinity Parish Church when she married her husband Colin there, in 1982. In 1990, they were both confirmed and have since become active members of the congregation.

She has worked as a primary school teacher for thirty-two years and has always had an interest in history and art, gaining an MA in 2002.

When the chance came to explore the history of the church, she naturally rose to the opportunity and has enjoyed researching the long line of Rectors from the Riland and Riland Bedford families, who played such a large part in the history of the church and town for more than 200 years.

CAROL HOARE

Carol Hoare is an associate priest attached to Holy Trinity Parish Church. She was a secondary school English teacher in Sutton Coldfield for twenty years, was ordained as a deacon in 1991 and was one of the first women to be ordained as a priest in 1994.

History has always been one of her major interests, particularly the history of the English Church through the centuries. When first ordained, she was very pleased to be attached to an 800-year-old church on the edge of Sutton, and it was a further satisfaction to move to the beautiful parish church in the town centre in 2002.

Carol is married to Terry, a former history teacher, and has two sons, four grandchildren, and two step-grandchildren.

ELIZABETH ALLISON

Elizabeth has a BA (Hons) in History from Reading University and an MA in English Local History from Birmingham University. Over the years she has given numerous talks on Sutton Coldfield's heritage generally, although her particular interest is in mediaeval church history. She has been awarded a British Empire Medal (BEM) for her work with several local groups but in particular with Sutton Coldfield Civic Society, which of course champions the cause of the town's built heritage.

LIST OF IMAGES

PROVENANCE

The abbreviations against each image are explained below. Where there is no further information, the picture is deemed out of copyright. Where abbreviations relate to an individual or company, permission has been secured for the image to be used in this book only. The authors and editor have made every effort to contact copyright-holders.

'qv' after a name means that their work is referenced in the list of references and further reading.

BA	Birmingham Archives (in Library of Birmingham). Original item created for Holy Trinity
BHD	Beacon Heights Digital – single use only in the book
Bluflame	Current floor plan created for Holy Trinity's use only
BM	Bob Moulder (artist)
CT	Christopher Tracy (qv)
Dugdale	Image originally in Dugdale 1656 (qv) and reused by Norman Evans
ED	Eileen Donohue
HTSC	Images created by the following members of the church for use on its website and in this book: Colin Ingley, Louise Jackson, Kristina Routh, Stella Thebridge
HWSO	Harold Osborne (qv)
KJ	Keith Jordan
KW	Ken Williams (SCL)
MB	Marian Baxter
NGE	Norman Evans – copyright for his work lies with Marian Baxter, and permission has been granted for acknowledged images to be used
R&C	Reilly and Constantine, photographers in Birmingham. Photograph used with permission of the family of the late Dennis Constantine. It appeared with others by this firm in a church guide book c1970.
SCL	In the collection of Sutton Coldfield Library and deemed out of copyright or permitted by the library.
ST from NGE	Stella Thebridge (editor) using information from Norman Evans (qv)
Strange	Image of Wild aquatint (out of copyright) was used from this book (qv)
WA	Warwickshire Archaeology – for images from report of 2019 (Coutts, qv)
WKRB	William Kirkpatrick Riland Bedford, specifically images in his book of 1889 (qv)
WM	Walter Midgley (qv)

LIST OF TABLES

1

EARLY HISTORY

Visitors sometimes ask, 'How old is Holy Trinity Church?'

The answer is often given as the famous question 'How long is a piece of string?' This is not to be facetious, but it is because it is not possible to give a single date. The current church building has seen a large number of additions and alterations over many centuries, and some rebuilding.

In addition, we do not know if a wooden church might have pre-dated the first stone one, nor do we know the construction date of the first stone church. We believe from documentary evidence that it was constructed around 1250–90.

The church building bears a certain resemblance to the faithful broom that has gone on for generations with only three new heads and two new handles.

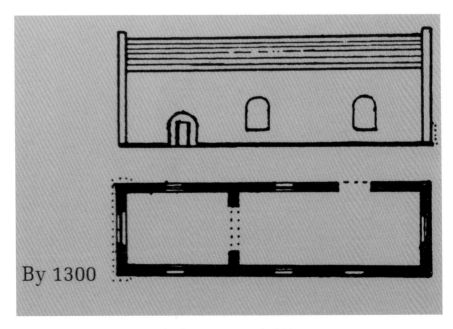

Fig. 1: *Floor plan and elevation of Holy Trinity to 1300 (NGE)*

In respect of the interior of the church, W Hobart Bird, in his guidebook *Old Warwickshire Churches*, wrote of Holy Trinity, 'restorations have robbed the fabric of much of its antiquarian interest' (Bird, 1940, p. 104).

This sounds harsh, but does reflect the fact that the continuing advantage to Holy Trinity of sufficient funds to extend the building and 'improve' it may have been at the expense of losing some very fine features as we might now think of them, though at the time the decision-makers may have thought they were modernising and improving at every step. In the twentieth and twenty-first centuries there have been many safeguards in place with better understanding of ecclesiastical heritage, the listing of ancient monuments (Holy Trinity is Grade 1-listed) and the involvement of specialist groups for different periods of architectural history. While it irks some to have to make cases for change to outside bodies, it is important that examples of good craftsmanship are not lost, especially where they are unique to a particular building. While Holy Trinity has sadly lost features of its interior fabric, many are preserved, and there are still examples of all the different eras of woodwork, especially pews that were installed in the eighteenth and nineteenth centuries. The church also bought woodwork being discarded by Worcester Cathedral in the nineteenth century which we now know to be not only rare but probably unique.

So, to return to the church origins in the latter thirteenth century, these need to be set in the context of the town of Sutton Coldfield and its much longer history.

EARLY SUTTON COLDFIELD

A key researcher of pre-Roman times in the town is Dr Mike Hodder, for many years Birmingham City Council's planning archaeologist and also archaeologist on Birmingham's Diocesan Advisory Committee (see Hodder, 2004, pp. 96ff, 2008 and 1989).

Finds from archaeological digs show evidence of settlements before the Bronze Age and then in Roman times.

The best remaining evidence of the Roman era is in the Ryknild or Icknield Street, which runs across what is now the western edge of Sutton Park, moving on into the area neighbouring the residential street known as Roman Road in Streetly.

It is probable that the land on which the church stands was used at least from Roman times for arable or grazing land. Margaret Gardner, Parish Archivist at Holy Trinity in the last part of the twentieth century, wrote in an article in the parish magazine about a water point in the Fordrift, a driveway opposite the east end of the church which was latterly the driveway to a former church hall. She writes:

Farmers on the Glebe land and Barn Field (the current Rectory Road cemetery) behind the street would have brought their animals to the Fordrift for water.

Water pipes from this source may well have gone back to Roman times, when wooden pipes were used.

(Gardner, 2000, p. 27)

DOMESDAY BOOK

Domesday Book of 1086 refers to Sutton Coldfield, and William Dargue has written about it on his churches website as follows:

> In the time of Edward the Confessor, the manor of Sutton was held by the Anglo-Saxon Earl Edwin of Mercia, and in 1086 by King William himself. For tax purposes it was a manor worth four times the value of Birmingham with land for 22 ploughteams against Birmingham's possible six. However, in Sutton only eight ploughteams were at work after the Conquest. With 10 acres, c4ha, of meadow it had more than any other Birmingham manor. And only Yardley with 100+ hectares had a greater amount of woodland than Sutton. However, the taxable value of Yardley's woodland stood at 40 pence, while Sutton's, when exploited, was worth 30 shillings i.e. 360 pence.

(*William Dargue,* https://ahistoryofbirminghamchurches.jimdo.com/)

So the town is mentioned but not a church. This may seem a clear indication that there was no church at this point, but recent work on the contents of Domesday Book in other areas of the country has apparently revealed that churches were not routinely listed in the book, as they were not central to the business of assessment for revenue collection.

Whether there was any church at that time or during the twelfth century has been impossible to prove to date.

There was certainly a chapel at the Manor House in Sutton (this area is now in the neighbouring parish of St Peter's, Maney), which was built in the twelfth century and dedicated to St Blaise. St Blaise was a Bishop of Sebastea in Asia Minor who was martyred in 316CE. He became popular in England. His festival is 3 February, and in 1222 the Council of Oxford forbade all work on his feast-day, such was his popularity. Services continued in the chapel until the fifteenth century when the house itself fell into disrepair and was demolished. Carved stones were reused by Bishop Vesey – see Chapter 2.

Evidence of further work near the church is the old sandstone quarry, thought to have provided the first mass of sandstone (a type known as Lower Keuper) in the twelfth century to make the dam across the valley for the Mill Pool (on the site of what is now the town's main shopping centre). Evans describes in detail the changes to this quarry area (now the upper car park of Sutton Baptist Church on Trinity Hill) and the measures taken to strengthen the wall with the stronger Upper Keuper sandstone in later years. (Evans, 1987, p. 77)

THE FIRST STONE CHURCH

There are several indicators that the first stone church was built before 1300. First is the mention in Vatican taxation records of Pope Nicholas in 1291, first noted by William Dugdale in his *Antiquities of Warwickshire*, where the church of 'Holy Trinitie' is valued at XX (20) marks. (Dugdale, 1730, p. 914)

The second indication is in a document researched by local historian Roger Lea, which suggests a very much earlier date. The chapel of St Blaise at the Manor House would have been served by one chaplain, yet a document dating from the early thirteenth century is signed by several clerics, whose number and titles imply that they would have served a more substantial church than a private chapel.

Roger Lea writes:

The charter of Waleran, Earl of Warwick from 1184–1204, has thirteen named witnesses, including Roger of Ullenhall who was probably his steward. Hugh, the Prior of Canwell Priory, was another witness, but both Roger and Hugh were alive during the whole of Waleran's earldom, so are of no help with dating the charter. Three of the witnesses, Henry the Priest of Sutton, William the deacon of Sutton, and John the clerk of Sutton are surprising because these three clergymen must have been attached to the parish church of Sutton. The charter must date from before 1204, but Holy Trinity Parish Church is generally thought to have been founded after 1250, and the spiritual needs of Suttonians prior to 1250 are generally supposed to have been satisfied by the Earl of Warwick's Chaplain, based at the Chapel of St Blaise in the Manor House on Manor Hill. These witnesses disprove this theory, providing evidence for the existence of a church in Sutton in 1200 served by three clergymen – perhaps it was a timber structure, replaced by the present stone church later in the century. (Lea, Witnesses, HS 345 16 January 2015)

Above left, Fig. 2: *Stonework beneath east end chancel wall (HTSC)*

Above right, Fig. 3: *Exposed foundations of mediaeval chancel wall – north side (AW)*

Mike Hodder concurs with this view, saying:

> the priest, deacon and clerk mentioned in the charter of 1184–1204 are likely to have been at a church on the site of Holy Trinity, demonstrating that there was a church there by 1204 at the latest and probably during the 12th century. (Mike Hodder, by email, 2019)

A third indication of the earliest building is the dating of the stonework beneath the window in the east end chancel wall. Described as the most ancient part of the church by Evans (p. 22) and visible only from the outside, the 'plinth and clasping buttresses' do appear to date from the thirteenth century (see Fig. 2).

Mike Hodder also notes findings from the archaeological investigation of 2016 as follows:

> I think it's important to emphasise that the oldest visible part of the church is 13th century – and predates the first mention of the church in the taxation of 1291, perhaps by as much as half a century. The archaeological work recorded the north side of the original chancel (now within the Vesey chapel) which has an identical plinth to that of the east end, showing that this is the original extent of the 13th century chancel. (Mike Hodder, by email, 2019, citing Coutts, 2019). See Fig. 3.

Agnes Bracken, in her history of Sutton Coldfield of 1860, gives some detail about the site of the village of Sutton and the chosen site for the church on Oker Hill as it appears to have been called, rather than Manor Hill (the site of the Manor House). The main reason appears to have been the favourable water supply, another the conspicuous position of the church, its being visible from 'Barr Beacon, the Park, the Manor, Maney Hill, Walmley, Whitehouse Common and the upper end of Hill Village'. (Evans, 1987, p. 119)

RECTORS' BOARD

One of the most useful historical records in Holy Trinity is the list of Rectors from 1250 to the present day, whose names are painted in gold on a wooden board. This board used to be in the south porch until the new entrance was created from the west side, and it was placed in 2016, beautifully restored, to the right of the entrance as people come into the church.

It is not known when the board was first erected or the source of dates for the early names listed there. Many sources, following Dugdale, give Gregory Harold as the first incumbent of Holy Trinity in 1305, but the board starts with Simon de Daventry in 1250 and then a lengthy gap before Richard de Bello in 1294, who reappears just three years after Gregory Harold, in 1308.

Dugdale refers to 'a certain Chantrie founded by one Thomas Broadmeadow (but the time when appears not) for one priest to sing Mass, and to pray for the soul of the said Thomas and his parents;' (Dugdale, 1730, p. 914). Dugdale gives as his source 'Willis Hist. of Abbies, v 2 p 253.' This refers to one of the books written by Browne Willis (1682–1760), an antiquary and Member of Parliament, who hailed from Dorset but devoted much of his attention in adult life to his home parish of Fenny Stratford in Buckinghamshire.

The designation 'Rectors' Board' is a misleading term. Strictly speaking the names refer to incumbents of the living, yet this is also confusing in the early days, as the 'advowson' (also called the living or the patronage) was owned by local noblemen (in Sutton's case, the earls of Warwick) or the Crown. Early incumbents (priests) may have been one and the same as the patron, the role being nominal and possibly also without involving the performance of any priestly duties.

Before the re-ordering work there was a preliminary archaeological investigation in 2015 and a further full investigation at the start of 2016. The report from the second investigation (Coutts, 2018) indicates that the original stone church does indeed roughly equate to the nave and chancel as they now appear, but that the pillars which currently delineate this space are not directly over the foundations of the earlier church. There is also an anomaly with a mediaeval burial of a priest in one case, which would appear to be beyond the church boundary at that time. This seems out of keeping with the standard practice to bury priests within the walls of the church:'Located within the church in supine position head at west end of grave cut. Thought to be a mediaeval priest due to the individual found with Paten bowl. Truncated by foundation of a stone pillar.' (Coutts, 2018, p. 2, 6:18)

A later chapter of this book (Chapter 11) looks in more detail at the role of the clergy through the centuries and some of the key names in the long list of incumbents since 1250.

FROM THE ELEVENTH TO THIRTEENTH CENTURIES

Whether or not a timber church preceded the first stone church in Sutton, worship would have taken place at the chapel at the Manor House. In terms of wider local history, William the Conqueror executed the last Saxon Earl of Warwick in 1071 and confiscated his lands, making them Crown property. Norman earls succeeded to the title, and ownership of Sutton was restored to the earls of Warwick in 1126 under Henry I. who exchanged his Crown property in Sutton for two estates he wanted in Rutland owned by the then earl, Roger de Newburgh.

The building of a stone church at this point (noted in Vatican records of 1291) fits well with the timing of changes to the status of the town, coinciding with the granting of a charter to the Earl of Warwick from Edward I in 1298 to enlarge the village and hold a market on Tuesdays and an annual fair beginning on the eve of Holy Trinity (Evans, 1987, p. 6)

Mike Hodder confirms that market and fair charters are a context for more building activity at the church. In his book *The Archaeology of Sutton Park* he suggests that the park originally extended right up to the town centre and was later reduced in size, when the town was being developed by the earls of Warwick. (Hodder, 2013)

Hodder confirms by email that the stone chancel of Holy Trinity, and a nave accompanying it, were already in place at this point.

Local historian Roger Lea has written about the site of the current church at this period as follows:

> If you stand on the Vesey Memorial looking across Vesey Gardens to High Street, you see a wide triangle of space enclosed by Mill Street and Coleshill Street. If you were standing here 800 years ago, you would be looking at the Earl of Warwick's newly-laid-out town of Sutton with its large triangular market-place in front of you. (Lea, Church Hill, HS 98, 2 April 2010)

[The steep cobbled drive called Church Hill has, since the 1990s, become the main approach to the church from Mill Street. It now has the Sons of Rest building on the right, as one progresses uphill, and the Vesey Gardens on the left. At the top it opens out onto a cobbled 'piazza' with the church on the left and the Trinity Centre on the right, and the car park at the rear just above Trinity Hill.]

Norman Evans notes that cottages were erected on Church Hill and Trinity Hill during this time, surrounding the church, and in adjacent roads – Coleshill Street and High Street. Mike Hodder writes that there have been very few excavations in Sutton town centre. (Hodder, 2004) However, mediaeval remains including an oven and a wall footing were found in Coleshill Street and a building there still has a mediaeval smoke hood.

THE FOURTEENTH CENTURY

While there is a lack of records generally for this century, former Parish Archivist Margaret Gardner reflected on the period of the Black Death and how it might have affected Sutton Coldfield. She noted that for the period 1345 to 1361 there were five Rectors in post. The Black Death itself is deemed to have arrived in 1348. Combined with the effects of famine following ruined harvests, the plague claimed huge numbers of lives and the clergy were heavily committed to looking after parishioners and administering last rites. At this point some dioceses had lost half of their monks and clergy, and a few dioceses were without any priests at all. It is difficult to establish how Sutton was affected, and it seems to have been quite sparsely populated at that time. (Gardner, 2000, p. 5)

One feature of the church that may have survived from this century is the arch over the south entrance (now within the newer porch). Norman Evans reports the date as suggested in *The Victoria County History* (p. 242) and he writes that this is proved by the 'chamfered jambs ... and its two-centred head of one chamfered order'. (Evans, 1997, p. 71) He suggests the arch was moved from the original south wall when the aisles were built (though he ascribes this to Vesey's time in 1533, whereas the accepted view now is that the aisles were added earlier, in the fifteenth century). He goes on to explain in relation to the porch:

This supposition is supported by the presence of the hood mould – a raised part of the stonework forming the arch on the external side for the purpose of preventing rain running down the outside of the wall falling on people passing beneath – thus confirming it was an outside door in the 14th century. (Ibid.)

Fig. 4: *Mediaeval pewter chalices found in 2016 (AW)*

Mike Hodder has confirmed:

> Archaeological evidence from the dig of 2016 revealed one of two priest burials (both of which were accompanied by pewter chalices) to be datable to between the late 13th and early 15th centuries. Both of the burials were within an earlier south aisle, narrower than at present – a short stretch of wall footing was found which ran parallel to the present south aisle wall. The arch now in the present south door and described by Norman Evans could have been from a doorway in this earlier, narrower aisle – which of course predates the aisle that was extended by Vesey. (Hodder, by email, 2019)

Fig. 4 shows the pewter chalices found in the dig of 2016.

EXTENSIONS TO THE CHURCH

The first major extensions to the nave and chancel were the tower and the two aisles, north and south, which extended to the end of the nave but not as far as the chancel's east end. Historians believe these were all executed in the second half of the fifteenth century, though not necessarily at the same time. The evidence for the aisles being built at this time is in the line of mediaeval 'stringing' – a narrow strip of protruding brickwork still visible on the south side of the church between the porch and the (later) SE chapel exterior, showing the original height of the aisles. This stringing is, of course, no longer on the north side as that original exterior wall was demolished as part of the church extension of 1879.

Some sources have Bishop Vesey constructing these aisles in c1530. It is now thought that confusing terminology has led to this mistake. The term 'iles' (aisles) used in some sources does not relate to what we would denote as the south and north (now Vesey) aisles but the *extensions* to these. This is not only confirmed by a contemporary local historian, Andy Foster, who has reminded us of the evidence of the mediaeval 'stringing', but also by William Kirkpatrick Riland Bedford who wrote that Vesey 'built two aisles or side chapels to the chancel' (Riland Bedford, n.d., p. 15). Vesey's work, taking both the north (now Vesey) aisle and the south aisle to extend either side of the east end of the chancel, made the church outline more of a rectangle. The separation of these two extensions from their aisle lengths into distinct chapels, as we see them today, came much later.

In terms of the walls themselves, we now only have the original south wall remaining but there is a photograph taken in 1878 and another in 1879 of the north wall. This was prior to the knocking down of the wall to make way for the north aisle extension, noted by Norman Evans (Evans, 1987, p. 202). As part of Evans' observation of the addition of a new window in the north wall in 1760, he remarks that it is curious that the windows in the north and south walls of the late fifteenth century were not placed diametrically opposite each other. (Ibid.)

The Victoria County History suggests the south porch also dates from 1530, making it part of the Vesey legacy. (VCH pp. 230–245 www.british-history.ac.uk/vch/warks/vol4/pp230-245 downloaded 30/6/19)

In the archaeological dig of 2016, fragments of fourteenth- and fifteenth-century decorated floor tiles were found which would have come from those parts of the church floor which had such decorated tiles.

WORSHIP

Evans confirms that before the Reformation, the chancel would have been separated from the nave by a rood screen across the chancel arch. There are two reasons for this. Firstly, the chancel was occupied by the priest only, who would also administer and take communion in that space, quite separately from the people, and the second is that the nave would also have been used by the people for secular (community) activities. (Evans, 1987, p. 15 and pp. 136–7). There was also the legal distinction that the priest paid for the upkeep of the chancel and the people for the upkeep of the nave. (This explains the quite different stone used in churches in some areas of the country for these two parts – a more expensive stone for the chancel and the local rough stone for the nave – in East Anglia the latter would be the local flint still visible in many of the churches there).

We know that the congregation would stand for worship as a rule. There might be some kind of step or bench against the wall where the more infirm could sit (hence the expression 'the weakest go to the wall'), but most would stand. They would apparently be saying their own prayers while the priest in the hidden chancel spoke the Latin words of the Catholic liturgy, a tongue not understood by the majority of the people. Many of the people could not read so would say extempore prayers or those they knew by heart (e.g. The Lord's Prayer). Those who could read might do so from their own copy of a book of hours.

The effect of all of this would be quite startling to modern congregations. Evans says that 'it has been commented that while a modern congregation can be likened to a class with a teacher, a mediaeval one was like a class when the teacher is out of the room' (Evans, 1987, p. 137). Quiet would only be achieved when the priest preached – from a platform or stage by the rood screen, a 'pulpitum', from which our modern term 'pulpit' is derived.

An artist's impression of a service in Holy Trinity in mediaeval times has been created by Bob Moulder as part of a commission of four paintings during the heritage project in 2018 (Fig. 5).

Fig. 5: *Artist's impression of Holy Trinity interior in mediaeval period (BM)*

THE TOWER

There is consensus that the style of the tower at Holy Trinity places its construction in the late fifteenth century. The exterior appears little changed in the succeeding centuries and the 'grotesque' spouts are thought to be original. (Evans, 1987, p 62)

The seventy-one steps to the top of the tower take in the entrance to the bell-ringing chamber, which has been at different heights in the tower over the centuries. There was presumably a single 'sanctus' bell (to call the faithful to worship) when the tower was built, but records show that Bishop Vesey added four bells in 1530 from Canwell Priory nearby (dissolved by Henry VIII in 1525).

Further changes and additions to the bells are noted in the relevant chapters as they happened chronologically.

The external height of the tower from ground level is about 70ft, with the height from the internal floor noted by Evans as 59ft 4in. Externally the tower looks higher in earlier pictures of the church, but that is because the roof of the nave was raised when it was rebuilt in 1863. Chapter 7 includes an image showing the differing heights of the floors in the tower over the centuries.

ST MARY'S HALL

An important building with stone foundations on the south-east corner of the churchyard was known as St Mary's Hall and is recorded as early as 1480 in the record of the estates of the Duke of Clarence, who was also Earl of Warwick and patron of the church.

Evans surmises that this might have been linked to church use, given its dedication to Mary, and possibly in use as a rectory at this time. (Evans, 1987, p. 74)

Its use in connection with the Grammar School is discussed in more detail on pages 51 and 52.

DIOCESAN OVERSIGHT

In Anglo-Saxon times the diocese of Lichfield covered the whole of the area of Mercia, a vast part of the middle of England from the Mersey in the north-west and the Humber in the north-east, then covering Wales across to East Anglia and extending south to the Thames.

In the eleventh century a Benedictine monastery was founded in Coventry and the then Bishop of Lichfield, Leofwyn, also claimed the title Abbot of Coventry, in 1054. The diocese was now named Coventry and Lichfield (1090), swapping to Lichfield and Coventry after the Civil War. This situation remained unchanged until the nineteenth century.

RECTORY TITHES

Based in biblical law (Deuteronomy 12:6), the tithe is an early form of tax, a tenth of the produce of the land, not an estimated rent as such. When the incumbent of a parish was entitled to the whole tithe of a parish he was known as the Rector, and it was then his duty to repair the church. As noted above, this duty extended only to the chancel and sanctuary; the congregation would be responsible for the nave and any other parts of the church. This division of responsibility has continued to the present at Holy Trinity, as at other long-established churches, that the Church Commissioners pay for the upkeep of the chancel, and the parishioners for the rest of the building including the contents such as pews and galleries. In Sutton this can be seen in the deliberations of the Warden and Society, whose Minute books record the transactions to pay for these items and repairs. (Evans, 1987 p. 121)

Some of the topics discussed in the general chapters like this one (which deal with the chronological development of Holy Trinity) are dealt with in more detail in later chapters, as listed in the Contents.

2

JOHN VESEY

The inclusion of another account of the story of Bishop John Vesey might appear superfluous to some readers. There have been many chroniclers of his life, and, because of his enormous influence over his native town, there has been much discussion and unpicking of the anomalies in the history as it has been passed down, as well as an element of controversy over the nature of his generosity to Sutton Coldfield viewed against the apparent financial losses to his See of Exeter.

No history of Holy Trinity Parish Church would be worthy of the name without some attempt to present the facts as we currently understand them and with the benefit of the weight of research that has been undertaken over the centuries since Vesey's times.

The weight of that research leads the current writer to attest that this far-sighted man changed the course of Sutton Coldfield in both its church and civic life. He set about his design using his wide experience as a courtier at the court of Elizabeth of York (queen to Henry VII) and subsequently with that of Henry VIII, whom he accompanied on many state occasions, notably to the Field of Cloth of Gold tournament and display in France in June 1520. He used his wisdom acquired through his university education in law and theology as well as in acting as tutor to Princess Mary, who would subsequently become Mary I.

Among the useful friends he made at Oxford were Thomas Wolsey and Thomas More, and it appears to have been his reading of More's *Utopia* that led to his enlightened view of local government, which he set about introducing to his native town.

His other achievements included the founding in 1527 of the grammar school, which still bears his name, and the introduction of improved housing and road infrastructure. He also gave some thought to the local economy, establishing a cottage industry known as 'kersey knitting', a type of weaving with wool. This process is explained more fully later in this chapter. He also provided grazing land for animals. This was all enabled through his successful petition to Henry VIII for the granting of a royal charter for the town, including the deforestation of Sutton Chase and granting the Chase to the new Corporation, eventually to be given to the people as Sutton Park, in 1528.

Fig. 6: *Face of John Vesey on his tomb effigy (HTSC)*

BIOGRAPHY

Vesey's early biography is problematic, as his birth date is not at all clear. In earlier centuries, births were not generally recorded, and baptisms only started to appear in church records later on in the fifteenth century. There are records of his death, and while these also differ, it is now generally agreed that the records of Exeter Diocese are reliable, which note that he died in 1554 (as we would now refer to it). His tomb states he was in his 103rd year. This would set his birth date as 1451.

But other known dates throw doubt on his date of birth. Vesey entered Magdalen College in 1482. This would make him 32 years of age, when the more usual age was 17. He might therefore have been born as late as 1465. His father, William Harman, died in 1471 and John is recorded as being the eldest of four children.

A CHANGE OF SURNAME

Vesey was born John Harman to parents William and Joan. Local historian Roger Lea suggests that at some point John's father (William) took the name Vesey. Fryer (1997) states that John was using the name Harman at Oxford until the year 1487–88, when the records start to give his surname as Vesey. This is very much later than if he had been using it concurrently with his father, as William had died in 1471. However, it may also be that Vesey was in occasional use by John as his surname, but he only used it in every respect from a point where he thought it might help his future prospects, that is, as he neared the end of his time at Oxford.

One theory is that it was the name of another branch of the family, possibly including someone responsible for John's early education. Fryer gives a full explanation of research into the will of one John Vesey of Lincoln College, proved in 1492 and including a bequest to a 'John Vesey of Sutton Coldfield' (Fryer, 1997, pp. 33–7). This explains some quite complicated family links and proposes not only the support John Vesey would have received to study at Oxford, but also his subsequent appointment to the court of Elizabeth of York. Fryer's useful book also gives the wording of the will at Appendix C (Fryer, 1997, pp. 231–4). He also notes that Vesey was a relatively common surname at this period.

John retained the name of Vesey through his life. However, his brother Hugh retained the name Harman, and tributes to both Vesey's parents and this brother are in the church above the Bishop's tomb in what is now called the Vesey chapel. Fryer describes Hugh as 'the brother that stayed at home, made a success of his life and sired the family's descendants'. (Fryer, 1997, p. 234)

HIS LIFE

It is believed that John was born in a house on the Moor Hall estate. His father, William, is described as a yeoman having lands at Wakers or Watters (though it is not clear where this place was). William Kirkpatrick Riland Bedford, the long-serving Rector of Holy Trinity who published a number of titles at the turn of the nineteenth to twentieth century about the history of Sutton, wrote, 'according to the pedigree of the family in *Camden's visitation of Warwickshire* 1619, he held lands at a place called Wakers or Watters and lived at Morehall'. (Riland Bedford, n.d., p. 4)

Riland Bedford goes on to quote from the same source that his marriage to Joan connected William to the family of Mountfort, 'to one of whom the manor of Sutton had been granted by Henry VI'. (Ibid.)

Records confirm that John Vesey entered Magdalen College, Oxford, in 1482, where he gained a doctorate in canon and civil law. Magdalen was relatively new then, its foundation dating from 1458. A fellow student who became a friend was Thomas (later Cardinal) Wolsey. Fryer writes that Wolsey's part in Vesey's advancement is 'undisputed'. (Fryer, 1997, p. 39) Another influential friend, not so much for advancement, but for the influence of his ideas in his well-known book of 1516, *Utopia,* was the law student Thomas More. Fryer points to an incident later in his life concerning Vesey's appreciation of the erudition of More's daughter Margaret who, with her sisters, was educated to the same high level as their brother. Margaret wrote a piece in Latin entitled 'Four last things' and More described how Vesey came to see it in a subsequent letter to his daughter, as follows:

> I happened this evening to be in the company of his Lordship, John Bishop of Exeter, a man of deep learning and a wide reputation for holiness. Whilst we were talking, I took out from my desk a paper that bore on our business and by accident your letter appeared. He took it into his hand with pleasure and examined it. (quoted by Fryer, 1997, p. 41)

The coincidental nugget of information in this account is More's summary of Vesey as a man of learning and with a reputation for holiness. It is a rare example of his character being described by a contemporary, and it supports the supposition from John's long life as a Bishop that he was able to adapt to changes of religious persuasion, unlike More himself, who could not suspend his strongly-held beliefs that wrong had been done to Catherine of Aragon by Henry VIII's reasoning for divorcing her, and who would lose his head for refusing to compromise on his position.

At Oxford, Vesey became Professor of Civil Law, and in 1489 he joined the court of Elizabeth of York, queen to Henry VII (and parents of Henry VIII). His clerical career began in 1495 when he became a chaplain to the chapel of St Blaise at the Manor House in Sutton Coldfield. Many more clerical appointments were made. Local historian Roger Lea has noted these and court appointments from a book about the Bishops who served under Henry VIII (Chibi, 2003), as follows:

Vicar of St Michael's Coventry 1507–20

Rector of:
St Blaize, Cornwall, 1495 (probably Sutton!)
Clifton Reynes, Bucks, 1495–99
Brize Norton, 1497

Edgmond, Salop, 1497
St Mary's on the Hill, Chester, 1499
Stoke Teignhead, Devon, 1504
Meifod, Montgomery, 1518

Prebendaries:
Darlington, 1498
Exeter, 1503
Crediton, 1504
St Stanford's in Crediton, 1512
Liddington, Lincolnshire, 1514
St Stephen's, Westminster, 1514–18

Archdeaconries:
Chester, 1499–1515
Barnstaple, 1503

Deaneries:
Exeter, 1509
St George's Chapel, 1514
Windsor, 1515–19
Wolverhampton, 1516–21

Other ecclesiastical appointments:
Vicar-general to Bishop Arundel, 1498–1502
Chancellor to Bishop Arundel (Bishop of Exeter)
Precentor of Exeter, 1508
Warden, Clyst St Gabriel Chapel
His provision to the See of Exeter, 31 August 1519

Court appointments:
Councillor to Queen Elizabeth of York, 1489
Registrar of the Order of the Garter, 1515
Enclosure commissioner, 1517
President of the Council of the Marches of Wales, 1526

Riland Bedford writes of Vesey's appointment to St Michael's Coventry in 1507 (the first post listed above) that he was 'at St Michael's Church in Coventry, administering, as Vicar-General, the Warwickshire portion of that enormous See of Lichfield and Coventry which extended from Morecambe Bay to Banbury'. (Riland Bedford, n.d., p. 6)

This, together with the long list of appointments, serves to confirm that the day-to-day work of parishes and even dioceses was usually conducted by other clergy. Very often the nominated Rector would rarely visit the parish, sometimes not at all, and Bishops might well spend very little time in their diocese, whose bounds could be extensive at a time when travel was arduous and time-consuming.

BISHOP OF EXETER

Vesey was consecrated Bishop of Exeter in 1519 by William Warham, the Archbishop of Canterbury, and other Bishops including the Bishop of Rochester. He received from the king 'the temporalities of the see', worth about £1,500 a year.

Bishop Vesey became tutor to Princess Mary (Henry's daughter by Catherine of Aragon, and his first child, who would become Queen Mary I). This was in 1526, when the princess turned 11. Mary was based in Ludlow (Shropshire) and Vesey was appointed President of the Court of the Marches of Wales, based at Ludlow Castle (then in the Diocese of Worcester). This appointment has created an unexpected resonance for Holy Trinity, as, quite by chance, wood-work purchased from Worcester Cathedral in the nineteenth century and now in use in the chancel and side chapels has only recently been dated to the time of Mary I (for more information, see Chapter 10 on the woodwork at Holy Trinity).

Vesey was Bishop from 1519 until the reign of Edward VI, who became king in 1547 on the death of his father (Henry VIII). It is not clear whether Vesey's resig-nation was forced in August 1551, but this seems likely. He was, however, restored to the See of Exeter by Mary I in September 1553 (her half-brother Edward had died in July). This gesture shows that, despite Henry VIII's break from Rome and the reforms of the Protestant King Edward VI, Vesey adhered to the old faith in which he had been brought up. Roger Lea notes that the new monarch was also acknowledging her childhood tutor.

THE BENEFACTOR OF SUTTON COLDFIELD

In 1523, John Vesey returned to his native town for the funeral of his mother Joan Harman (8 March) and also had to witness the funeral of his brother Hugo

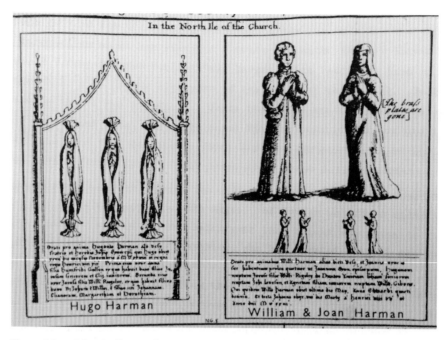

Fig. 7: *Memorials to William and Joan Harman (Dugdale / NGE)*

(Hugh) in November that year. Memorials to Vesey's parents, William and Joan, and Vesey's siblings, with a separate memorial to Hugh, are all to be seen above Vesey's tomb in the Vesey chapel in Holy Trinity. See Fig. 7 for an image from Dugdale, 1656, as used by Norman Evans.

It has been well documented that this return to his native town after a long absence shocked the Bishop. The population had decreased, and there was insufficient work available to support families. Housing and roads were poor, and travel was dangerous for those passing through on the old Roman roads which skirted the town.

Fryer gives a cogent reason for the decline of Sutton Coldfield from 'a prosperous little market town in the early 15th century' to a place which appeared neglected by 1523. (Fryer, 1997, p. 137ff). He ascribes the fall to the death of the Earl of Warwick (the Kingmaker) in 1471. The manor of Sutton was settled on the earl's daughters and their husbands, notably the elder daughter, Isabel, who herself died in 1476. Her husband was now Earl of Warwick but better known as George, Duke of Clarence (famously convicted for treason against his brother and allegedly drowned in a butt of malmsey). That brother,

Edward IV, was now the owner of the manor of Sutton Coldfield while Clarence's son was not yet adult. In 1487 Henry VII restored the Earl of Warwick's lands to the Kingmaker's widow Anne, and she immediately passed them back to the crown. While she did take possession again of Sutton Coldfield in 1489, she died a few years later and so the manor was back with the crown until Vesey secured the charter in 1528.

Fryer suggests that the constant changes of ownership would not have encouraged anyone to become too committed to the town or to wish to invest long-term in its economy. He estimates that the population at this time was around 1,000 people (some 200 families).

Vesey's achievements in and for Sutton Coldfield are well documented, including on the tomb in the church, but they bear repetition here. Fryer (1997, p. 141) also lists the costs of various works as recorded by Sir William Dugdale. These are repeated at Table 1 at the end of this section, together with the equivalent amounts in today's terms, for comparison.

Establishment of a Warden and Society

This has to be Vesey's major achievement for the town of Sutton Coldfield – the establishment of a system of local government, which remained until the late nineteenth century when the Warden and Society was formally changed to a corporation in line with other major towns and cities. The deliberations and decisions of both have not been faultless over the years, but the origins of this council of local men set up by Vesey following his reading of Sir Thomas More's book *Utopia*, have stood the test of time and appear to be a reasonable means of achieving democracy within the constraints of the age.

A moot hall was built, where local issues could be heard and discussed, with decisions made where necessary. A prison formed part of the new building.

Construction Work

A major improvement to the town was the paving of roads in the High Street area just by the church. The cost was £40 3s 8d and related specifically to High Street, Mill Street and Coleshill Street. Vesey also had a new marketplace constructed at the junction of these three roads at the top of the hill.

Stone bridges were built over the River Tame at Curdworth and Water Orton, the latter still in use today.

Vesey arranged for fifty-one stone houses to be built, some to enable kersey weaving to be carried out, others to give protection to travellers on through roads at the edges of the town where they were prone to attack. By housing townspeople in strategic places, Vesey ensured there was a measure of safety in an era where there was no formal public protection of this kind.

Vesey also constructed a tithe barn in High Street (the road going north towards Lichfield). He used carved stones from the ruined chapel of St Blaize to decorate a number of buildings, also the bridge at Water Orton (these ones have been removed to Curdworth church for protection from the elements). The tithe barn was photographed in 1855 by William Grundy (in its more recent guise as a malthouse, and the gable end clearly sports four separate carvings. The one directly under the gable is of a man supported by a stag, thought to be St Hubert, patron saint of hunters, which would fit with its previous home: a hunting lodge.

Two carved figures stand below this, either side of a figure in monk's clothing. The two side pieces were subsequently put into the church wall on Church Hill when found loose in the churchyard in 1939. They subsequently went missing at the time of the building of the Trinity Centre in the 1990s. Two stones were put at this time into the care of Sutton Library, but when these were retrieved at the request of the library in 2017, they were found to be much smaller and of a different design from the ones in Grundy's photograph (see Fig. 8).

Fig. 8: *Carved stone from Manor House on tithe barn (SCL, Grundy)*

Promotion of 'Kersey' Weaving

This was a less successful venture. Vesey was trying to find a cottage industry that could regenerate the area and bring in both employment and money to the town. He chose a trade based on the successful kersey weaving carried out in Devon and Cornwall (the name actually derives from a village in Suffolk called Kersey), but it had the following potential disadvantages in Sutton, as charted by Fryer (1997, pp. 149-155):

- The high land of Birmingham was not known for producing wool of high quality.
- Wool produced from sheep in other parts of Warwickshire to the south did not fetch as high a price as that from other parts of the country, including the nearby Cotswolds.
- While kersey weaving was more suited to the lower-quality wool produced in Sutton, people had to be trained in the trade, and weavers were brought from Devon to do this. The whole family would need to be involved in different aspects of the work. This all added to the costs of setting up and carrying out the work.
- As a cottage industry, good housing was required, and this led to Vesey's decision to build the fifty-one stone houses across the town. This was also a considerable investment.
- A fulling mill was required for shrinking and thickening the wool fibres. Water power was harnessed from the pools in Sutton Park to power a mill in Witton (four miles away). It may be that the local streams were unable to provide enough water in the long term.
- The industry relied on exports, notably to Antwerp. Sutton Coldfield is a long way from the sea and haulage would have been a further expense.
- It is possible that Vesey's contacts with the merchants in London, necessary to enable foreign trade, declined with the years.

Whatever the reasons, the industry did not take off as envisaged, but Vesey's plan was indicative of his strategic vision for the town, and the legacy in road infrastructure and bricks and mortar is evident to this day.

Sutton Park

A major and long-lasting legacy of John Vesey's work for the town was the inclusion in the charter of the 2,400 acres of Sutton Park for the people of the town. The deer park had been established in the twelfth century by King Henry I within the Manor of Sutton. The Royal Forest of Kank, designated by William the Conqueror, extended over the whole area between the rivers Tame and Trent, governed by strict laws to facilitate hunting. A quarter of this forest, known as Sutton Chase, was granted in 1126 to the Earl of Warwick along with the Manor of Sutton, and was still in existence 400 years later, subject to the forest laws, and administered by keepers appointed by the Crown. The 1528 charter disforested (abolished) the Chase to the great benefit of Suttonians, who could now graze their sheep on the 5,000 acres of common land.

A story has been passed down over the centuries that Henry had been hunting in the park, his own hunting ground at the time, and was saved from the attack of a wild boar by an unknown archer. When the king called the archer to him it was revealed to be a woman. The king was apparently so grateful that he asked the woman what she would like as a reward, and she was prompted by Bishop Vesey, who was with the hunting party, to ask for the park to be given to the people of Sutton. This story is not in older histories but may contain a grain of truth.

Part of Vesey's endowment to the town was the provision of mares, colts and horses in the park to enable employment through animal husbandry.

Vesey also set about a programme of hedging, ditching and enclosing the coppices which, again, have shaped the park as we know it today.

Additions to the Church

Vesey's two main contributions to Holy Trinity were an organ in 1530 and the two aisle extensions to the south and north. He also provided the first set of bells to add to the single 'sanctus' bell, which would have already been in the church.

Norman Evans refers to the pillars (still extant) between the chancel and Vesey's aisle ends as being based on a design seen in his travels through Devonshire. They are apparently similar to pillars in the nave at St Andrew's church in Cullompton, East Devon, where the arms of Bishop Vesey are also cut into the stonework. (Evans, 1987, p. 196)

In his account of 'The Vesey buildings at Sutton Coldfield', William Kirkpatrick Riland Bedford clarifies the description of the organ as 'a pair of organs' in some sources. The pair just means the two parts of a whole, manuals and pipes. (Riland Bedford, 1893, p. 33)

Riland Bedford also clarifies the confusion in some sources around the extensions Vesey made to the church. (See Chapter 1 on the early history of the church for further information.)

The School

John Vesey established a school close to the church on the south side near the present Sons of Rest building in Mill Street. The schoolmaster's house, known as St Mary's Hall, stood on the same level on Trinity Hill, and the school-master's garden, now incorporated in the churchyard, extended along the hillside between the house and the school. Trinity Hill was formerly known as Blind Lane.

A key chronicler of the history of the school is Kerry Osbourne, a local solicitor (now retired) whose firm has practised in the High Street, Sutton Coldfield, since 1800, and who was clerk to the governors of Bishop Vesey's Grammar School for forty years. Mr Osbourne found early documents relating to the school in the attic of his firm's premises (known as Sadler House) and this led him to a thorough investigation of the school's history, published in two volumes, the first covering the first 375 years (1527 to 1902) and the second covering the twentieth century. Those wishing to know the full history of the school are encouraged to seek these sources out (see references). A few salient points in relation to Vesey and the history of the church are included here.

Although the Foundation Deed was 1527, there were difficulties in col-lecting funds and securing teachers. Osbourne notes in his chronology that 'a yearly rent of £7 per annum payable out of certain properties in Sutton Coldfield [was] given to 21 trustees to pay a fit person to teach grammar and rhetoric in Sutton Coldfield'. (Osbourne, 2000, p. 249). This person was to be a priest and to say Psalm 130 (*De profundis* – out of the depths) each day with the scholars in thanksgiving for their dead benefactors. Vesey also stated (perhaps aware of the small size of Sutton Coldfield as compared with other places which boasted schools) that if such a clergyman could not be found, then a layman might be appointed. Nothing appears to have happened as the rents were not universally forthcoming. There is no record of a master being appointed in 1527, but Osbourne suggests a possible candidate for the post, one 'Nicholas Mogg, the chaplain who lived at Okerhill next to the Parish Church.' (Osbourne, 1990, p. 7) He suggests that as Vesey was in Sutton at the time he would have made efforts to find a master. Times at court were turbu-lent in this period and it seems the Bishop was not able to enforce payment. It took until 1540 for Vesey to try again to secure the rents, this time making them payable to the Warden and Society of the town to secure the teacher. Significantly, the teacher now was to be a layman.

The headmasters were varied in their commitment and popularity.

The first to be appointed was John Savage, c1540, when the school appears at last to be fully in operation. According to Fryer:

His house was known as St Mary Hall and was at the top of Blind Lane, now named Trinity Hill. It was a stone house similar to the Vesey houses in Maney and Wylde Green Road, but larger. The rent was 8 shillings (40p) a year. The adjacent St Mary House at the corner of Coleshill Street was used for boarding pupils. Another nearby house 'The old grammar school' was used as the school. Vesey presumably provided these buildings. (Fryer, 1997, p. 163)

Osbourne notes that a deed of 1543 refers to St Maryhall being 'now in the tenure of John Savage schoolmaster'. (Osbourne, 1990, p. 6) He suggests that this places his appointment at an earlier date. 1540 is the date attributed by the school.

Presumably the old grammar school was the original building designed for the school but which was only now coming into use as such.

A contentious appointment also during the lifetime of Bishop Vesey was of Lawrence Noel (or Nowell), who succeeded Savage when he either retired or died in 1546. Nowell was in his twenties, a scholarly man but, despite good paper qualifications, he appears to have neglected his duties. Fryer quotes Dugdale, 'his dexteritie and diligence in teaching scholars fell far short of what they expected'. (Fryer, 1997, p 164). Osbourne refers to his concentrating on research work, particularly in relation to the Anglo-Saxon language (Osbourne, 1990, p. 8). Nowell may also have felt that his salary was not sufficient to encourage him to put the effort required into his teaching. He was also about to take holy orders, so may have seen this as another reason to wind down his school work. Either way, he was not popular locally, but, as he had been appointed for life, the Warden and Society could not now remove him without appealing for a court order. Fryer quotes the judgement from the register of Acts of the Privy Council of 28 February 1550, which shows that he could not be removed unless some notable offence had been committed. While Nowell had thus won his case, he subsequently resigned, however, accepting arrears and a lump sum, as we would now describe it.

According to Riland Bedford, again quoted by Fryer, this may have had repercussions in the dismissal of Vesey from his See the following year. Vesey was conspicuously absent from his diocese of Exeter, so could not fairly judge an absent schoolmaster back in Sutton Coldfield. A high-profile friend of Nowell and his family was the reformer Hugh Latimer (who would subsequently become a martyr for the Protestant cause). Latimer had a score to settle with Vesey, who had been one of the Bishops to judge him in 1532 after he had been pronounced 'contumacious' and imprisoned at Lambeth. Latimer now took the opportunity to denounce Vesey in a sermon before the Protestant king (Edward VI) in March 1550. This must have been a factor in dismissal from his bishopric when Vesey was an elderly man at this point. (See Fryer, 1997, pp. 205–6).

Nowell, as a Protestant priest, fled to Germany when Mary I acceded to the throne in 1553, but returned under Elizabeth I, moving on to become Archdeacon of Derby and Dean of Lichfield. He died in 1576.

The school's fortunes are referred to in later chapters as they link to the church in later periods. It survives to this day, and despite times when its finances were less assured, especially around the turn of the nineteenth to the twentieth century, in the twenty-first century it continues as a thriving grammar school whose pupils achieve excellent results academically. The link between the school and the church remains strong, with students attending a service every October near to the anniversary of Vesey's death, to commemorate their founder and lay flowers on his tomb in the church. As Bishop Vesey's Grammar School, it looks forward to its 500th anniversary in 2027.

Benefactions of John Vesey	Cost	Cost today*
Premises for Warden and Society – moot hall and marketplace	£35 5s 7d (£35.28)	£15,567.88
Weights and balances and first 'leet'	£2 1s (£2.05)	£904.62
Paving roads	£40 3s 7d (£40.18)	£17,730.14
Procurement of Sutton Park	Not known	
Provision of mares, colts and horses in the park …	£40	£17,651.20
… and ditching and quicksetting thereof	£27 5s 6d (£27.27)	£12,035.83
Enclosing the Seven Heys coppices etc	£43 2s 7d (£43.13)	£19,022.72
Provision of an organ for the church	£14 2s 7d (£14.13)	£6,234.88
Building two aisle extensions on the church and 'finishing'	£96 18s 2d (£96.91)	£42,763.42
Construction of two stone bridges at Curdworth and Water Orton	Not known	
Promotion of 'kersey' weaving	Not known	
Construction of 51 stone houses	c£500	£220,638.50
Foundation of a school (now Bishop Vesey's Grammar School)	Not known	

Table 1: *Benefactions of Bishop Vesey to Sutton Coldfield (Original 'List of Vesey's main works in Sutton', with original costs only, in Fryer, 1997, p. 141)*

Note: the currency converter of the National Archives was used:
www.nationalarchives.gov.uk/currency-converter

MOOR HALL

John Vesey had been born on the Moor Hall estate. In relation to the Bishop's return to Sutton Coldfield, local historian Roger Lea describes the Moor Hall of 1525 as 'the old family home, but not for much longer'. He continues:

> In 1527 the King gave Vesey the Moor Hall estate, and the Bishop proceeded to build a splendid new mansion on the hill above the old house, where he lived in style with a household of 140 retainers dressed in red livery. The old Moor Hall was rebuilt in stone on a more modest scale – it was known as the Dairy House in 1550, and later as Moor Hall Farm.

Lea notes that, after his death in 1554, Vesey's brother Hugh Harman lived at Moor Hall for a time, although by 1600 it was in new hands (see Chapter 6 for more information on Moor Hall). (Lea, *Moor Hall,* HS 62, 17 July 2009)

END OF LIFE

There are reliable records at Exeter Cathedral of Vesey's restoration to the See of Exeter by Mary I and of his death a year later, although this actually took place at his home in Sutton Coldfield. Oliver (1861) lays out the facts and also quotes the record in Latin on Vesey's death made at the time by the registrar in Exeter. This extract reads as follows:

> King Edward VI, dying on 6th July, 1553, no sooner was his sister Mary settled on the throne, than she restored, on 3rd September that year, the nonagenarian prelate to his see. On 13th November that year we meet him at his palace here, where he remained nearly two months arranging the affairs of the diocese. The Register of his probate of wills commences with 21st November, 1553. By 28th January, 1554, he had returned to Sutton Coldfield, where he continued till his death, as I imagine at the age of 92. His Registrar thus concludes his acts: — 'Vicesimo tertio die Octobris, anno Domini MDLIV, in manerio suo de More Place, infra Parochiam de Sutton Collfyld, in Com. Warwick, Dominus ab hac luce migravit. Cujus animae propitietur Deus, Amen.' His tomb is still to be seen in the north aisle of the parish church, and is engraved in Dugdale's 'History of Warwickshire.' (Oliver, 1861, pp. 124–5)

To clarify the allusion to Mary being 'settled on the throne', her accession was not immediate because of all the difficulties of the various children of Henry VIII by different wives laying claim to the throne (with varied Roman Catholic or Protestant allegiance). There was also the brief sad period when Lady Jane Grey was confirmed as the next monarch.

The wording on the tomb in Holy Trinity is inaccurate, but this is partly explained by the fact that the original has seen two substantial changes both in its design and its place in the church, in 1687 and 1748.

Taking the Exeter records above, we know from the Latin inscription that Vesey died on 23 October 1554, and can conclude from other sources that he was aged 93 or so.

THE TOMB OF BISHOP VESEY

The effigy on the tomb is thought to have been carved soon after Vesey's death and as a likeness of his face. Monuments researcher Jon Bayliss writes:

> The effigy to Bishop Vesey at Sutton Coldfield was probably commissioned in the late 1550s, although the bishop had died in 1554. Pevsner commented that it had been 'handled over the centuries with too much care' and that it was difficult to determine how much of it was mid-sixteenth century under the paint. The Royley provenance is clear from the distinctive ears and the treatment of the drapery, which is very close to that on some female effigies, including one of the wives of Sir Edward Littleton at Penkridge. The placing of the top cushion diagonally on the lower cushion under the effigies' heads is an indication of a relatively early date. Between the erection of the two very similar tombs at Brewood (dates of death 1556 and 1560), cushions began to be placed square to each other. (Bayliss, 1991, pp. 26, 29)

The vestments shown are Catholic (as befitted the era of Mary I) with the following garments:
- An Alb – a white robe reaching to the feet.
- A Dalmatic – a wide-sleeved loose garment with slit sides.
- A Chasuble – a sleeveless vestment worn to celebrate Mass, with a colour according to the feast of the day. (on the tomb this is green, the colour of 'ordinary time', which means the majority of Sundays – those that are not in the Advent or Lent seasons (purple) or feast days (red or white).
- A Mitre on his head.
- A Crozier (shepherd's crook) in his hand.

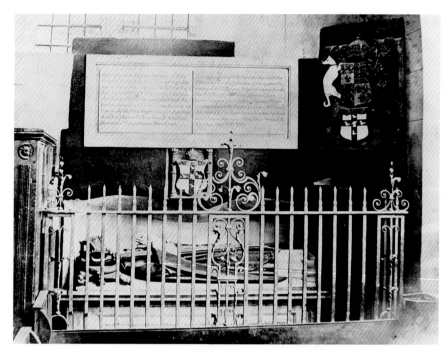

Fig. 9: *Bishop Vesey's tomb c1895 (SCL)*

Norman Evans (1987) must be acknowledged for his description of the garments in his *Investigation of Holy Trinity Parish Church*. In this section of his publication on Vesey's tomb, he also notes that 'until recent times it was the only monumental effigy of a Bishop in Warwickshire and is visited from afar because of the very rare display of pre-Reformation vestments'. (Evans, 1987, p. 23). All these garments and the mitre and crozier are still part of a Bishop's dress in both the Roman Catholic and Anglican traditions. Fig. 9 shows the tomb c1895.

In a detailed appendix to his investigation of 1987, Norman Evans notes that Mary I was strongly supported in her Catholic revival by the then Bishop of Coventry, the Rt Revd Ralph Bane, who granted the faculty for Vesey's effigy on the tomb in his pre-Reformation Roman Catholic vestments. Evans writes:

> The fact that his likeness in such robes was not destroyed a few years later under the orders of Bishop Thomas Bentham, or during the subsequent extreme Puritan era in Sutton shows the very high esteem in which Bishop Vesey must have been held by the Suttonians. (Ibid., p. 138)

The first known renewal of the effigy was in 1687. At this point the effigy was on a slab on the floor over the grave, as it had been since the Bishop's burial (in the north-east corner of the church, now known as the Vesey chapel). It is probable that the effigy was damaged by iconoclasts in the early seventeenth century, when some followed strictly Puritan values, seeking the removal of 'graven images'. Certainly the grand-nephew of Vesey, Sir John Wyrley of Hamstead, paid for repairs at this point.

In 1748 a much greater change took place when the effigy was restored and placed in a niche in the north wall by the Warden and Society of Sutton Coldfield. The whole was protected by iron railings.

The final major change was in 1875. The current clergy vestry had been built beyond the north wall the previous year and major change to the decoration of the chancel and tomb area (Vesey chapel) was now imminent, following the acquisition of woodwork from Worcester Cathedral.

The effigy was removed from its niche in the north wall and thoroughly renovated. The opportunity was taken to open the vault and note the findings on 25 August 1875. These were recorded as 'part of a skull and jawbone in which two teeth remained, and various bones which had obviously been previously disturbed'. (Evans, 1987, p. 24).

The *South London Chronicle* of 4 September 1875 records the grizzly detail in a report entitled 'Re-opening of an ancient tomb'. The reporter notes the decision was made in order to see if the tomb did indeed house the remains of the Bishop. The Rector and other officials were present. As well as the skull parts noted above, there were various larger pieces of bone (arm, thigh). There was no trace of a coffin or of any of the adornments of a Bishop (e.g. the ring all Bishops wear). The writer notes, 'it was quite evident that this was not the first occasion on which it had been opened'.

The report mentions a theory of the time, which was that the opening of the tomb in the previous century had, by exposing the remains to the air, caused them to crumble to dust, so other remains had been interred in their place. The report explains what happened next:

All the remains of the prelate were carefully collected and placed in an earthen vase, accompanied with a bottle containing a parchment bearing the following inscription:

This writing is to commemorate the fact that on the 25th day of August, AD 1875, the vault wherein the remains of John Harman, alias Vesey, were interred, was opened on the occasion of the restoration of the monument by the Warden and Society of Sutton Coldfield, and the bones were deposited in an earthen pan, within which this writing is also enclosed. They were the only remains discovered beyond the dust and earth covered by them, which were also replaced in the tomb.

Evans writes that 'an arch was constructed over the grave to carry the weight of the alabaster slab and the present altar tomb which was erected over it, the effigy of the Bishop being laid on top'. (Evans, 1987, p. 24).

Jon Bayliss has written as follows about the tomb itself:

The effigy of Bishop Vesey is one I identify as being made in the workshop of Richard Royley in Burton-upon-Trent. The chest on which it rests is a replacement of the original except, I suspect, for the shield on the west end. There are a couple of panels in the church that I suspect were part of the original chest. (Jon Bayliss, by email, May 2019)

VESEY THROUGH HISTORY

Undoubtedly, the influence of John Vesey on the church and town of Sutton Coldfield has been far-reaching and long-lasting. His memory has been kept alive through the varied fortunes of his tomb in the church, and the Reverend William Kirkpatrick Riland Bedford must be credited for writing about him in a number of his publications. In the twentieth century, local people were mobilised into action by an enthusiastic Sutton Coldfield councillor, John Willmott JP, whose work ultimately brought a lasting legacy, more visible to the town than the tomb within the church, in the creation of the Vesey Gardens including a memorial to the Bishop.

Alderman John Willmott led celebrations in 1928 for the 400th anniversary of the royal charter secured by Vesey from Henry VIII. A pageant was held in Sutton Park with a large number of activities. When the time came for the town to consider appropriate celebration of the Silver Jubilee of George V in 1935, John Willmott again led celebrations by writing a play.

Following these celebrations, Willmott set about the creation of the Vesey Gardens in earnest. The site just in front of the north side of the church on Church Hill was at the time populated with houses and two pubs. There had also been some cottage industry on the hill, but the houses were not fully occupied at this point. Willmott saw this as the ideal place to have memorial gardens. He outlines the process in a two-page article in a church guide written by a one-time Rector of Holy Trinity, George Harvey, some time after 1945

(Willmott, n.d.). The alderman acknowledges the generosity of Ansells Brewery in facilitating the purchase of land by the corporation, enabling the transformation of the hill to take place, though nowadays one wonders how difficult it might have been for those tenants still living on the hill, who presumably had to be found alternative accommodation.

In 1989, KM Kendall, a member of the Sutton Coldfield Local History Research Group, published an excellent booklet on the history of the site entitled 'From Church Hill to Vesey Gardens'. This brings out the detail of the individuals who occupied the houses and includes census information, photographs and details of the planning and final execution of the gardens. (Kendall, 1989).

Willmott had been concerned that John Vesey might be forgotten. The tomb in the church, the memorial in the Vesey Gardens and the name Vesey, used as part of the school he founded, all ensure that his memory is very much alive in the minds of people in Sutton Coldfield, the city of Birmingham and beyond.

Following the re-ordering of the church interior in 2016, the name is further commemorated with the new church entrance to the north-west named the *Vesey entrance,* as it leads directly to the Vesey aisle and the Chapel at the far end which houses the Bishop's tomb.

Fig. 10: Vesey memorial in the Vesey Gardens (SCL)

3

FROM VESEY TO 1800

Fig. 11: *Former tailor's cottage, Coleshill Street. Drawing by Ken Williams (KW)*

Vesey's death in the middle of the sixteenth century coincides with the start of a great deal of religious and political turbulence. Politically this would last into the subsequent century – into the Civil War, Protectorate and re-establishment of the monarchy with the accession of Charles II. A further century would be required before there would be any softening of polarised views about Roman Catholic and Church of England doctrinal positions. Specifically those of Roman Catholic persuasion were driven underground in terms of their ability to practise their faith; priests were outlawed, and 'inter-marrying' was not tolerated. Many who refused to renounce their Roman Catholic allegiance would be hunted down and tortured, often also imprisoned. Many were executed. The Gunpowder Plot has gone down in history as something rather exciting, celebrated with fireworks, yet it was a desperate act by desperate men to try to reclaim some measure of justice for Roman Catholics and the right to practise their faith alongside their Protestant brothers and sisters. It represents a dark time when religious tolerance and Christian charity were both lacking. Furthermore, those of us now worshipping as Anglicans in churches like Holy Trinity need to be mindful of the long period of our church's history when the building must have been perceived as out of bounds to part of the population. Many will have continued to worship there as the only church in the town. Probably there was no perceptible difference in worship styles or expressed beliefs at the outset, soon after the death of Vesey, when Mary I, who had tried so fervently (and in some cases brutally) to reinstate her brand of Roman Catholicism, died and was succeeded by her half-sister Elizabeth, the Protestant daughter of Anne Boleyn. The long reign of Elizabeth I ensured that the Church of England would remain the established church of the United Kingdom, as it does to this day. Over the next century, Anglican practice started to diverge more noticeably from Roman Catholic styles of worship and belief, and some key tenets of the Catholic faith, notably the authority of the Pope, became areas over which there could be no foreseeable reconciliation. There is more about this in Chapter 14.

CHANGES OF EDWARD VI

Until Henry VIII's death, services would have continued according to the rites of the church of Rome, even though the monarch was now head of the Church in England. When Edward VI became king in 1547, these rites were suppressed. WK Riland Bedford, in his history of Sutton Coldfield, notes that the interior of the church would have been whitewashed to obliterate superstitious pictures and that the royal coat of arms would be erected in place of any image of the Madonna and Child. (Riland Bedford, 1891, p. 75) One of the tablets showing the Tudor coat of arms is still in the church, currently on the north wall of the tower.

According to Norman Evans, in 1551, Edward VI issued instructions that altars were to be replaced by a simple table to emphasise that the Eucharist symbolises the Lord's Supper, not the offering of a sacrifice. The custom would have been to bring the altar table away from the east end wall to the middle of the chancel and turn it at right angles. At this time the chancel of churches would have been empty of furniture, and at Holy Trinity this would also have been the case, with the organ and choir accommodated in the side end chapel (the floor of the chancel being at the same level). (Evans, 1987, p. 16)

During the reign of Edward VI, the Rector, Ralph Wendon, made an inventory of items at Holy Trinity, quoted by Norman Evans as follows:

> one oon chalice; [which Evans describes as meaning a worn-out chalice] four bells and a saint's bell; [these would be the four bells brought to Holy Trinity by Vesey from Canwell Priory in 1530 with the pre-existing sanctus bell] three vestments all in silk, a silk cope, four fronts to altars, all silk; [Evans notes the word altars in the plural] six altar cloths and six towels. (Evans, 1987, p. 138)

THE SEVENTEENTH CENTURY

The seventeenth century saw the upheaval of the Civil War when Charles I was beheaded (1649) and Oliver Cromwell became the first Lord Protector. This role passed to his son Richard at his death, then the monarchy was restored with tighter restriction of the role, and Charles II acceded in 1660 until his death in 1685. Sutton Coldfield was, to the surprise of some citizens of today, a Puritan stronghold during the Civil War. This had repercussions in 1642 when James Fleetwood was put forward to be the next Rector. This was unacceptable to the town as he had Royalist allegiance. He was duly sent elsewhere, subsequently becoming Bishop of Worcester (a city with Royalist sympathies).

But Fleetwood is remembered at Holy Trinity as one of the four Bishops commemorated in the stained glass window in the east end of the Vesey chapel (see Chapter 9).

It is likely that any traditional scene of the Last Judgement (also known as a 'Doom' painting) which might have been painted on the chancel archway at Holy Trinity would have been whitewashed during the Puritan era, when images were covered or removed. After the restoration of the monarchy, in line with practice in churches across the land, three large wooden tablets were erected in the chancel archway at Holy Trinity showing the Lord's Prayer, the Ten Commandments and the Creed. Above them was placed a further tablet depicting the royal coat of arms of Charles II. These tablets no longer exist. Following the changes of 1662, the altar table (brought forward by decree of Edward VI) would have been moved back to its position against the east end and had a communion rail added (Evans, 1987, p. 16)

A far-reaching change in church practice during the period of the Commonwealth was the change to baptisms, marriage ceremonies and funerals, shown in the detail of registers of the time. There is detail about this in Chapter 14, but it should be noted here that in 1657 the Rector, Anthony Burgess, reinstated the practice of conducting weddings in church.

In 1667 and 1678 legislation was introduced, presumably to support the wool trade of the Cotswolds and other areas, that 'no corpse of any person (except those who shall die of the plague) shall be buried in any garment other than what is made of sheep's wool only'. Non-compliance would lead to a steep penalty fine of £5. More is written about this and other burials in Chapter 8.

The seventeenth century appears to have seen less upheaval to the church in terms of extension or re-building. This may, however, be explained by the lack of documentation and the political turmoil creating repercussions with the Civil War and its aftermath. Certainly none of the histories mentions any substantial work at this period.

One addition to the churchyard was the sundial, still standing today. The exact date of its construction is not known, but it is first recorded in the account in the parish register of the burial on 9 September 1671 of Thomas Dawney, whose grave (the tomb is now demolished) was described as being 'on the north side of the dyall post' (see Chapter 8).

THE QUEEN ANNE RECTORY

The decision by John Riland to commission a new rectory in 1701 in what became known as Rectory Park, beside what is now Rectory Road, led to the first purpose-built house, which remained the rectory until 1909. The date of its demolition has been variously 1929, 1935 and 1936, but a press cutting from the *Warwick and Warwickshire Advertiser* of 8 August 1936 confirms it to be that year: '[William] Wilson is believed to have been responsible for the design of Sutton Rectory, which is now being demolished.'

Fig. 12: *The Queen Anne Rectory, built 1701 (SCL)*

This article is in fact about Wilson's home, The Moat House, built on the Lichfield Road in the 1680s and refused permission for demolition to become the police court and offices at this point in the 1930s. It does confirm that Riland is thought to have commissioned local stonemason William Wilson, but this is not apparently proven. More of William Wilson's story can be found in the chapter on parishioners (Chapter 13).

'The house was made to the specifications of 45 feet long, 35 feet deep and 23 feet high and included a wall (later pulled down in 1823) around a forecourt with a large garden,' writes William Kirkpatrick Riland Bedford. (Riland Bedford, 1891, p. 19) He also records that John Riland provided the timber for the house and that its total cost was £239 11s 3d (£239.56p), a sum equivalent to about £25,629.19 in today's money.

A New Vault in the Church

We learn that Sir George Sacheverell of New Hall secured a faculty to install a family vault in 1706 below the floor in the south-west corner of the church. The faculty had to be read to the congregation, in order for any objections to be voiced, by the Rector, who had to swear at the Court in Lichfield that this had happened. According to Norman Evans, there is no mention of any alteration to the windows, so he suggests the monument was wider than originally anticipated as one light from each of the adjacent windows was subsequently blocked in. The memorial was erected in Sacheverell's lifetime with blank space ready for the name of the first burial to be inserted.

The vault itself has been exposed to view in recent times when the floor was replaced in 2016. Archaeological investigation showed:

> The vault contained five coffins in various stages of collapse, four laid with their head ends at the west end of the vault … and the fifth, a rectangular coffin with a circular depositum plate which read 'G S DIED 1715 AGED 82', presumably the coffin of George Sacheverell himself … The remaining coffins (nos 1–4) belonged to his descendants, possibly including his great nephew Charles Sacheverell Chadwick, who inherited his estate in 1715; New Hall remained in possession of the Chadwicks until 1897. (Coutts, 2019, pp 11-12, section 5.14)

The detail continues:

Coffin no 1, in the south-west corner of the vault, belonged to Mary Chadwick (unmarried daughter of Charles Chadwick), who died 1770 aged 70 and had a lead depositum plate above her single break lead coffin … The wooden coffin case had completely disintegrated, leaving oval gilt cherub lid motifs. Coffin no 2 was a fish-tail shaped coffin with no depositum present, but it can be assumed to belong to another member of the Chadwick family, possibly the Charles Chadwick who had inherited New Hall in 1715; he died in 1756. Coffin no 3 belonged to Frances Chadwick, wife of (a later) Charles Chadwick, died 1804. The brass depositum lay on the remains of the wooden coffin case, which had oval gilt cherub motifs and a gilt coronet motif at the head of the coffin, indicating her status as sister of a Baronet … The coffin was badly damaged at the foot end. Coffin no 4, on the northern side of the vault, had a lead shell incised with criss-cross decoration and belonged to Charles Chadwick aged 76, died 1829. The wooden case was covered in black Utrecht velvet. The depositum plate was decorated with an 'all-seeing' eye. (Coutts, 2019, p. 12, section 5.15)

This investigation records that some of the coffins found in the vaults were 'fish-tail' design, an unusual shape not often revealed (see Fig. 13).

Fig. 13: *Fishtail design coffin in Sacheverell vault (AW)*

When Sir George himself died, his name was added to the memorial – a reasonably lavish affair with a skull at the foot, no doubt a customary 'memento mori' of the time. Sir George traced his family roots to a Norman knight fighting alongside William the Conqueror. The poignant part of his story is that he died without issue. He was so concerned to preserve the family name that he insisted his nephew add the name Sacheverell to his own (Chadwick) so that it could still be carried down the generations. Sadly, this nephew also died without heirs, followed by his sister (also childless), and this accounts for the relatively few burials in the vault.

In 1708 a small gallery was erected at the west end of the church in front of the tower for the Ffolliotts of Four Oaks Hall. Henry, Lord Ffolliott, who had built the hall, was married to Elizabeth Pudsey, daughter of Henry and Jane Pudsey, all of whom are buried in the Pudsey vault in the Vesey chapel and commemorated in the Pudsey memorial on the north wall. (However, there is no record of Elizabeth's burial in the parish records of that time). Henry Ffolliott wished to have an uninterrupted view of the chancel, which a gallery in the west end would afford, and duly went through the process of obtaining a faculty for his gallery. Some have questioned why Sir George Sacheverell did not request a gallery himself, but it is thought that he might have seen his box pew in the chancel as being suitably central and adequate for his needs.

In 1745 the roof was found to need extensive repairs (Evans, 1987, p. 9), and the box pews, which had either been replaced or repaired in 1739, appeared again to need renovation. Two further galleries in the south and then north (now Vesey) aisles were built at some time before 1755.

The railings currently outside the south porch entrance to the church were originally installed in 1748 by John Wyrley around the newly restored tomb of Bishop Vesey to protect it.

THE WORKS OF 1760

Following the surveys of 1745, in 1758 the Warden and Society of Sutton Coldfield decided to undertake major repairs and alterations to the church. Norman Evans writes:

£100 was allocated from the Corporation's funds for 'new pewing' … but soon after that had been completed, holes appeared in the floor of the nave and the carpenters were blamed. The building was examined in 1759 when it was discovered that 'the Breach in the Church was occasioned by the Badness of the Foundations of the Arches or Walls in the Middle Isles' [quoting Warden and Society Minutes of 14 May]. (Ibid.)

The corporation instructed a local architect, William Hiorn, to create a plan. Hiorn, together with his brother David, had taken over the illustrious Warwick firm of Francis Smith and his two brothers, who had rebuilt Warwick town centre after the fire of 1694.

Once it was confirmed that the collapse of the nave was owing to the pre-existing poor state of the foundations, not the result of any work by Hiorns or his team in preparing for the new pews, the firm set about the necessary rebuilding, erecting the octagonal pillars in the nave, as we see them today, and surmounting them with round arches to match those in the chancel.

The Warden and Society ordered the felling of further trees in Sutton Park, to the value of £657 (£67,317.73 in today's terms). These also allowed for further woodwork to create the south gallery with its eleven box pews, and the final bill of William Hiorn was settled in 1761. While the work was carried out, the chancel area became a temporary whole church boarded off from the nave. Temporary benches were placed across the chancel and both adjacent side aisle ends.

In total, 146 new box pews of different sizes were created in the church including the chancel (the choir at this point would have sung from the special gallery at the west end of the church). The church could now seat 750.

Roger Lea writes about the aftermath of the new work:

Box pews were regarded as belonging to specific Sutton properties, and there were angry scenes when some householders found that their new pews were less favourably placed than their previous ones. The eleven box pews in the new gallery seem to have been highly rated, box pew no. 7 belonged to Joseph Duncumb of Moat House, William Jesson had no. 6, and 9 went to Mrs. Mary Riland, the Rector's widowed mother. (Lea, Hiorn, HS467, 2017)

Information about the pews has been largely gathered from both Lea, 2017, HS 467 and Evans, 1988, pp. 12–13. In addition, Janet Jordan has researched the story of the complaints about the new pew allocations in a thorough account entitled 'The box pew rumpus of 1762'. Jordan notes that with an emphasis in worship at that time on preaching, the congregation would wish for an unobstructed view of the preacher. She records that the gentry who were now to be seated in the galleries were offered new larger pews, with which they were clearly satisfied. However, the pews in the main body of the church had been paid for by the corporation, which drew up a plan for this area, and this was the cause of dissent, when Hiorns's plan was unveiled in 1762.

Jordan describes the four main causes of the discontent, which dragged on for some time, as follows:

- Unauthorised people claiming some of the seats; just sitting where they liked.
- Some applying directly to the Bishop for permission to occupy some of the most favoured new pews (this was passed to the Spiritual Court in Lichfield to be settled).
- Four former occupants of the north gallery – Richard Whately, Abraham Oughton, Abrahem Jones the younger and Thomas Bonell – complained about the new position of their pews. Jordan notes this was probably reasonable as one of the carpenters referred to the north gallery box pews having been 'built upon a slightly different position' and, specifically, that Box Pew No. 3 in that Gallery was 'slightly larger than the former one and that from part of it the view of the pulpit was obstructed by the new pillar'.
- William Davenport wrote to the Warden and Society saying they had deprived his daughter of a seat formerly hers of right. (Jordan, 2019)
- The Warden and Society refused the complainants and the plan had to be adhered to by all the occupants. The gentlemen of the society cannot have endeared themselves to their community when a minute of one of their meetings referred to 'several greedy people of low rank, intending to take to themselves some of the best seats in this Parish Church'. (Ibid.)

A faculty was finally prepared in 1766 in which the seats were assigned, and this plan lasted until the re-pewing of 1874 (Riland Bedford, 1891, p. 37). As a last word on the pews of that time, these were allocated not to individuals but to residences. The first instance of pews being rented out at Holy Trinity is noted in minutes of the Warden and Society in 1781 when two parishioners each agreed to pay 6*d* (2.5p) for their respective pews annually on Easter Day. (Evans, 1987, p. 195)

Evans notes that the light from the early sixteenth-century window in the tower at the west end of the church has been obscured at two periods of its life, the first being from 1760 to 1879. The stained glass memorial in the window was not added until 1863.

The work of 1760 also entailed the installation of a new organ and the appointment of a contentious organist Dr John Alcock, who had come from Lichfield Cathedral. The organ was a gift from John Riland II, the younger brother of the Rector and, at that point, the curate at Holy Trinity. Dr Alcock had not been popular at Lichfield and was unhappy at Sutton Coldfield with his salary.

A vestry for the choir was added to the tower space behind their gallery. Evans notes that the gallery at the west end and added vestry must have made this

Fig. 14: *The South gallery and box pews of 1760 (HTSC)*

side of the church very dark, especially for those allocated the pews beneath. He writes, 'This was at that time considered to be of little consequence as they were allocated to cottagers who were uneducated and unable to read or write.' (Evans, 1988, p. 13). The stairs to the Four Oaks gallery and choir vestry ascended from the floor in front of the west window at the end of the south aisle (near the Sacheverell monument).

The new gallery in the south aisle is the one that remains in Holy Trinity today exactly as it was constructed, with the box pews still in place (see Fig. 14). The gallery erected in the then north aisle now enabled the portion at the east end to be reserved for the master and pupils of the Grammar School. (ibid.)

One final piece of work is worth noting, as it relates to the former north wall (before the north extension was built). It was decided to take the opportunity of all the work going on at this point to improve the natural light in the north-west corner of the church. Accordingly, a new window was inserted on the north wall (near the west end) and the window on the west wall was enlarged. (Evans, 1987, p 182-4) The north wall was demolished in 1879 and the appearance of the north-west area was changed then and again in the re-ordering work of 2016.

OTHER FIXTURES

The font of the time was placed in the middle aisle under the Four Oaks Gallery. According to Norman Evans, it consisted of a marble basin on a classic pedestal. (Evans, 1987, p. 56)

The pulpit was made as part of this work and positioned on the south side of the chancel with the tester (roof) supported by two Corinthian columns. More information about the pulpit is in Chapter 10 on the church woodwork.

The external clock on the tower is said by WK Riland Bedford to have been installed at the time of the 1760 work. A guide to Sutton Coldfield states that it was erected in 1758 and made by John Height of Pershore (Sidwell and Durant, 3rd edn, 1900, p. 10). The clock was on a square surround and faced High Street (on the north side of the tower). The mechanism was in the bell-ringing chamber with a weight at ground floor level held in place in a groove still visible today. The clock was removed in 1884.

The other alteration of 1760 was the replacement of the west end (Ffolliott) gallery by a larger one for the new owner of Four Oaks Hall, Simon Luttrell, and his bigger family.

In 1779 a further small gallery measuring 20ft by 9ft (c600cm by 270cm) containing three box pews was erected between the Four Oaks Gallery on the west end and the north gallery for Robert Lawley of Canwell, a worshipper at Holy Trinity, and his family. This was accessed from the staircase then in existence in the northwest corner for access to the 1760 north gallery. The building of the gallery is not recorded, but Norman Evans cites a faculty with plan in Lichfield Record Office of 25 May 1779 for this information (Evans, 1987, p. 13), and Riland Bedford records its being demolished in 1879 (p. 74). Evans both translates the faculty and has an image of the original in the appendix to his work. (Evans, 1987, p. 197–202)

THE PARISH OF HOLY TRINITY IN THE 1770S

In 1772, the Rector, Richard Bisse Riland, described his parish in a letter to the Bishop (of Lichfield and Coventry). This is worth quoting in full, as it describes not just the physical layout of the parish at this time, but also the families 'of note' and the different Christian denominations now emerging at this point. Riland Bedford quotes it as follows:

> The parish of Sutton Coldfield is nearly of an oval figure, whose longest diameter is seven miles, and shortest four, it comprehends several hamlets, viz. Maney, Hill, Little Sutton, Warmley (*sic*) and Wigginshill, besides several single farmhouses and cottages dispersed at considerable distances from each other and from the church. The whole number of houses is 376. The families of note are those of Simon Luttrell, Lord Irnham, at Four Oaks Hall, Charles Sacheverell Chadwick, Esq., of New Hall, R. Lawley Esq., only son of Sir R.L. Bart, A. Hacket, Esq., John Hacket, Esq., of Moor Hall, second son of the former (the lineal descendants of Bishop H. of Lichfield and Coventry), T. Duncomb, Esq., W. Jesson Esq., and many other gentlemen.
>
> There are three Roman Catholic families in my parish, the master of one of them is a carpenter, and hath several children, the other two are day labourers.

But none have been lately perverted to popery, nor is there any place in my parish where they assemble to worship. No Popish priest hath resorted to the parish of late years, or exercised any ministerial functions that I know of.

There is only one family of Quakers in my parish, and a meeting house at the aforesaid hamlet called Wigginshill, but a congregation is very seldom assembled there, the building being small and ill convenient. I know of no Anabaptists nor Moravians in my parish, nor of any Presbyterians who abstain from the church as such, there is one meeting house of Independents within the town of Sutton Coldfield, which is duly licensed at the sessions, whither they who are called Methodists do also resort, to the amount (I believe) of eight or ten families, and their number is rather increased lately, because they have now a regular teacher, Mr. Abraham Austin (Riland Bedford, 1891, p. 40).

RB Riland goes on to bemoan the poor attendance at some services; no more than 120 at festivals and seventy at monthly sacraments. From a population of 376 households this actually sounds a reasonable figure by today's standards, especially as the frail would have been unable to walk the distance, and some would not have been released from work. He does say that all have been baptised either by the Parish Church or the non-conformist communities (see also p. 202ff).

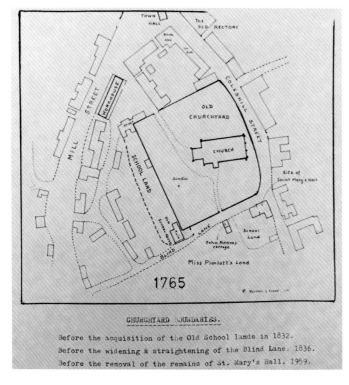

Fig. 15: *John Snape's map of Church Hill 1765 (NGE)*

Fig. 16: *Artist's impression of Church Hill based on Snape's map (Fig. 15) (BM)*

Figs. 15 and 16 represent respectively a map of Church Hill in 1765, as redrawn by Norman Evans, and an artist's impression (Bob Moulder) of that view.

CHURCH BELLS

It is thought that the bells installed in Bishop Vesey's time (from Canwell Priory) had become a ring (set) of six bells by 1778. A new ring of bells of 1784 was replaced just a few years later (1795).

A website called 'Church bells of Warwickshire' records the detail:

There was a ring of 6 cast by Thomas Mears in 1795, tenor 22cwt. These were the successors to the four bells and a saunce [sanctus] bell that was in the tower at the time of the 1552 inventory. These became 6 by 1778, at the latest. Rudhalls supplied a ring of 6 in 1786, Tilley and Walters note that the Corporation voted 100 guineas for a new ring in 1784 and that a certain William Hughes was killed by a piece of timber which fell while the workmen were preparing to put up the bells. They therefore speculate that this ring was short lived. This speculation is accurate, as Mears provided a new ring less than 10 years after the Rudhall ring was installed. Two of these bells remain in the present ring. (www.warksbells.co.uk)

GLEBE LAND

A feature of the seventeenth and eighteenth centuries at Holy Trinity is the recurrence of formal information about the 'glebe' – a portion of land assigned to the incumbent of a parish. For the Rector of Sutton Coldfield, this territory extended from Coleshill Street along what is now Rectory Road as far as open common land beyond the current Hollyfield Road. Successive 'terriers' (records of the land held, field names, etc.) were created in 1612, 1698, 1705, 1767 and 1779–92. Norman Evans provides further detail about this in a section of the appendices to his book entitled 'Sutton Coldfield Rectory tithes'. (Evans, 1987, pp. 121–127). This is followed by a section entitled 'The glebe and the parsonage' (Ibid., pp. 128–133). A map of the glebe land by John Snape created in 1761 provides

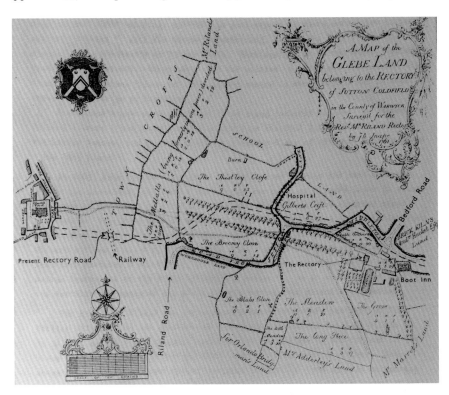

Fig. 17: *Snape's map of Glebe land overlaid with newer landmarks by NG Evans (NGE)*

useful detail of this area. Norman Evans has overlaid it with the names of land-marks and additions from a later date (the railway, 1701 rectory, Good Hope Hospital and even the Boot Inn opposite the hospital). This helps to add context to the earlier map (Fig. 17).

In his study, Evans describes the various elements of the tithes paid in 1698 in a table, reproduced below, an example of the tithe system at this period (Table 2).

The parish of Sutton Coldfield is divided into eight areas, most of which are recognisable to us today, although 'Beyond the wood' refers to the area beyond Fox Hollies Road. The tithes from 'liveings' were from the various businesses, such as they were, mainly the larger farms and the mills. These would be paid in the equivalent amount of goods, with hay being stored in the tithe barn which Bishop Vesey had built the previous century in High Street. Cottagers with small-holdings paid a fixed tithe (two pence per cottage per annum) equivalent to about one day's pay. Landed gentry would pay varying amounts between four pence and one shilling.

Areas of the Parish	'Liveings'	Cottages	Houses	Received by the Rector £ – s – d.
Great Sutton	10	54	20	2 – 4 – 4.
Hill	7	30	5	7 – 11.
Hill Hooke	–	22	–	3 – 8.
Little Sutton	12	26	10	10 – 4.
Moore & Ashfurlong	14	36	13	1 – 5 – 10.
Beyond the Wood	7	14	12	17 – 10.
Wormley	20	14	8	2 – 4 – 7.
Many and the Wild	5	14	11	3 – 12 – 9.
Wigginshill	11	–	–	1 – 0 – 8.
Total:-	86	230	79	12 – 7 – 11.

Signed: John Riland, Rector
Table 2: *Record of the tithes to the Rector in 1698 (from Evans, 1987, p. 122)*

Evans notes that part of the corn tithe in Wigginshill would go to the 'impropriator of Curdworth' and that the New Hall estate and mill, in the area of Maney, required George Sacheverell in this year to pay a tithe of £3.00 – a sum which appears to be a major proportion of the total received from this area. (Evans, 1987, p. 122)

4

THE NINETEENTH CENTURY

Following the significant amount of building and renovation work of the later eighteenth century, one might be forgiven for thinking there would have been a lull in changes to Holy Trinity in the succeeding century. However, this was a period of expansion to towns, and this century would see increased population, industrialisation, the coming of the railway, improved road networks and greater social change. All this would have an impact on both the church and the town of Sutton Coldfield.

Administratively, the old diocese of Lichfield and Coventry, which covered a huge expanse of the country, was reduced in size in 1836, and the old area of Mercia was distributed among the following dioceses: Lincoln, Peterborough, Ely, St Alban's, Oxford, Gloucester, Worcester and Chester. The Archdeaconry of Coventry, which included Sutton Coldfield, was transferred to the Diocese of Worcester. Lichfield remained as a diocese, with Coventry relinquishing its diocesan status at this point. (Evans, 1987, p. 120)

EDUCATION – THE GRAMMAR SCHOOL

The grammar school founded by Bishop Vesey was undergoing changes, and a new headmaster, Charles Barker, was appointed in 1817 at the age of 25. He had previously taught at Rugby School. He does not appear to have been universally liked, and Kerry Osbourne, chronicler of the school's history, writes that he:

> was content to have a handful of classical scholars and to devote the rest of his time to the management of the estates, and his private affairs. In addition to his political interests and enthusiasm for the chase, Barker turned his hand to writing poetry. (Osbourne, 1990, p. 79)

Fryer, in his biography of John Vesey, notes that Barker favoured the Classics over the English class.

Fig. 18: *Watercolour of High Street with Holy Trinity c1850. By AE Everitt (SCL)*

The background to all of this is the introduction of more elementary education in addition to the teaching of Greek and Latin in a grammar school. Osbourne gives the context as follows:

Back in 1727, when the old school by the church had fallen into disrepair and the School moved to its present site in Lichfield Road, the land was bought by the Sutton Corporation and the cost of building the school was shared by the Corporation and the Master, Paul Lowe. The Corporation granted Lowe a lease of the land and it was a condition of the lease that he taught a class of twelve parish boys English and Mathematics. Barker took over this lease when he was appointed as Master in 1817, together with the teaching obligations. In 1828 Barker suggested that the school trustees should give the old school site near the church to the Corporation to enlarge the churchyard in exchange for the Corporation transferring the freehold interest in the new school to the trustees. For the future of the School this was the best thing that could have happened, but Barker's motive was that once the Corporation no longer owned the freehold the lease became of no effect, and the teaching obligation in the lease came to an end. In this way Barker managed to get out of any responsibility for elementary education. (Email to the author, 2019)

Osbourne's chapter, tellingly entitled 'Charles Barker, parents' complaints', charts some of the dissent with his headmastership of the school.

In relation to Holy Trinity, Barker also divided up the pews in the former north gallery of the church (previously reserved for pupils and masters) and sub-let them to parishioners at two guineas (£2.10) a year. Barker did become Warden of the Town in 1836 and 1837, so must have resolved any difficulties there.

There is a memorial plaque in marble to him under the tower in Holy Trinity (moved in 1879 from the former north wall). His death was untimely in 1842; he had fallen from his horse and was later found on the road, the horse having returned home without him. (See Evans, 1987, p. 59)

EDUCATION – A SCHOOL FOR YOUNGER CHILDREN

In 1825 the Sutton Charities had sufficient funds to establish schools for poorer children in three areas – Sutton Town, Hill and Walmley. The pupils would be expected to attend church, and in Holy Trinity provision was made for those at the new town school to attend. Extensions were made to the south and north galleries of the time over the aisle extensions (current Vesey chapel and choir vestry) at the east end of each. It was not deemed suitable for the children to be part of the general congregation, so their galleries (separated for boys in the south gallery and girls in the north) were separated from the main galleries by curtains, and spiral staircases to each were constructed in the aisle ends, leading off new small external arched doorways in the east wall.

The galleries were demolished again in 1868. The doorways were bricked in, although the one to the south side was in use from 1901 to 1950 as a side entrance to the organ at that time. Both outlines can be seen externally, but only the door-way for the north side can be seen internally – by looking between the upper and lower parts of the Jesson memorial in the north-east corner of the Vesey chapel. Parishioner Harold Osborne took a photograph of the church exterior from the east in 1910 which clearly shows the external door to the children's gallery on the left-hand (south) side, which at this point was in use for access to the church so that maintenance of the organ could be undertaken (Fig. 19).

Fig. 19: *Holy Trinity in 1910 showing small doorway in east end (HWSO)*

CLERGY VESTRIES

With the building of the gallery extensions, the vestry in the south-east corner chapel was abandoned and a new one built in the floor of the tower. The west door was replaced by a cast iron tracery window, and a new door fitted on the south-west side of the tower (now visible externally with its replacement in ashlar stone). The floor was at a different height from now.

It may be presumed that this new arrangement was not entirely satisfactory, as a new clergy vestry was built in 1874 in the north-west corner beyond the Vesey chapel. This is still in use today and is probably much more practical, being nearer the chancel and at the same floor height as the main church floor.

CHURCHYARD

In 1832 it was necessary to look at enlarging the burial ground, and this was achieved by incorporating land under the ruins of Bishop Vesey's original school of 1541. An old brick wall, demolished at this time, marked the boundary of the old school and ran from the east corner of the Sons of Rest building to near the single sycamore tree in the churchyard.

The path from Coleshill Street on the south-east side, which leads to what was until 2016 the main entrance through the south porch, came into existence in 1817 for easier access to the churchyard. Prior to that there was an entrance further down Trinity Hill called Blind Lane.

Further churches were built in other areas of Sutton Coldfield as the century progressed, each with their own burial grounds, and this eased the increasing demand for space. The churches were St James Hill (1835), which had been a chapel of ease of Holy Trinity, St John's, Walmley (1845) where Lucy Riland, the daughter of the previous Rector, gave £1,000 towards the new building, and St Michael's, Boldmere (1857).

In 1876 the Burial Board for Holy Trinity (with the approval of the Secretary of State) considered locations for a new burial ground as the extended graveyard was now full. The board bought 6 acres of Barn Field off Rectory Road for £1,500 and paid half the cost of building the Rectory Road site. The new cemetery was consecrated by the Bishop of Worcester on 4 May 1880 and the first burial was on Monday 1 November. More information about the churchyard changes and burials in this period are in Chapter 8.

FONT

The font is much older than Holy Trinity, dating at least from Norman and possibly Saxon times. It had been removed from the church of St Leonard's, Over Whitacre in North Warwickshire, when that church had a considerable refurbishment. Subsequently it was discovered by Richard Sadler, a resident of High Street in Sutton Coldfield, upside down in the churchyard, where it was used by customers of the neighbouring inn as a mounting block to climb onto their horses. Richard took it home and put it in his garden. On his death in 1856, his son (also called Richard, and a churchwarden at Holy Trinity) gave it to the church, where it replaced the previous font thought to date from the eighteenth century. The bowl of that font was transferred to the newly-delivered one.

WORKS OF 1863

In 1863 there was a need for the church to be re-roofed. A decision was made also to enlarge the clerestory windows (just under the roof in the nave) and both to raise and increase the pitch of the roof. When the work was begun, a further complication arose with the window at the tower end. Its position on the east wall of the tower was not central, meaning that the roof needed to be raised higher than was originally planned to accommodate this. The slit window is now also obstructed on the inside by the roof timber. (Evans, 1987, pp. 62–3)

Richard Holbeche commented unfavourably in his memoirs as follows:

> Now comes the dear old church, much altered now, and, it must be admitted for the better, though I cannot think that some of the alterations have been carried out without a great deal of taste, notably the peaked roof of the nave, which from outside dwarfs the noble tower. (Holbeche, 1893, p. 11)

The Four Oaks Gallery in front of the tower had become neglected since the estate had been sold, and the decision was taken to demolish this and the choir gallery and to move the choir into the south chapel, where a new organ (by Gray and Davidson) would be installed. This enabled the west archway to be cleared and the west window high in the tower to be visible again (though this would be plain glass at this point).

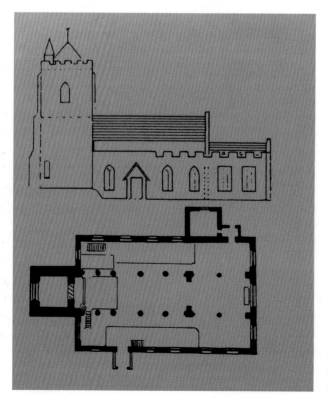

Fig. 20: *Floorplan and elevation of Holy Trinity to 1874 (NGE)*

Another major work of 1863 was the installation of the stained glass into the main east end window (in the chancel), dedicated to the memory of William Riland Bedford, the Rector who was father of William Kirkpatrick Riland Bedford and who had died in 1843. This is described more fully in Chapter 9 about the stained glass in the church.

VESEY CHAPEL

In 1870 the children's benches were removed from the Vesey chapel and replaced by pews for adults facing the chancel. One presumes these children's benches had been moved downstairs from the children's galleries demolished a couple of years earlier. The stained glass was installed in the east end window, known as the Bishops' window as it commemorates four Bishops who had some association with Holy Trinity. Full detail about this and the other window in the chapel is in Chapter 9.

CHANGES TO THE CHANCEL

In 1875 the chancel floor was raised. This was presumably to give a better view to the congregation of that area and also to accommodate the choir, as cathedrals were now tending to do, bringing them from the west end galleries to the east end where worship is focused, especially Holy Communion.

Another reason for this change was that woodwork had been acquired from Worcester Cathedral, which had undergone internal changes in 1864, releasing large amounts of woodwork which were then sold to other churches. Holy Trinity paid £100 for the substantial amount that came to the church and was used across the two aisle ends and the chancel in the east end. The story of this woodwork and our new understanding of its provenance is given in more detail in Chapter 8.

The raising of the floor meant that brasses commemorating burials were moved to the walls on the north-east and south-east corners of the chancel. The vault under the floor was the burial ground for Rectors, and for two centuries all members of the Riland and Riland Bedford families. The two brasses which were moved are, however, of others: Barbara Elyot (d. 1606), the wife of Rector Roger Elyot, and Josias Bull, who was buried in 1621. More detail about these is in Chapter 8.

The year 1875 also saw work on the tomb of Bishop Vesey, and at this point the wrought iron railings around the tomb were removed and made into gates outside the porch on the south entrance, where they are still in place today.

HOLY TRINITY RECTORY

During the nineteenth century the rectory in Rectory Park continued to serve as the home of the Rector and his family. Discussion has arisen at various times about the cottages in Coleshill Street, now numbered as 1, 3 and 5, which had been thought to be an earlier rectory for the church. Roger Lea has researched this and writes as follows:

> The reference to the barn as a tithe barn [in the diary of Sarah Holbeche], and the earlier purchase of the property from the Rector, gave rise to the belief that it had once been the Rectory of Sutton Coldfield (the build-ing of a new rectory in Rectory Park in 1701 is well documented). The Victorian Rector and historian of our town, W.K.Riland Bedford, himself believed this, writing 'The Rectory house itself was in the main street, close to the Church.' Recent research has thrown doubt on this, however, as it can be shown that the property was purchased, probably in 1757, for the widow of the Rector Richard Riland, whose son Richard Bisse Riland became Rector that year. The previous owner of 1,3 and 5 Coleshill Street was Thomas Woodhouse, Warden of Sutton in 1752; the 1742 Rental refers to the property as 'The Swan', so it may have been an inn at one time. (Lea, The Holbeche Swan, HS 398, 22 Jan 2016)

Sarah Holbeche quoted the price paid by her father in 1817 for the house as £1,700. (Jordan, 2001, p. 11)

Further confusion is sometimes made with the house which served as a rectory following the transfer of the patronage to the Diocese of Birmingham in 1907 until 1998. This was a house in Coleshill Street on the other side of Trinity Hill from the church. It was built in the 1840s, and the date of its construction as well as its location in the same street as these other cottages has sometimes created further confusion about when it served as the rectory (not during the nineteenth century, in fact).

THE LAST EXTENSION OF HOLY TRINITY

The coming of the railway to Sutton Coldfield, with the station relatively close to the town centre, encouraged a rise in the population, along with increasing industrialisation. It was felt that the church needed to be enlarged to accommo-date more people, despite the addition of churches in growing areas of population on the outskirts of the town in Hill, Walmley and Boldmere. This major work began with the addition of the clergy vestry to the north wall of the Vesey chapel in 1874, which has remained unchanged following the re-ordering of 2016. The vestry covered part of the churchyard, including the grave of Sir William Wilson. A new memorial to him was made and put in the vestry in 1879 where it can still be seen on the wall adjoining the Vesey chapel.

That year also saw the last major extension to the church with the replacement of the north wall by pillars to match those in the nave, and the erection of a further aisle and gallery, now named the north aisle and gallery. The previous north gallery and wall were demolished, and the aisle became the Vesey aisle leading to the Bishop's tomb in the north-east end.

The box pews were removed from the church with the exception of the south gallery where they remain to this day, and were replaced throughout the church with open pewing characteristic of the Victorian era. The north gallery also extended across the west wall, cutting some of the light from the west window. The stairs led from the base of the tower in a wide spiral to the end of the western edge of this gallery. A press cutting from the *Leamington Spa Courier* of 11 June 1892 notes that the church at this point 'contains sittings for 909 worshippers, including 10 chairs and 263 in galleries'. It also usefully gives the dimensions of each part of the church at that point as follows:

Nave	57ft x 18.5 ft	
Chancel	28.5ft x 18 ft	
North chancel aisle	27.5 ft x 16 ft	(now the Vesey chapel)
South chancel aisle	15 ft x 13 ft	(now the choir vestry / south chapel)
North aisle no. 1	54.5 ft x 16.5 ft	(now the Vesey aisle)
North aisle no. 2	54.5 ft x 15 ft	(now the north aisle)
South aisle	54.5 ft x 13 ft	
Porch	12 ft x 7.5 ft	
North vestry	12 ft x 11 ft	
Organ chamber	16 ft x 13 ft	(built into the tower, with the ringing chamber above, hence the same dimensions as the tower floor beneath)
Western tower	16 ft x 13 ft	

These dimensions confirm our description of the church today as looking 'as broad as it is long'. Similar dimensions given at a later date are in Chapter 5 on the twentieth century.

During these alterations, the ceiling in the Vesey aisle was raised to its present level. Its former height would have been the same as the current ceiling height in both the Vesey chapel and the south aisle where the gallery remains (as would have been the look in the Vesey aisle with its gallery before the extension of 1879).

In 1879 Rectory Road was created, giving a properly surfaced road between the rectory and the church.

ALTAR TABLE

On the death of his wife Amy in 1890, the Rector, William Kirkpatrick Riland Bedford, gave a new communion table in her memory (still in use). The wood of the previous table was used to form part of the screen to divide the south chapel (now choir vestry) from the south aisle. To begin with, it formed a handrail on top of lower panels (4ft 6in high), which hid the organ housed there from the rest of the church. (Evans, 1987, p. 42) Wording on the screen explains this. It was subsequently raised higher.

The Popular Guide to Sutton Park of 1900 includes a picture of the Revd William Kirkpatrick Riland Bedford, suggesting he had a hand in the content although it is by Sidwell and Durant. The section on the church (Sidwell and Durant, 1900, pp. 9–11) includes a reference to the Vatican taxation valuation of 1291 and cites 'authority Mr Bloxam'. Riland Bedford quotes this authority, describing him as an architect, although Wikipedia describes him as 'a Warwickshire antiquary and amateur archaeologist'. Matthew Holbeche Bloxam (12 May 1805–24 April 1888) hailed from Rugby and was a member of another branch of the Holbeche family (see Ince, 2012).

BELLS AND CLOCK

Norman Evans writes that by 1884 the current six bells at Holy Trinity 'had become cracked and the clock had begun to disturb Divine Service by "groaning".' (Evans, 1987, p. 65) A quotation was sought for replacing the bells and the clock, which came in at about £680. After discussion it was agreed that the clock was no longer essential as there was now a reliable clock on the Town Hall. So a fund was opened to raise money for the bells alone, and this secured sufficient funds for not just six, but a ring of eight bells in total, thanks to the 'liberality of several gentlemen' (Ibid.).

The work was completed by November 1884 by the Loughborough-based firm of Messrs John Taylor at a cost of £410 6s 6d. A frame was constructed in the tower to enable an extra tier to be built for two bells above the space for the other six. A special peal was rung in December by a band of ringers from Birmingham, who declared afterwards that 'the go of the bells was all that could be desired'. (Ibid.)

EXTENSION PLANS OF 1891

The archives in the Library of Birmingham contain a number of boxes of papers and plans relating to Holy Trinity. An interesting series of drawings by Birmingham architects HR Yeoville Thomason (in Birmingham Archives – ref: MS 1460/86) show plans for a further extension to the church on the eastern end, which were drawn in 1891. These are stamped 'Not executed', which would

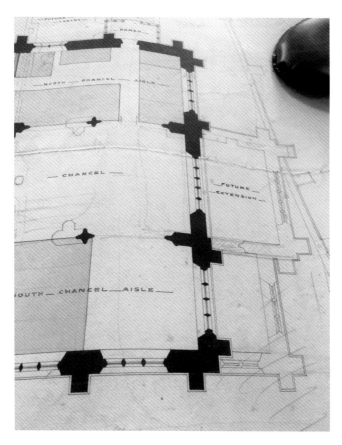

Fig. 21: *Extension plan of 1891 (part) by Yeoville Thomason (not executed) (BA)*

appear with hindsight to be a blessing for a number of reasons. The church was already the largest in the area, with 909 spaces, and with additional churches being provided, it seems now that it would have been a mistake to make it even larger and potentially even darker. With the coming of electricity to the town just a few years later, there would have been further drains on the coffers to pay for heating and lighting too. It is hard from the twenty-first century perspective to gauge exactly how such an extension would have affected what now looks like a limited amount of space on the eastern side before a sheer drop to Coleshill Street, a narrow street anyway and with beautiful buildings on its opposite side which might have had to make way for this. Furthermore, it would have disturbed both the only extant brickwork from the thirteenth century in the church (below the east window) and the window itself, which had not very long had stained glass added to its sixteenth-century frame. A part of the plan is shown at Fig. 21.

Fig. 22: *Artist's impression of Holy Trinity interior in 1850 (BM)*

The Reverend William Kirkpatrick Riland Bedford retired in 1892. He was the longest-serving of any Rector (forty-two years) and his incumbency saw these major changes to the church from 1863 onwards. He also wrote extensively about the church and town, was active in civic and political life – being warden in 1854 and 1855 – and was celebrated toward the end of his life (1898) when the townspeople erected the lychgate on Coleshill Street. The inscription reads, 'Erected by the parishioners and friends of the Revd WKR Bedford as a memorial of his 42 years occupation of the rectory of Sutton Coldfield. Easter 1898.' (Evans, 1987, p. 82)

The final work of the century was to raise funds for a new choir vestry and organ. This was facilitated during the tenure of Revd William Campbell Riland Bedford (who had succeeded his father as Rector in 1892) by a fund-raising bazaar in the town hall in 1899. More information about this and other fund-raising efforts is in the information about the church in the town (Chapter 6).

The bazaar helped to raise the necessary funds, and the new choir vestry was designed by William Henry Bidlake (1861–1938), a leading figure of the Arts and Crafts movement, who later became director of the School of Architecture in Birmingham. It was constructed at the north-west corner of the church and had two doors, one accessed from a corridor to the tower and the other from steps up from the recently added northern aisle. The work was completed in 1901, along with a new organ, and fuller details on that instrument follow in the next chapter. Fig. 22 shows an artist's impression by Bob Moulder of the interior of the church in 1850.

THE DEATH OF MARY ASHFORD – A FOOTNOTE TO THE NINETEENTH CENTURY

The story of Mary Ashford has been much written about in the 200 years since her death, and some might prefer not to see it in a history of the church as it is not about the building or even a member of the church congregation. But some account of the story should be recorded, as Mary is buried in the churchyard at Holy Trinity; her gravestone is still accessible and the inscription still partially legible for those who wish to view it. Moreover, following the trial of Abraham Thornton, accused of her murder, two landmark changes in British law were made, and this is also worthy of record.

Mary was young (aged 20), when she was found drowned in a pool early one morning in 1817 following an evening spent at a dance, after last being seen in the company of Abraham Thornton. The investigation was of its time, with inadequate and misleading 'evidence', inconsistent witness statements and the whole mired in pre-Victorian preconceptions about innocent girls, the reputation of young men and ignorance of scientific investigation or the workings of the human body. Money was raised by a clergyman in another part of the town for an inscription for Mary's tomb extolling her virtues. The public were outraged that Thornton was acquitted and his throwing of the gauntlet to challenge Mary's brother set legal minds buzzing that this form of legal challenge was still on the statute books. This law was soon removed, as was the previous right to charge someone for the same crime twice, also used in this case.

Many are the writings about the Mary Ashford story and there are some sources for further reading in the references to this volume. Richard Holbeche, in his diary about life in the 1850s, noted that 'The Church yard was very badly kept, and sheep grazed it. It was unincloaed and the Birmingham roughs used to sit and make a noise about Mary Ashford's grave during service'.

Fig. 23: *Nave looking East c1881 (SCL)*

Fig. 24: *Church Hill in 1906 (SCL)*

5

THE TWENTIETH
CENTURY AND BEYOND

INTRODUCTION

The momentous changes of the twentieth century could not fail to leave marks on Holy Trinity. While changes in liturgy and in the role of women as leaders in worship, theology and pastoral work affected the spiritual life of Christians, there were also further changes socially with family life, social structures and technological advances from cars through aeroplanes to information technology. In terms of the building, Holy Trinity benefitted in the twentieth century from the introduction of electricity, a major programme to embellish and decorate four large areas of the ceiling, and the refurbishment work and formation of the Vesey chapel in 1929. More stained glass was introduced, including a memorial to a parishioner killed in France in the First World War. The 'war to end wars' spawned further conflicts and the two world wars would forever change both church attendance and social structures.

More Anglican churches were built in other districts of the town, and churches of other denominations were added in every district too. A major change at Holy Trinity was the end of the patronage of the Riland and Riland Bedford families, meaning that the church was now under the oversight of the newly created Diocese of Birmingham.

Diocesan changes were also completed locally with the reinstatement of Coventry as a diocese in 1910. Following the break-up of the large diocese of Lichfield and Coventry in 1836, there was for a while a suffragan Bishop of Coventry, and early thoughts were for the diocese of Birmingham to cover Coventry too. This was not workable, and it was owing to the planning of the new Bishop of Worcester in 1902, Charles Gore, that the Diocese of Birmingham was finally established in 1905, with Gore as the first Bishop. His replacement at Worcester completed arrangements to re-establish the diocese of Coventry.

Further changes to Holy Trinity included the closure of the churchyard and the establishment of a new cemetery off Rectory Road. The memorial headstones

Fig. 25: *The Hope-Jones organ console in the Vesey chapel c1910 (HWSO)*

around the church were moved in 1950. At the end of the century the unsatisfactory and changing arrangements for church meetings and community group activity were resolved with the opening of the purpose-built Trinity Centre.

In the twenty-first century the re-ordering of the church was finally realised in 2016–18, with changes to equip the church building for the new century, making it accessible, warmer, lighter and more flexible to meet the varied needs of the congregation and community.

THE FIRST DECADE

The Rectory Act of 1907 precipitated the move to be part of the diocese of Birmingham. This is discussed in more detail in Chapter 11 about the Rectors of Holy Trinity.

During the incumbency of William Campbell Riland Bedford, electricity was installed in the church and this enabled a new organ using electricity to be installed in the south gallery and chapel in 1901, made by organ-builders Hope-Jones.

Fig. 26: *Nave looking west c.1930 (SCL)*

Former parishioner Harold Osborne wrote a good deal in his memoirs about playing the Hope-Jones organ. (Osborne, 2017, pp. 43-4) He describes meeting Robert Hope-Jones and reflects on his pioneering work in developing an organ to work on electricity, noting the pitfalls of the Hope-Jones system and how the organs he built (including those at Worcester Cathedral and Holy Trinity, Stratford-upon-Avon) were subsequently overhauled by the firm of Norman and Beard.

This information and the photograph at Fig. 25 have only recently come to light in the publication by Osborne's grandson, Geoff Howell, of the memoirs in 2017. (The memoirs were written in the 1940s and described the period when Osborne worked in Birmingham from 1906 to 1913, although Osborne stayed with family at 'The Knoll' on Coleshill Street, so knew the area before that time).

Stained glass was added to the two lights of the window in the western end of the north wall of the church wall after the First World War to commemorate the young son of a church family. Details of this are in Chapter 9.

DECORATIVE WORK OF 1914 AND 1929

In 1914 Charles Bateman was commissioned to paint the ceiling of the Chancel. This was duly completed (full details are in Chapter 7), but the remaining ceilings were not completed until 1929, because of the interruption of the First World War and subsequent period of economic depression.

In 1929 the painting was incorporated into a major programme of work, comprising the following:

- A screen, given in memory of Canon Charles Barnard by his daughter, which divided the area at the east end of the Vesey aisle into a separate chapel, renamed the Vesey chapel.
- Painting of the Vesey chapel, nave and tower ceilings, to complete work started in 1914.
- Removal of the Lord's Prayer and Ten Commandments boards from the nave arch.
- Fabric hangings and riddle posts placed either side of the main altar table in the east end (removed in the 1990s).
- Re-decoration of the whole church.

Minor restoration of the tower ceiling, which was uncovered in the re-ordering of 2016, revealed the names of the workmen who had undertaken the painting, tucked into the north-west panel of the ceiling and discovered when the ceiling was cleaned of extraneous paint in October 2018:

Fig. 27: *Architect and others who worked on decoration of 1929 (HTSC)*

DECORATIONS ETC. BY
JOHN WOOD LTD
C. E. BATEMAN (ARCHITECT)   FRANK Hughes
C. G. GRAY (DESIGNER)   PHIL Holmes
SEPT. 1929

This can no longer be seen, but two photographs taken in 2018 show the whole as illustrated at Fig. 27.

At the end of the work of 1929, a service of thanksgiving was held on 19 October, after which bell-ringers from St Martin's-in-the-Bullring rang *a* peal of 'Stedman Triples', conducted by George Swann. See Fig. 26 for an image of the nave at this time.

POST-1945

After the Second World War the pulpit, columns and tester were moved just 5ft further north than the previous position in the nave, which was nearer to the chancel steps. The entrance steps were from the chancel floor. The pulpit occupies the same position today, albeit with new steps on the north side, allowing for more space in the chancel area. These steps were created in 2016 as part of the major re-ordering of the interior of the church.

The tower floors have changed height several times to accommodate the ringers' floor, and, between 1950 and 2018, to incorporate the pipes and electrical mechanism of the organ used at that time for worship. The new organ replaced the 1901 Hope-Jones instrument.

A service of dedication led by the Lord Bishop of Birmingham, E. W. Barnes, was combined with a 650-year celebration of the founding of the church (deemed at this point and in the year 2000 to have been 1300) on Saturday 9 December 1950 at 3 p.m. The order of service has a description of the new organ written by the then organist and director of music, Harold Gray, a noted Birmingham organist and conductor who served at Holy Trinity for fifty years. He notes the provision of a main organ sited under the west arch and a separate organ in the chancel to support the choir, especially when singing alone. The main console had three manuals and the specification was as follows:

Great organ	512 speaking pipes
Swell organ	598 speaking pipes
Choir organ	464 pipes
Pedal organ	5 x 16ft stops
Chancel organ	268 speaking pipes.

The last of the four artist's impressions of the church is shown at Fig. 28, of the interior in 1950, with Canon Boggon as Rector.

Fig. 28: *Artist's impression of church interior in 1950 (BM)*

CHURCHYARD

In 1950 or thereabouts, the gravestones immediately around the church were making it difficult for maintenance of the grounds to be effected, and some stones were no longer being cared for. At first it was agreed they would be laid flat so that mowing could proceed around them, but later it was decided to move them completely and they were moved to be upright against the perimeter wall of the churchyard. They are currently in this position around the car park area. Sadly, no one thought to record the names at any stage, and many are no longer legible. More information about the extant gravestones is in Chapter 8.

In 1959, the Georgian house, which had been built in the 1720s on the site of the former St Mary's Hall on the south side of the church, was demolished to allow the corner of Trinity Hill and Coleshill Street to be widened. The ownership of this land passed briefly to the corporation to allow this to happen, but then reverted, along with the cottage at the top of the hill next to the former rectory, to church ownership. The cottage was used at various times as a curate's house from c1990 until it was sold in 2016.

A new cemetery for Sutton Coldfield was built off Lindridge Road at the far end of Rectory Road in 2002, as the Rectory Road site was itself full. In 1987 Holy Trinity sought permission to inter ashes in an area on the south-east side of the churchyard, but there are no external memorials where this takes place.

LIBRARY

Two stained glass windows were added in the 1960s to the south chapel (now choir vestry), and these are described in more detail in Chapter 9. Major alterations were made to this chapel in 1960 with light oak panelling installed to create cupboards for a library, and two chairs and a table in the same oak. The whole was dedicated to William Douglas Edward Clayton, a dental surgeon in the town and churchwarden for many years. The library was not a hugely successful designation, because the entrance required steps up and over some heating pipes, so it was not easy to access. Originally parish records were stored here, but latterly there have just been back issues of the church magazine and one or two books (mostly Bibles) that had been given to the church. In the 1980s it became an overflow repository for the choir music, which has made more sense for its use following the re-ordering, where the space as a whole has become the choir vestry. The large oak chairs are now in the chancel of the church.

Fig. 29: *Bell-ringing chamber in tower (HTSC)*

BELLS

As early as 1929 disquiet was expressed about the bells (installed in 1884 in two tiers), as they had become difficult to ring. By 1965 quotations were sought and the recommendation was to remove them all, retune them and then hang them in one space, specially strengthened for the purpose. This would not only help the bells to ring better, it would rectify deterioration in the main lower chamber, which was thought to date from 1795. The major problem with this plan was that the organ installed in 1950 was now blocking the best exit route for the bells, as the only window was too small for the largest bell. Somehow the plan was effected but not until 1973 under the tenure of Canon Alaric Rose. The current bell-ringing chamber in the tower is at Fig. 29.

FURNISHINGS

From 1969 to 1970, tapestry hassocks were made by a group of congregation members for the Vesey chapel which incorporated various arms seen on the stained glass and screen there. More hassocks were made in the 1990s for the main church area. Many of these are now in the south and north galleries of the church, boasting a wide range of designs, many individually created for the church.

After the re-ordering of 2016, new cushions were designed and made by local embroiderers to act as kneelers on the step of the new dais when it was in use as a communion rail. A new permanent pulpit frontal was also made. These new furnishings are in purple to match the colour of the fabric used for the main church chairs.

MOSAICS

In 1991, altar hangings in the Vesey chapel (at the east end under the window) were removed, exposing the four stone niches which at one time had housed memorial stones (now on the north-west wall of the church). In 1992 students from the college on Lichfield Road (at that point named Sutton College) were commissioned to make four mosaic panels for the stone niches. Left to right, these depict Christian symbols as follows:

The loaves and fish of the famous miracle of Jesus.

The Lamb of God.

The self-wounding pelican. (This story is an ancient one which preceded Christianity. The legend was that in time of famine, the mother pelican wounded herself, striking her breast with her beak, to feed her young with her blood to prevent starvation. This was sometimes used to represent Christ's giving of himself – his body and blood – to save mankind. In fact, the pelican only appears to be stabbing itself – it is actually fully emptying its pouch).

Three fish in a triangle suggesting the Holy Trinity. (The fish is an early Christian symbol – the letters in the word for fish in Greek – *ichthys* – spell out the Greek first letters of the phrase 'Jesus, Christ, Son of God, Saviour'. The fish was a coded way for early Christians to identify themselves to each other. It is often found on early Christian coffins where lettering might otherwise have been defaced).

OTHER WOODWORK

In 1985, the inner light oak doors to the south porch entrance were added in memory of Alaric Rose, a popular Rector who had retired just two years earlier. These have panels of stained glass to let the light through and afforded useful additional protection against the elements when the south porch was the main entrance to the church.

In the 1990s, the first two rows of pews at the front of the nave were altered to make them removable. This allowed for a platform to be put in place so that there was adequate space in front of the chancel steps for participative worship, whether for musicians or a performance piece of some kind. For a while the pews were replaced when a full congregation was expected. A more permanent platform was then put in place which looked attractive but kept some of the already inadequate underfloor heating at bay as well as creating a step across the central aisle, making a trip hazard.

In the twenty-first century, the platform was removed but the open space remained. A consequence of the removal of those particular pews was the loss of the mace-holder, which had been fixed to the front pew for the mayor when in attendance (though there was no mayor from the period of local government reorganisation of 1974 until a new town council was established in 2016). This had been given in memory of R. A. Reay-Nadin, who served for thirty-three years as town clerk. The bracket for the mace is no longer attached, but the enamel and wrought iron memorial can be seen fixed to one of the Victorian pews now kept as an example in the south-west corner of the church. More information about this memorial and Robert Reay-Nadin is in Chapter 8.

Again in the 1990s, a ramp was made from the south porch entrance to the main nave floor to facilitate access for wheelchair and pushchair users. The first ramp was particularly steep, so was replaced. This was far from ideal for a number of reasons, but such attempts to improve the accessibility and flexibility of the church were the first stage of what was to become a full re-ordering of the interior.

RE-ORDERING

A programme to re-order the church interior was first mooted during the tenure of Revd E. G. (Ted) Longman from 1984. He commissioned the head of the Department of Theology at Birmingham University to undertake a report on the church and potential changes that might be made. The resulting report of June 1985 from Prof. J. G. Davies makes interesting reading, not least for his consideration of changes in worship style and the need for changes to the church interior to make this work better, but also his consideration of the space required for the social functions of a modern church.

The options for change included the re-orientation of the church from the traditional east-facing orientation so that the pews would face north. This change has been effected in other churches, particularly where extension has taken place and, as is the case at Holy Trinity, the main area of the church is now more or less a square rather than a rectangle. While this might have been feasible architecturally it was not the professor's preferred option and was also unacceptable to the PCC at the time. Other ideas were also rejected, but although the church re-ordering took a further thirty years before coming to fruition, a number of the ideas in that initial report were taken up, notably the dais extension of the chancel and the consideration of a refreshment area in the church. More immediately, the altar table was moved forward from the east wall, enabling the clergy to adopt the more usual west-facing stance (i.e. facing the congregation) as they presided over the communion service. (This change had come about in Anglican churches over time since the 1960s).

However, as at this point the ideal plan did not seem to be in place, efforts were redirected in the first instance to building a new hall on the church site to replace the one then in use (Church House). This was on the other side of Coleshill Street facing the east side of the church. This facility had a number of drawbacks:

- An unattractive poorly heated hall with high ceiling and windows, not large enough for whole church social gatherings.
- A tiny kitchen with limited facilities and a notoriously ill-sited hatch which meant people either side of it had to duck their heads to address each other.
- Minimal parking.
- No provision for church business meetings.
- Division from the church by Coleshill Street, making the hall too far away for Sunday school groups to spend parts of the service there in terms both of the time taken to walk back and forth and the danger of crossing the road.

While the site had been a useful facility in its day and represented a great deal of time and effort on the part of church members to raise the funds for purchase in the first instance, it was now felt to be inadequate for the needs of a modern church. Furthermore, the rectory was increasingly used by the church for its business meetings and on Sundays for the Sunday school groups and refreshments after the family service. This was not a long-term solution, being reliant on the goodwill of the Rector and family, and the rectory, being owned by the diocese, could not be guaranteed as such in perpetuity either.

THE TRINITY CENTRE

Feasibility studies now began in earnest to design a hall that would provide adequate accommodation for church and community needs, that would be on the Church Hill site, and that would be both in keeping with the church building and sensitively designed in line with the needs of the designated conservation area of which it is a part.

The first hurdle was to establish an appropriate site. This involved investigation of the churchyard, which had not seen any burials for many years, but such an investigation was, understandably, a sensitive issue for some members of the community who did not feel it appropriate for graves to be disturbed. While the headstones had been moved to the edge of the church site in 1950, the graves beneath were still in situ.

An archaeological evaluation was undertaken by members of the Birmingham University Field Archaeology Unit in April 1992 (Leach and Sterenberg, 1992) 'to investigate the survival, character and period of human remains and of any other surviving archaeological evidence' and to assess the impact of the church's proposals to build a hall as well as vehicular access and a car park. (Ibid., p. 1)

The excavators noted that bone preservation was poor and recorded a number of multiple burials. (Ibid., p. 3) Although a number of metal coffin plates were found, none was decipherable in terms of the name of the deceased. All the burials uncovered were of eighteenth- or nineteenth-century origin, implying that much earlier burials had been overlaid by more recent ones, as is to be expected.

There was controversy over the use of the proposed site for the new hall as evidenced in newspaper reports at the time. Inevitably some people misunderstood the proposals. For example, the area to the south-west of the church, where graves and their headstones were still in situ, was never proposed as part of the new site, but descendants of some of these deceased families were vocal about the fact that they did not want the remains disturbed. The Rector assured people that 'every family that had a plot in the churchyard would be allowed to object and no permission would be given to exhume or re-bury remains until everyone had been consulted.' (*Sandwell Evening Mail*, 14 June 1990).

The church community was understandably anxious to be sensitive to the wishes of the local community, and there were attempts to discuss and move forward. Ultimately, where required and mainly on the western side of the church, bones were removed and re-buried. This was undertaken sensitively and a service was held to mark the interment.

Meanwhile, plans were being drawn up and numerous options were proposed not only for the hall itself but for the access route for vehicles and the car park site. Again, this necessitated a great deal of discussion, proposals and counter-proposals with objections along the way.

A church building on a hill surrounded by main access routes to the town, all of which are fairly steep, was not the ideal place from which to begin this process. But while people had managed in the era before cars to walk to church (and had had to miss worship if they were unable to walk), this was no longer a realistic option for worship in the late twentieth century, particularly in the case of large-scale services at Christmas, or weddings. Nor did it allow for the justified increasing demands for access for the less able, also being enshrined in law in the Disability Discrimination Act of 1995. While historic buildings have always been able to claim exemption, it was felt that churches should do their utmost to welcome all, regardless of disability, and especially to avoid discrimination in terms of who might be able to attend worship and participate fully.

Fig. 30:
*Foundations of
the Trinity Centre
(HTSC)*

The many facets of the planning were finally approved, with give and take on both sides, and the next phase was to raise the necessary funds. A professional fundraising campaign was set in motion and the foundation stone of the new facility was laid in June 1995 during a service attended by representatives of the church and community, including the then MP, Norman Fowler. A time capsule of memorabilia was also buried in the foundations, which are shown at Fig. 30.

The building was opened in May 1996, with two floors offering large halls for different types of function and a basement below for storage. The aim was always to serve church, commerce and community. A car park was created to serve both the church and the centre. While the thirty places secured might not have been as many as the congregation would have liked, this represented a huge improvement both on the initial permission for just a few spaces and the previous situation of having none at all.

The site was sensitively landscaped with cobbled areas to blend in with the tone of the church building, and the newly named Trinity Centre matched the design of the new building for the Sons of Rest alongside the centre (whose old building was demolished).

RE-ORDERING THE CHURCH

The building of the Trinity Centre was a huge piece of work for a number of members of the congregation, many of whom had also given generously to the fundraising campaign. Many were reluctant to start planning for the church re-ordering (always anticipated as Phase 2 of the project) and it was some years before this could be considered. The difficulties of re-ordering the church were much as they had been in 1985 – how to make the building accessible, to create appropriate and flexible space for worship, to cater better for children in church services and to increase comfort, notably around seating and heating.

A further difficulty was around the tower in the west end where the organ of 1950 had been installed, blocking both the painted ceiling and the stained glass window of 1869 in the west wall. To remove this would involve demolishing the still serviceable pipe organ, with the inevitable consequence that there would not be enough money to replace like for like, nor a place anywhere else in the church where it (or a replacement pipe organ) could be adequately accommodated.

Reluctantly, those who would have liked to see a pipe organ remain in the church had to concede to the majority view that a digital organ could be more easily accommodated and allow the tower to be opened up as envisaged in the plans.

The new century saw preliminary work undertaken by the Rector from 2000–04, James Langstaff, but the project was not undertaken in earnest until the tenure of Revd John Routh (from 2006). The architects, Brownhill Hayward Brown of Lichfield, drew up plans incorporating a number of features which had been recommended in the 1985 report by Professor Davies. These included a dais to open up the chancel area and the introduction of a café area. However, the major change was the removal of the Victorian pews throughout the building and the replacement of the floor over new underfloor heating.

Other major changes were the lowering of the floor on the north side of the tower, enabling a new entrance on one level from the car park to be created. The new floor was now mainly at one level within the church, with ramped access to the dais and chancel area. The only areas to remain inaccessible for wheelchairs are the two galleries to north and south, the internal access to the south porch (former entrance) and the steps up to the tower floor from the nave (and the tower itself). However, the tower floor can be accessed (externally) by wheelchairs from the new glazed doors in the west end, as can the south porch from the exterior door.

Other changes have been:

- New lighting.
- The removal of the portion of the north gallery on the west wall and the moving of the spiral staircase to the middle of the gallery on the north side (from the Vesey aisle).
- Moving of the font from the south-west side of the tower steps to the floor of the tower.
- Removal of the pulpit steps from the chancel, and creation of new steps to the north side of the pulpit.
- Creation of glass partitions under the north gallery (three spaces).
- A kitchen and café area.

- Upholstered chairs for the congregation.
- Additional stacking chairs.
- Re-design of the south chapel including old woodwork to form the choir vestry.
- New toilets in the new entrance – the 'ladies' uses an old oak door which was the door of the former choir vestry.
- New inner glazed and outer wooden doors at the west end.
- Re-gilding of the Rectors' board listing names of incumbents from 1250 to the present, and re-siting in the new Vesey entrance.
- Re-siting of the borough flag and Charles II coat of arms on the tower walls.
- Re-siting of the Commandments boards in the south-west corner.
- New items of furniture in light oak.

THE CHURCH NOW

The project funded by the Heritage Lottery Fund, called *Holy Trinity Parish Church: heritage at the heart of Sutton Coldfield* (2017–19), addressed the will of congregation members to make the church more available to the local community both as a resource and as a place to visit, whether for worship, or for personal reflection, or to absorb aspects of its history through appreciation of the many and varied features of this Grade I-listed parish church.

The church building is now open regularly during the week outside of service times and tries to offer site-wide open days with the Trinity Centre from time to time.

The needs of church members, local people and visitors from further afield are met by a new website which was developed as part of the project to include a large section of information and images about the history of the church and its place in the town.

As it now stands, the church floor plan is as shown in Fig. 31.

According to the Victoria County History of 1947, the measurements of each part of the church are as follows:

Nave	58 ft x 19 ft
Chancel	28 ft by 18 ft
Vesey chapel	16 ft wide
South chapel	13 ft wide
Vesey aisle	16.5 ft wide
North aisle	12 ft wide
Tower	13.5 ft square

(Source: Victoria County History pp. 230–245)

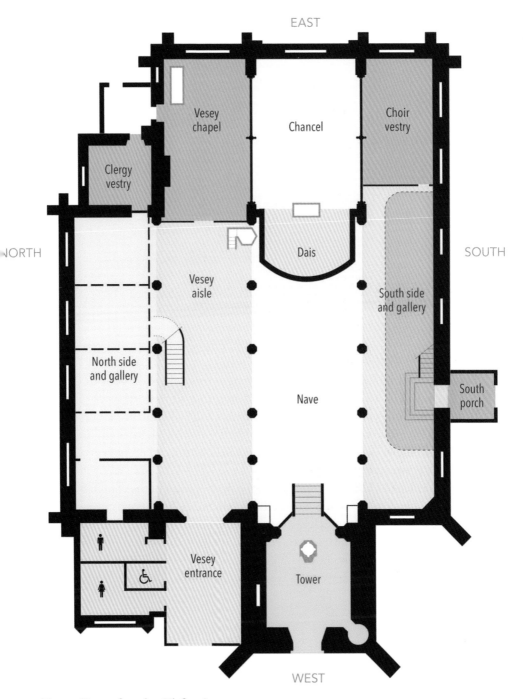

EAST

NORTH

SOUTH

WEST

Vesey chapel

Chancel

Choir vestry

Clergy vestry

Dais

Vesey aisle

South side and gallery

North side and gallery

Nave

South porch

Vesey entrance

Tower

Fig. 31: *Current floor plan (Bluflame)*

Fig. 32: *Celebration of heritage project in church February 2019 (BHD)*

From this we can deduce an overall length (from the west door to the east window) of 99.5ft (c30.3m) and a width (south wall to north wall) of 71.5ft (c21.8m). If one considers the floor area without the addition of the tower, then the church appears to be a square.

Fig. 32 shows the church being used to celebrate the end of the heritage project in February 2019.

These chapters have concentrated on the development of the church building, associated buildings and the churchyard, in the main. Further chapters explore the key features of the church in more depth, as well as aspects of the church's life within the town. Two chapters are devoted to those who served as Rectors and another to notable parishioners. A final chapter examines a number of intangible changes, for example in worship, as well as controversies of different kinds over the centuries.

6

THE CHURCH IN
THE TOWN

<figure>⊱—⊰⟐⊙⟐⊰—⊱⟐⊰—⊱⟐⊙⟐⊰—⊱⟐⊰—⊱⊙⟐⊰—⊱⟐⊰—⊱</figure>

This chapter focuses on the relationship between the church and the royal town of which it is a part. Church and town are intertwined, for reasons not only of geography – the church holds a commanding position at the top of the hill overlooking the town centre – but because of the strong links between the two from the charter for a market in 1300 through the benefactions of Bishop Vesey to civic occasions from coronation and jubilee celebrations to fundraising bazaars and flower festivals. It should also be noted that until the second half of the nineteenth century, Sutton Coldfield was a single parish extending from Walmley across to Wylde Green and up beyond the church to Four Oaks.

Fig. 33: *Junction of Coleshill St, Mill St and High St 1887 with 'pepperpot' (weighbridge) (SCL)*

In many histories of the church it is described as being founded at the same time as the charter for a market on the eve of Trinity Sunday in 1300, the first incumbent being cited as Harold Gregory in 1305 (Dugdale, 1730; Riland Bedford, 1891). Later historians follow these sources.

However, as explained elsewhere, the church and first incumbents are listed earlier than this in other sources, not least on the Rectors' board in the church porch.

Suffice it to say in the context of the town, the licence for a market on the eve of Trinity Sunday does provide a link to the dedication of the church to the Holy Trinity, so that there would probably have been commemoration of the dedication festival on Trinity Sunday in church at the point where the town was hosting its market.

Local historian Marian Baxter has written a history of the Trinity Fairs from their inception, to the periods when they lapsed, to their final demise in the 1930s.

FAIRS AND MARKET OF SUTTON COLDFIELD – MARIAN BAXTER

Many markets and fairs were already flourishing before the dates of the earliest surviving record mentioning them. They were held by virtue of a specific royal grant, usually embodied in a charter, or by prescription right based on immemorial custom. In the case of the manor held by the king in demesne, the initiation of a market or fair would not normally be recorded in a charter.

During Roman times in England, markets were small, well-organised and thriving, giving a good return if additional farm products were sold there. It seems likely that with the Roman settlements at Metchley (near the University of Birmingham), Mancetter (near Grendon) and Wall, and with the junctions of the two main Roman roads near Shenstone, there may well have been a market town, which has not been identified.

In Edward I's time the prices at markets were usually as follows:

Item	Price	Equivalent	Today's price
Best Fat Ox (grass-fed) alive	£0 16s 0d	80p	£567.20
Best Grain-fed	£1 4s 0d	£1.20	£850.83
Best Cow (fed alive)	£0 12s 0d	60p	£425.40
Best Hog, two years old	£0 3s 4d	17p	£118.17
Best Shorn Mutton	£0 1s 2d	6p	£41.30

Best Goose	£0 0s 3d	1.5p	£8.85
Best Hens, each	£0 0s 1½d	1p	£4.42
Wheat	£0 6s 0d	30p	£212.70
Rye	£0 5s 0d	25p	£177.25
Barley	£0 3s 0d	15p	£106.35
Beans and Peas	£ 0 2s 8d	13p	£94.50
Oats	£0 2s 0d	10p	£70.90p
Eggs (20)	£0 0s 1d	0.5p	£2.95

Table 3: *Prices at market in the reign of Edward I (1272–1307)*

NB: it is not known in the case of the meat or grain what quantity is indicated. If it were a whole cow or sheep, this might explain an equivalent price today of hundreds of pounds, which would appear expensive, as high-quality meat at that time was a luxury.

With the growth of the English economy in terms of population and markets in the two centuries before the Norman Conquest, a market may well have been established at Sutton Coldfield. Markets tended not to be more than 8 miles apart so that farmers would not need to travel more than 4 miles to the nearest market, and Sutton Coldfield is about 8 miles away from neighbouring market towns. The development of Sutton as a market town was as much in the interest of the local lord of the manor as a general will to foster the growth of agriculture. There is good evidence that with Sutton's increasing importance in the thirteenth century, it had a market and some specialised tradesmen long before the first market charter.

By 1300, the Lord of the Manor of Sutton, Guy de Beauchamp, Earl of Warwick, granted a royal charter whereby Sutton could hold a weekly market on Tuesdays and a fair to last four days, an annual fair on the eve of the Holy Trinity and two days after, and the other on the eve and day of Saint Martin's (November).

The weekly markets were held in an open area at the junction of High Street, Mill Street and Coleshill Street, serving the local area up to 4 miles around and attracting trade from further afield. There was still a tendency for markets to be 8 miles apart, and Lichfield, Coleshill, Birmingham, and Walsall, which also held markets, were all about this distance from Sutton Coldfield, and from each other.

As the church at Sutton Coldfield was dedicated to the Holy Trinity, the fair or wake was held in honour of that day. An old manual of Ecclesiastical law describes how such church festivals came into existence. There would be celebrations with people waking at night-time. The church fathers would urge people to abstain from the wake and fast, yet they still used the same term, 'vigil', for remaining awake:

> The people came to the church with candles burning and would wake and come with lights towards night to the church, in their devotions: and after they fell to lechery, and songs and dances, harping and piping and also to gluttony and sin, and so turned the holiness into cursedness. (Burn, 1842, p. 337)

Sutton was a thriving town at the time of the fair but it is conjectured that the Tuesday market fell into abeyance, as in 1353 a new charter was granted to Thomas, Earl of Warwick, to hold a market on the same day, with fairs on the eve, feast and morrow of Holy Trinity, and on the eve and feast of Saint Martin (10 and 11 November).

It seems that both the market and the fairs lapsed and that Sutton became somewhat run-down: 'ere long the mercate [market] being utterly forsaken, the Town fell much to ruin; and the Mannour place was totally pulled down.' (Dugdale, 1730, p. 913)

According to both Dugdale and the Victoria County History of Warwickshire, Bishop Vesey came to the town's rescue in 1519. The inhabitants of Sutton were given a licence to hold a market on Monday (instead of Tuesday), with one fair on the eve, day and morrow of Holy Trinity and another on the morrow of Saint Crispin and Saint Crispinian and the eve of the day of Saint Simon and Saint Jude (26–28 October). These were confirmed in 1528 when the town was incorporated, and the newly constituted warden was empowered to act as clerk of the market. He was forbidden to exact any tolls from persons attending this market.

The two annual fairs were big occasions, each lasting three days. The Trinity Fair was in May or June (Trinity Sunday is always the week after Whitsun or Pentecost, which in turn signifies fifty days after Easter. As Easter is variable, Trinity Sunday can fall from the end of May, but frequently occurs in June). The October fair took place on the feast of Saint Simon and Saint Jude (28 October). The Tudor courts ordered the archery butts to be set up in advance of the Trinity Fair, everyone being required to be able to handle a longbow in Elizabethan times, and the constable was ordered to see that the fairs were properly policed. Horse-traders came to the fair, paying a market fee or toll on every transaction.

In 1554 the court ordered all inhabitants of the town to clean their street frontages before the feast of Simon and Jude.

By the first half of the eighteenth century the fairs again seem to have fallen into disuse. In 1757 fairs are noted for 8 November and Trinity Monday in Rider's 'List of Fairs', and these continued until at least 1850. The tradition of the fairs was continued in one form or another until the 1930s.

The word 'fair' is ancient British, signifying a market: in early times frequently kept on Sundays, until, in 1448/9 during the reign of Henry VI, a statute prohibited fairs and markets on that day.

It is difficult today for us to realise the importance and popularity of these mediaeval fairs. When shops were few and small, people bought all their goods for the year at these great local markets, and immense stocks were disposed of during the few days they lasted. Special courts were established on the spot to settle the disputes between the traders, to regulate weights and measures, and to certify to the purity of the goods sold. These were called Pie-Powder Courts, from *pieds poudrés*, or dusty feet in French, in an allusion to the pedlars who used them. The fairs provided large profits from the tolls to the lords of the fair who granted special privileges to the people who attended them. The lords would open the fair in full state followed by a procession of retainers with their banner, and preceded by the town/bell crier or the 'court baron', who would proclaim the 'laws of the fair'.

A useful website describes the origins of the Stourbridge Fair in Cambridgeshire, which was one of the largest in mediaeval Europe and dates from 1199. This records the full wording of the 'cry', which was given at the start of the fair. The law declared that the people must leave their weapons at their homes so that 'the King's peace may be kept', and describes in detail all the goods to be sold and the respective measures of each. (www.gwydir.demon.co.uk/jo/walks/fair.htm)

The reader might conjure a picture of the fairs at Holy Trinity, which took place on Holy Trinity Eve and the three following days, with worshippers bringing lighted candles and the graveyard full of traders, minstrels, storytellers and jugglers. Beyond the churchyard there might have been booths of mercers, vintners, potters and cattle dealers. There may also have been shows and miracle plays from time to time. Some of these early performances presaged the menageries of more modern fairs.

By 1850, a market was still held on Mondays, for cattle, sheep and pedlary, and this continued at least until 1902. From 1897 to 1902 stock sales for cattle, sheep and pigs were held at Sutton Coldfield on the first Tuesday in every month, but in 1903 the date was altered to alternate Mondays.

The diary of Richard Holbeche describes the Trinity Fair of the 1860s:

Early in the morning on a fair day, people came and tied hurdles all along the footpaths to make sheep pens. There are still staples in the barn wall, which was used for this purpose; the barn was at Number 1–3 Coleshill Street ... Sutton was 'en fete' in those days. Cattle and sheep and pigs hustled about and horses trotted up and down the hollow. Booths occupied the middle of the town hall ... in the stalls were yellow rock, ginger bread, brandy soup and nuts teefee caffirs ... and all sorts of wild animals. There were shooting galleries, roulettes, merry-go-round and freak shows and the crowds poured in from all directions. If you desired to see real pomp you should have seen the fair proclaimed. The Sergeant at Mace and certain crippled friends with halberds, and the crier, undertook this responsible duty (Holbeche, 1893).

The *Parish Magazine* of July 1898 gives an account of the Sunday School and Benefits Clubs' Annual Festival, Trinity Monday, 1898:

At 10am a service in church, followed by a long procession with three bands along the High Street, Lichfield Road, Anchorage Road and back to the school in Mill Street (now the Baptist Church) for a good dinner: sixty prizes were presented, rain poured down but cleared by where sports were held and tea was served at the Rectory [this was the Rectory in Rectory Park].

By 1900 two fair days had been added to the former 8 November and Trinity Fair, namely 14 March and 19 September, but these two lapsed after a few years.

In the 1920s Trinity Monday had taken on the air of a carnival with a parade through the town, with all the local dignitaries, bands and uniformed organisations, and all the horses and carts were decorated and dressed up for the event.

By 1937 some of the traditional processions through Sutton Coldfield centre had disappeared. One of the most notable was Trinity Monday. So once more and this time forever, the Trinity Monday traditional event had faded away. [End of section by Marian Baxter]

In the 1990s a series of fairs was held at the church on the Saturday immediately before Trinity Sunday. These were again called Trinity Fairs but lapsed, partly because of the changing date of the Trinity Sunday festival making it difficult to adjust arrangements each year.

LOCAL GOVERNMENT

Bishop Vesey's establishment of a Warden and Society to look after the affairs of the royal town was both a far-sighted initiative for its time and one that lasted until the change to a town council in 1886.

The list of wardens from 1529 to 1890 is given by Riland Bedford in his history (1891, pp. 81–85). It is perhaps not surprising how many of these names have links to Holy Trinity church. The first, William Gibbons, was Vesey's brother-in-law, and we see other family relations (Gibbons and Harman) and also many of the Rectors of the church, especially the Rilands and Riland Bedfords, and some curates (including Blick, Mendham and Packwood), churchwardens, headmasters of the grammar school and prominent parishioners – titled and untitled – all taking their place. The warden appears to have been elected annually until 1541, then every two years, and then the length of office varies, probably because they could be re-elected year on year. Some served several times in a number of different years.

The first mayor of the new council in 1886 was Benjamin Stone, and this council remained in place until the large national reorganisation of local government in 1974, when Sutton Coldfield was moved from the overall jurisdiction of Warwickshire County Council to the City of Birmingham. A new town council was established, again headed by a mayor, in 2016.

LEGAL BUSINESS

It has been noted that Bishop Vesey enabled the building of a moot hall near the church which allowed local disputes to be heard and settled more formally. It is thought that the Holy Trinity Church porch, at the entrance on the south side, dates from around this time too. This space would have allowed people to settle spiritual matters with a priest without coming into the sacred space of the church. However, Sally Dixon-Smith writing about marriage in mediaeval times notes:

> All that was required for a valid, binding marriage was the consent of the two people involved. In England some people did marry near churches to give greater spiritual weight to proceedings, often at the church door (leading to some rather fabulous church porches being added to earlier buildings), but this still did not necessarily involve a priest. (Dixon-Smith, 2016)

Perhaps the porch at Holy Trinity was also seen as a way to bridge the gap between the secular and spiritual worlds for a variety of reasons. Further information is at www.historyextra.com/period/medieval/love-and-marriage-in-medieval-england

LIGHTNING

The porch played a part in a distressing incident at the church in 1907 when a freak storm caused lightning to race through the building, putting out the electric lighting which had only been installed a few years before. It is worth quoting the press report from the *Tamworth Herald* of 6 July 1907 in full:

Church struck at Sutton Coldfield

On Sunday afternoon a thunderstorm of unusual severity passed over Sutton Coldfield, and lasted for nearly an hour. At the Parish Church, where a service was being conducted by the Rector (the Revd Canon Bedford), the south porch was struck by the lightning. The glass of the window on the Coleshill Street side was smashed and the woodwork twisted and broken. From the window the lightning passed to the box enclosing the electric bell connected with the vestry, smashing it to pieces. The lightning then went through the church putting out the electric light. Several ladies fainted and much alarm was occasioned. The gas was immediately lighted and the service carried through to the end. Mr Matthews (the deputy clerk) and Mr Riley were seated in the porch, and both received severe shocks. The storm was one of the worst that has passed over this neighbourhood for some years.

From our perspective, the fainting might seem rather typical of the time, but electricity was mistrusted by a lot of people and the force of the storm might well have been quite frightening. One wonders how severe were the shocks to the two gentlemen in the porch. The Rector alluded to as Canon Bedford was Revd William Campbell Riland Bedford, the last of that family's line.

FUNDRAISING BAZAARS

In July 1854, a bazaar was held in Sutton Park where local aristocratic and untitled ladies manned stalls and raised hundreds of pounds for a new local church:

Bazaar in Sutton Park in aid of the erection of a new church in the Parish of Sutton Coldfield

Contributions in work or saleable articles are solicited and may be sent to the Rectory, Sutton Coldfield; to Mrs Edwards, 39 New Street Birmingham, or to Mrs Thompson, Market Street, Tamworth, addressed to the Committee; or to any of the following ladies who have kindly consented to preside at Stalls:-

The Rt Hon The Countess of Bradford	The Rt Hon Lady Chetwynd
Lady Hartopp	Mrs Chavasse
Lady Scott	Mrs Holbeche
Mrs Newdegate	Mrs Sadler
Mrs Chadwick	Mrs Riland Bedford
Mrs Baron Webster	Miss Steele Perkins

This announcement in *Aris's Birmingham Gazette* of 12 June 1854 does not state the area of Sutton where the church was to be built, but from the date it can be inferred this was for St Michael's Boldmere, which was consecrated in 1857.

Such notices tell us a great deal about the parishioners and the social structure of the time. While the men are remembered for their role in the town, the wives, who were no doubt equally able and in many cases as well educated, would busy themselves with such good works.

This is the first bazaar which appears in the records, indicating that this kind of public fundraising by the sale of small-scale items was a new development of the nineteenth century, compared with previous times when money would have been raised solely by appeal to those men with disposable incomes, as was the case with the fundraising for new features in the church in the eighteenth century, like repair of the bells and new pews.

Now men and women would be encouraged to enjoy a day of browsing and probably children came along too. Perhaps there would have been refreshments of some kind on sale as a further way of raising funds.

This bazaar was in the park, so it is unlikely that cover would have been provided in the event of rain, and maybe it was a warm June day. In the event, Norman Evans notes that 'hundreds of pounds' were raised. This was also before the coming of the railway. In 1865 the Royal Hotel was built above the new railway station to serve visitors to the town, but it was never financially secure, and in 1901, following a brief time as a sanatorium, it was bought to be used as council offices comprising council chambers, assembly rooms and a fire station. The earlier town hall in Mill Street closed in 1903 (when it became the Masonic Lodge) and an extension was added to the council offices at a cost of £10,000 to create a new town hall, which opened in 1906 (still in use as the town hall).

The fundraising bazaar of February 1899 would have been held in the earlier town hall in Mill Street (the building at the foot of Church Hill now the Masonic Hall), and the later one of 1928 in the current town hall in King Edward's Square.

The bazaar of 1899 was to raise funds for the new choir vestry and organ. The total amount required was £2,000, and the programme stated that half this sum had been raised by parishioners. An 'inflation calculator' suggests that £1,000 in 1899 would now equate to £120,000. The event was clearly successful, as both vestry and organ were in place by 1901.

The expensive printed programme for attendees would have secured a good amount of the funds raised.

The programme cover (Fig. 34) describes the sale as being 'a grand bazaar with scenic representations of an old English village'. The picture of the church on the

Fig. 34: *Cover of bazaar programme 1899 (HTSC)*

front cover is a useful reminder of the church aspect from the west at that point, before the choir vestry was added.

Each page of the programme is devoted to a different stall, giving the names of the ladies in charge and an idea of the goods for sale. The reader also finds not one but two encouraging quotations on each page, as in this example from William Cobbett on the page for stall no. 1: 'Women, so amiable in themselves, are never so amiable as when they are useful; and as for beauty, though men fall in love with girls at play, there is nothing to make them stand to their love like seeing them at work.'

This stall is run by Mrs W. C. R. Bedford (the Rector's wife), Mrs Q. C. Colmore, the wife of Quintus Colmore – who would after his death have a stained glass window installed to his memory in the south chapel – Mrs A. L. Crockford and Mrs E. Riddell. These last two names are not known to us, but the initials, of course, are of the husbands. It is comforting to know that they will be 'assisted by other ladies' and we also learn that their main sale items will be a bicycle, musical box, gramophone, toys, Norwegian china and 'a fancy assortment of work, dolls etc'.

For stall number 2 the stallholders are led by Mrs J. C. Skelton, the church-warden's wife. Here buyers are exhorted to snap up more china, brass artwork, wood carvings, tools and 'electro-plated goods'. On this page we read:

Men are more eloquent than women made,
But women are more powerful to persuade.

After a few pages of this, the modern reader feels ambivalent about the enjoyable period style and the unpalatable tone of some of the content, although by stall number 4 we may be wondering about some private jokes being played out: 'Timid persons are advised to bring an escort of friends or ask for the Secretary.'

The other major bazaar, for which there are still copies of the programme to be found in local records, was held over three days in November 1928, and styled 'in a Japanese garden', perhaps nodding to the exotic attraction of the Far East at that time. This would have been shortly after some significant fundraising for the town pageant held in the previous July.

The funds were required this time for the final painting of the ceilings, formation of the Vesey chapel (the screen had been given in memory of former Rector Charles Barnard and his wife) and the redecoration of the church.

Interestingly the amount raised is noted in a press cutting from the *Birmingham Daily Gazette* of 21 February 1929 (£4,680) which is principally reporting on the quantity of threepenny bits received in the church collection over the year – some 2,884. This equates to £36 10s in old money (£36.50p) and would today be worth approximately £1,671.17p. The £4,680 raised at the bazaar equates to a staggering £214,275.67p.

OTHER FUNDRAISING

Two major fundraising campaigns were held for the building of the Trinity Centre in the 1990s and for the re-ordering of the church in the early twenty-first century.

In both cases money was raised where possible from grant-making bodies, including the Sutton Coldfield Charitable Trust, which is a hugely beneficial trust offering funds to individuals and community groups across the town. This was supplemented by campaigns led by professional fundraisers to help maximise donations from congregation and community. In both cases, the church also used any available funds that could be expended in this way, including sale of property in the case of the re-ordering work. It is to the credit of the congregation and community that many individuals gave generously to support both these building projects and to enable the church better to serve its community for the longer term.

The grant from the Heritage Lottery Fund for the project which ran from 2017 to 2019, entitled 'Holy Trinity Parish Church: heritage at the heart of Sutton Coldfield', is described more fully in the introduction to this book. Of the many benefits of the project, the new church guidebook and this history book were two.

Smaller-scale fundraising has always been a feature of church life, and, as with most churches, the congregation is committed to raising funds via community events for charitable causes every year rather than for the church building or running costs. (For this work it tries to secure funding from the donations of congregation members.)

For example, a flower festival was held in the 1990s, and on two further occasions in 2000 and 2011. Community groups were invited every time to contribute displays. In 2000 it was an opportunity to celebrate both the millennium and approximately 700 years of Holy Trinity. The festival in 2011 was on the theme of 'Creation' and then two successful Christmas Tree festivals followed in 2013 and 2014.

A major fundraising event until the 1990s was the annual September garden party in the grounds of the rectory in Coleshill Street. This relied very much on the good-will of the Rector at the time but was an effective way of attracting the public who wished to see the otherwise private gardens, which were really quite stunning. A number of attractions, stalls and even donkey rides, and a water slide for children, ensured fun was had and money was raised, always for good causes beyond the church.

As part of the heritage project, the church has begun to run heritage open days every September as a way of encouraging more visitors. For these, fundraising is a sideline.

SUTTON COLDFIELD LIBRARY – SUE INGLEY

It is interesting to note that the initial setting up of a permanent public library in Sutton Coldfield was by Dr Richard Williamson, Rector of Holy Trinity from 1843 till 1850. As a former headmaster of the prestigious Westminster School, it is probably not surprising that any project that could promote learning and education, particularly within his parish, would be close to his heart.

Today, in Sutton Reference Library, his proud handwritten opening address of Sutton's first 'Permanent Library', on 3 April 1850, can be found. In it, he explains how the project came to fruition and speaks of his hopes and aspirations for its future. He states: 'This institution goes far to fill up a void long felt by many of us in this parish'. (Williamson, 1850, p. 7). He clearly saw the establishment of a library as an opportunity for people to extend their limited school education, as well as the spiritual goal that it would 'assist and direct the humble learned along the path which leads to heaven'. (Ibid., p. 8)

Dr Williamson was fervent about the exposure to books that would feed both mind and body. He also claimed at the opening ceremony of the library that 'The true philosopher is humble' and 'the ignorant or shallow-learned is the conceited man'. (Ibid., p. 11)

The first Sutton Library was originally set up by the Sutton Book Club, with a committee to spearhead the project. The Society (Corporation) donated £50 towards initial book stock, and at first, with the warden's permission, a book room was set up in the Town Hall.

While Dr Williamson was initially keen to combine the library with a museum, which did not happen, he also hoped for provision for lectures, and this is how the subsequent Sutton Coldfield Library evolved, with exhibition space and loans of pictures and sound recordings.

A permanent home for the library took some time. Both the church and other premises were used at different times, and it was not until nearly ninety years later that a permanent site was found. This was after a £3,500 grant from the prestigious Carnegie Trust was turned down (many Carnegie libraries are still serving the public across the UK. The trust was funded by the businessman turned philanthropist Andrew Carnegie).

Finally the former Methodist church was purchased and reopened as a public library on Saturday 6 March 1937, serving in this capacity for thirty-eight years. In June 1964, the council began to search for a site that could accommodate a modern library more effectively. In February 1967, plans to develop what was the ABC Empress cinema site were issued, and, five years later, work began on the new building.

On 26 October 1974, the old library was closed and its jurisdiction was transferred (along with other local authority functions) from Warwickshire to Birmingham Public Libraries. The new library opened officially on 14 December 1974 and is still used today, currently supported by a vibrant Friends organisation – FOLIO (Friends of Libraries in our Sutton Coldfield). [End of section by Sue Ingley]

SOCIAL ACTIVITIES

Churches have always offered premises and often leaders too for a range of clubs and activities to support the community of church members and non-members alike. From youth groups such as Scouts and Guides to general youth clubs and interest groups for adults, Holy Trinity has also supported a range of these over the years. Some church-focused activities such as the choir, bell ringers, flower-arrangers or fellowship groups continue to welcome both church members and others who feel they wish to serve the worship of the church in this way, while fellowship groups centred around crafts or hobbies might also spring up from time to time. Past issues of the magazine recount the exploits of various drama groups, ad hoc choirs, an under-35s group, the Church Fellowship, and in the 1990s there was even a series of 'men's breakfast' meetings.

One group, called Church House Guild, was expressly set up to raise funds in the longer term for an adequate church hall. This culminated in the purchase of Church House on Coleshill Street, which served for many years in the twentieth century as a hall and office accommodation. The group continued to meet and raise funds for church needs, changing its name to the Trinity Guild and meeting in the Trinity Centre once that was built and the old Church House was sold.

The Scout Troop was started in 1926 and the Guides some years later, both extending to cover all age groups, though there is not currently a Rainbows section (for 5-to-6-year-old girls) meeting at the church.

The Scouts were pleased to be one of the 'home' troops for the 50th anniversary World Scout Jamboree in Sutton Park in 1957, and many local people still have memories of being involved in some capacity with the camp.

A Boys' Brigade unit was set up in 1905, but only lasted a few years, owing to the death of the captain, Greyson Wynn James (1881–1906), only a young man at the time, and also of the curate at the church who also died young, who is listed as the lieutenant of the group, Revd George Warburton White.

It is also thought that they may have had brigade meetings at the crystal palace, which was in Sutton Park at that time, but suffered a collapse of the floor in 1905. Although it was not demolished at that point, it was not used for group meetings of this kind again.

TRIBUTE TO QUEEN VICTORIA

A splendid book, now in the church archives, is the programme for the coronation celebrations in Sutton Coldfield for George V in 1911.

Not only does it contain a full listing of the rich programme, it also includes a full history of the town by the then mayor, one T. H. Cartwright.

But the gem is the full account by Cartwright of the town's celebrations for the coronation in 1838 of 'the beloved King's grandmother'. This is reproduced in full as follows:

Coronation Celebrations in 1838

As this Book is intended as a Souvenir of the Sutton Coldfield Coronation Festivities, it is fitting to give an epitome of what was done in the Royal Town when the King's beloved grand-mother, Queen Victoria, was crowned in 1838.

The records show that a meeting of the Parishioners was convened by a notice "affixed on the Town Hall and stuck about the Parish." and that such a meeting, on the 15th June, 1838, was attended (among others) by the Warden, Mr. Oughton, Mr Horton, Mr. Packwood, Mr. Grimes, Mr. Wm. Wilkins, Mr Oates, Mr. Vincent Holbeche and Mr. Richard Brown.

It was resolved "That Mr. Oates be requested to take the trouble of writing to Mr. Charles Webster, of Walsall, to provide ten musicians to be in attendance on the morning of the Coronation by ten o'clock, for the whole of the day, at ten shillings each man."

"That immediate steps be taken to collect subscriptions."

A further meeting was held on the 18th June, when it was decided to meet at the Town Hall at 11 o'clock and move in Procession at 12 o'clock; Dinner at 1 o'clock; Park at 3 o'clock; Fireworks 9 o'clock.

A subsequent meeting was held, at which Mr. Horton reported that the meat would be furnished by the butchers in the Parish.

Five hundred Medals were to be provided, at a halfpenny a-piece, for the children, by the Warden.

The Ale Committee reported that the Ale could be found from ten public-houses and the four beer-houses in the Town.

£5 was to be spent in Tea Drinking, and the Warden and Mr. Horton were appointed a Committee to manage it.

The Estimate presented to the meeting gives the cost of the Festivities as under:-

800	people at 1b. each.
7d.	per 1b., including roasting.
£2368	Meat.
06134	Bread; 200 Quartern Loaves, 4 lbs. 6 ozs.
0 0 0	Pudding.
1 13 4	Sheep Roasting.
25 0 0	Ale.
25 0 0	Do. for the Park.
5 0 0	Band.
5 0 0	for Prizes.
5 0 0	for Fireworks.
10 0 0	Ball Expenses.
1 0 0	Potatoes.
£107 13 4	

Various committees and officials were appointed; among others, Mr. Hollis and Mr. Baylis as Conservators of the Peace.

The Dinner was laid out on twenty tables in Coleshill Street for which forty Carvers were appointed, including the following:-

The Warden	Mr. Cooper
Mr. Horton	Mr. Pepper
Mr. Grimes	Mr. W. Wilkins
Mr. Perkins	Mr. Solomon Smith
Mr. W Perkins	Mr. James Hughes
Mr. Edward Sadler	Mr. Kempton
Mr. Oughton	Mr. Harry Smith
Mr. Geo. Brown	Mr. Hartopp
Mr. V. Holbeche	Mr. Holbeche
Mr. R. C. Wiloughby	Mr. Ryan
Mr. Jacob	Mr. Buggins
Mr. Brockhas	Mr. Boddington
Mr. J. Holbeche	Mr. Stephenson

Beer Stewards were appointed, consisting of –

Mr. G. Brentnall	Mr. J. Cooper
Mr. W. Brentnall	Mr. John Brown
Mr. Clive	Mr. Harper
Mr. Pipe	Mr. Crabtree
Mr. Barton	Mr. Joseph Wilkins
Mr. Hayward	Mr. Brindley
Mr. Griffis	

The Sports in the Park consisted of Races for Boys under 12, under 14, and under 16; Swarming a Pole, Sack Racing and Collar Grinning; and the prizes were waistcoat pieces, silk handkerchiefs, hats and smock frocks.

The Subscriptions included £10 from the High Steward and £50 given by the Warden and Society. £5 each from Sir F. Lawley, Bart., and Sir E. C. Hartopp, and totalled £144 18s 0d. In addition, S. F. S. Perkins Esq., Sir E. C. Hartopp and the Rev. W. R. Bedford each made a gift of a Fat Sheep.

GOD SAVE THE QUEEN

Sung at the Coronation Celebrations in Sutton Coldfield in 1838.

God save our gracious Queen,	Let then our Royal Town
Long may Victoria reign,	True to its old renown
God save the Queen.	This day be seen.
Send her victorious,	Steady to England's Throne
Happy and glorious,	Be our devotion shewn,
Long to reign over us,	While in our hearts we crown
God save the Queen.	Victoria Queen.

[Source: This single page is the last in the programme (the first section) of Cartwright and Ellison (1911)]

So much can be gleaned from this of the way such functions were managed in a time before electricity. The total cost given of £107, 13s and 4d (£107.67p) would equate today to £8,416.54p.

It is not known if the food was cooked and then carved hot or cold. The names of the men who carved or were beer stewards appear to give an initial where the son is named as well as a father to distinguish them. The new verse of God Save the Queen is not something that has been seen elsewhere, and it would have been difficult to sing for subsequent monarchs except perhaps Elizabeth II, by which time it was probably forgotten.

OTHER ROYAL TRIBUTES

On 20 May 1910 a special peal of muffled bells (Stedman Triples) was rung at Holy Trinity on the day of the burial of King Edward VII at Windsor. A commemorative plaque at the foot of the church tower describes 'a last tribute to his late Majesty King Edward VII, and in appreciation of those Noble and Charitable qualities which earned for him throughout his world-wide Empire, the name "Edward the Peacemaker".'

This was during the tenure of Canon Charles Barnard, who then had to preside over the church's part in festivities for the coronation of George V in 1911.

The book cited above includes a full programme of activities, with school sports in Sutton Park, and lists naming every competitor in each school and the rota for tea to be taken. A special lunch for the 'old people' (over 60s) was given, and details

Fig. 35: *Remembrance Parade, King Edward's Square, 1950 (SCL)*

for a commemorative church service. This also includes instructions for the poor bell-ringers who had to start their first ring at midnight the evening before.

The next major celebration of this kind in the town was the commemoration of the silver jubilee of George V in 1935. More detail of this is given in the section below about the milestones which led to the establishment of the Vesey Gardens.

OTHER CIVIC OCCASIONS

Many of the royal commemorations have included a church service as part of the proceedings in the town, and there have also been many civic services, for example, at the start of a new year for the town council. Along with churches across the land, there has been an annual service of remembrance on the Sunday nearest to the anniversary of Armistice Day (11 November), which in Sutton Coldfield incorporates a parade to church from the war memorial in King Edward's Square, and a return after the service. Fig. 35 shows the 1950 parade in King Edward's Square.

This is currently one of only two occasions in the year when the church is regularly full to capacity, the other being the founder's day service for students at Bishop Vesey's Grammar School in October, when flowers are laid on the Bishop's tomb.

At the centenary of the armistice in 2018, around 1,000 people were in the church, which meant that some were standing. Most years there are between 750 and 900.

STATELY HOMES

A number of parishioners were landed gentry occupying (and sometimes building) large houses in the parish, notably New Hall, Four Oaks Hall and Moor Hall.

New Hall

The house which became New Hall is first recorded as early as 1200, though not recorded as New Hall until 1341. William Gibbons, the brother-in-law of Bishop Vesey, is recorded as living there from 1525, followed by his son, Thomas, warden of the town from 1542 to 1581. It was owned by the Sacheverell family from 1590, passing from his grandfather and father to Sir George c1709. The property passed to Sir George's nephew Charles Chadwick and remained in that family until 1897. In the 1890s it was used as a school and then purchased by a Walter Wilkinson, from whom it passed to the Owen family – Sir Alfred Owen, chairman of Rubery Owen and Co., being the last individual owner. Since 1988 the hall has been a hotel. The neighbouring flour mill had ceased operation in 1960, and in 1972 Sir Alfred Owen set about overcoming the water supply problem to make it a working mill again. The New Hall Mill Preservation Trust was formed in 1973 and its volunteer members not only keep it working but continue to open the mill to the public several times a year. (The story of New Hall).

Moor Hall

Two buildings on the Moor Hall estate are significant in the context of the church in the town of Sutton Coldfield – Moor Hall itself and the smaller house on Moor Hall Drive now known as Moor Hall Farm and described in the 1949 listing document of the house as the 'conjectured birthplace' of John Harman (Bishop Vesey).

William Dargue writes:

> The first written record of Old Moor Hall is in 1434 in the ownership of Roger Harewell. Believed to have been the birthplace of Bishop Vesey

c1462, the house on Moor Hall Drive is a Grade II★ Listed building in sandstone with surviving 14th-century roof timbers and lancet windows of c1520. It is in private ownership.

The house has a circular staircase and timber floor and must originally have been timber-framed, although no timber framework survived the rebuildings of 1527 and the early 20th-century. Traces of a medieval moat in the garden may barely be seen with a practised eye. (https://billdargue. jimdo.com/placenames-gazetteer-a-to-y/places-m/moor-hall)

Roger Lea notes that Vesey's niece, Jane Harman, was engaged to George Middlemore of Haselwell, near Stirchley, and that a marriage settlement document was drawn up in 1525, in which George's father agreed to give the Haselwell estate to the couple on their marriage. Bishop Vesey was required to give George's father, John, £400 in return, and the deeds were consigned to a chest with two locks, one of the keys to be kept by John, the other by Bishop Vesey or his brother Hugh Harman. The chest itself was to be kept at Moor Hall, Sutton Coldfield.

Bishop Vesey built a new mansion on the hill above the old house, where he lived in some style, dying there in 1554. Roger Lea writes:

After the death of Bishop Vesey in 1554, his brother Hugh Harman lived at Moor Hall for a time, but Gawen Grosvenor, a relative of the Pudseys of Langley Hall, was the owner in the early 1600s, followed by his son Leicester Grosvenor. John Addyes purchased Moor Hall, and the Addyes family occupied it for most of the eighteenth century. In the 1800s Moor Hall was the property of a branch of the Hackett family of Moxhull Hall. Over time the house had been greatly altered – writing in 1890, the Rector of Sutton, W. K. Riland Bedford, refers to it as 'now modernized'. Moor Hall was not modern enough, however for its new owner, the brewer Colonel Edward Ansell, who demolished it and built the present Moor Hall on the site in 1905. (Lea, Moor Hall, HS 62, 17 July 2009)

It has been a hotel and function venue since this time.

Four Oaks Hall

Four Oaks Hall was built by Lord Ffolliott on 60 acres of land next to Sutton Park in 1700. It was designed by William Wilson, who was the stepfather of Lady Ffolliott (née Pudsey). Following Lady Ffolliott's death in 1742, the hall was purchased in 1744 by Simon Luttrell, who modernised it in 1760, bringing it up to the height of Georgian fashion. It is probably no coincidence that Simon's daughter, Anne, married the brother of George III at this time – a marriage which apparently sparked the Royal Marriage Act of 1772. There is more about Anne's story in the section on the Luttrell family in Chapter 13.

An Act of Parliament in 1757 had enabled Simon to add 46 acres of Sutton Park to his Four Oaks Park, though the alterations depleted his finances and the hall was sold to a Dr Greasly in the 1770s and then bought by Sir Edmund, the first Baron Hartopp, in 1778. Succeeding generations of Hartopps occupied the house for some eighty years, and another 63 acres of Sutton Park was added in exchange for the land area now known as Meadow Platt.

Roger Lea sheds light on the household at Four Oaks at the time of the census of 1861:

> The family was at home at the time of the 1861 census, and the Census Enumerator recorded them – the 66-year old Baronet and his wife Lady Jane, daughters Matilda, Louisa and Julia aged 25, 19 and 18, and 14-year old Edmund …
>
> The Hall also accommodated 25 servants. There was a housekeeper, 32 years old, born in Northumberland, and twelve maids, the youngest a housemaid of 16 and the oldest a laundry maid aged 39. Then there were the butler and the under-butler, cook, coachman, two valets, two footmen, a groom, a postillion, a stable boy and a poster. None of the servants was native to Sutton Coldfield; places of birth included Scotland, Montgomery, Wiltshire and Dorset. (Lea, Hartopps, HS 46, 2009)

Four Oaks Park was later developed as a racecourse, when a consortium bought it in the 1870s, opening it in 1881. The circular course lay between Bracebridge Road and Four Oaks Road, with the hall in the centre; it was never a commercial success and closed in 1889. Four Oaks Hall and its park were purchased by Lord Clanricarde and the now derelict house was demolished in 1898.

Roger Lea gives more information about the subsequent demise of the hall and redevelopment of the site:

> Hubert de Burgh-Canning, second Marquess of Clanricarde was notorious for rack-renting on his huge estates in Ireland, a very wealthy man. A contemporary noted 'Few people know Lord Clanricarde personally. He lives the life of a hermit in London in a dingy set of chambers in the Albany, off Piccadilly, and never goes out into society'. The purchase of Four Oaks Hall was a purely business transaction, done with a view to making a profit, and his agents soon set out Hartopp Road, Luttrell Road, Ladywood Road,

Wentworth Road and Bracebridge Road with a view to selling the land off for building. (Lea, Briarwood, HS 108, 11 June 2010)

VESEY PAGEANT

This took place in July 1928 to commemorate the 400th anniversary of the granting of the Royal Charter to Sutton Coldfield by Henry VIII via Bishop Vesey.

It was a very large-scale affair, though preparations only started in April for the July event. Patrons included not only local dignitaries but peers and royalty (both the Duke of York and the Duke of Gloucester), and the prime minister, Stanley Baldwin. Congratulatory letters were received from both the King and the Prince of Wales.

Fig. 36: *Canon Golden (1928) as Bishop Vesey (SCL)*

With ticket sales and a lot of goodwill from traders, the event covered its costs.

A play about the history of the town, written by John Willmott, was performed in a series of tableaux covering key moments from 'The Icknield Street' (Roman road) in c100CE through the last struggle of the English (1070), various scenes from Bishop Vesey's time and the nineteenth-century incorporation of the borough.

The programme gives full details of the content of each scene and the names of the many local people involved in all aspects of the production of each scene. Many local people took part, dressing up as townspeople and characters of different eras, and the souvenir book gives not only the text of the play, but full detail of the various activities that took place.

There are images of actors playing the Bishop both from 1928 and from 1935. In 1928 this was Canon Frederick Stanley Golden, who was vicar of the neighbouring parish of St Peter's, Maney, from 1920–46 (see Fig. 36), and in 1935 it was John Willmott himself.

A website relating to town pageants across the UK offers a great amount of detail (see Bartie et al, website).

A similar event took place in 1935 when a play was performed for the Jubilee of King George V. It was these two events that catalysed interest (led by Alderman John Willmott, JP) in the formation of a lasting and visible memorial to Bishop Vesey. The Vesey Gardens were created in 1939 on Church Hill next to Holy Trinity, incorporating a memorial to Vesey. (see Chapter 2).

There is more information about the Rectors and clergy of Holy Trinity in chapters 11 and 12, and about prominent families associated with the church in Chapter 13.

7

CHURCH FEATURES: AN INTRODUCTION

The following three chapters give more details about key features of the church which deserve fuller description.

Chapter 8, by Marian Baxter, tells the stories of individuals and families commemorated in the stone memorials in the church and in the churchyard, though the tomb of Bishop Vesey is described in Chapter 2, which tells the story of John Vesey in full.

In Chapter 9 there is a description of the stained glass in the church, most of which was given in memory of clergy or parishioners and, in many cases, depicts biblical stories to amplify a characteristic or action of the person being commemorated.

Chapter 10, by Carol Hoare, brings together, for the first time, the full story of the significant woodwork in the church, notably the large quantity bought from Worcester Cathedral in the late nineteenth century.

In this introductory section there are brief descriptions of other notable features of the church which have not been described fully in the preceding chapters recounting the history of the building in chronological order.

THE TOWER AND FONT

The tower at Holy Trinity is little changed externally since it was built in the late thirteenth century, though internal changes have been many, from the formation of vestries to the installation of bells, an organ and stained glass.

The various changes have been noted in previous chapters in their chronological period, but an image by Norman Evans (Fig. 37) usefully depicts the internal changes from earliest times to the mid-twentieth century (Evans, 1987, p. 61).

Since the re-ordering of 2016–18 and the removal of the pipe organ installed in 1950, the space is now open again with an uninterrupted view (when the external wooden west end doors are open) to the east end window.

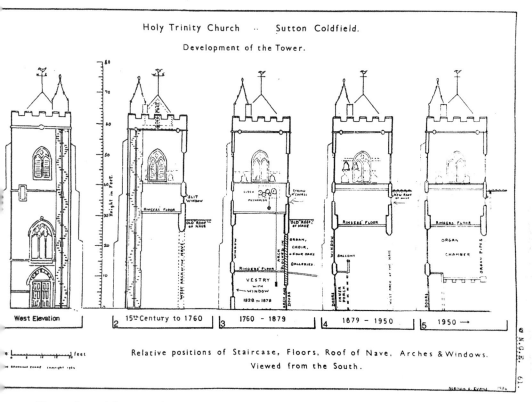

Fig. 37: *Internal changes in the tower to 1950 (NGE)*

The font was placed here in 2016 and is now in a flexible space for family members to gather at baptism services. Fig. 38 shows its former less convenient position near the south-west corner of the nave.

The ring of eight bells is maintained as required and the bells are rung for Sunday morning worship and by arrangement at weddings and other services.

The tower is also opened up to visitors from time to time to climb to the top and experience views across the West Midlands in all directions. The weather vane is at Fig. 39.

PAINTED CEILINGS

Four areas of the ceiling of Holy Trinity are painted in a highly decorative style, and all were executed by Birmingham architect Charles E Bateman.

Above left, Fig. 38: *Font in nave c2005 (HTSC)*

Above right, Fig. 39: *Weather vane on tower (HTSC)*

Fig. 40: *Chancel ceiling – detail (BHD)*

The ceiling of the chancel (1914) has thirty-six panels, many with a Tudor Rose design. The words of the 'Sanctus' (Holy, holy, holy) feature around the edge. The six panels at the east end show angels, each bearing a line from the words of the 'Gloria' (the words begin with the praise of the angels at the birth of Christ: 'Glory to God in the highest and peace to his people on earth.') Both the Gloria and the Sanctus feature in the liturgy of the mass or service of Holy Communion.

There are fourteen painted shields attached to the wall plate adjoining the vertical ribs of the ceiling. These depict symbols of the Passion of Jesus as follows, starting from the east end:

North side	Note	South side	Note
6. Nails	To pierce hands and feet (four of the five wounds of Christ)	**5. Pillar and cords**	Pillar where Jesus would have been tied and then whipped
7. Ladder and crossed spear, and sponge on reed	Spear used by the centurion to make the fifth wound (in Jesus's side) A soldier gave Jesus vinegar and gall on a sponge	**4. Robe**	Described in the Bible as seamless, so it could not be divided up
8. Hammer and pincers	The hammer to drive in the nails and the pincers to remove them	**3. Dice and cup**	The soldiers gambled to win the robe worn by Jesus
9. Crown of thorns	Placed on Jesus in mockery	**2. Scourges**	For whipping
10. Latin cross with INRI on top	INRI = letters traditionally written on crosses as indicated in the Bible. Abbreviation of Latin words meaning 'Jesus of Nazareth, King of the Jews'	**1. Lantern**	Soldiers came with lanterns to take Jesus (on Maundy Thursday)

Table 4: *Shields in chancel ceiling (Source: NADFAS, 2001, Woodwork, 397a)*

These are known generally as 'Arma Christi', the weapons of Christ, or the instruments of the Passion. There are others sometimes used but all will include the cross. They have been placed in a particular order to indicate the sequence of events in the Bible, and are numbered accordingly here, as they appear on the chancel ceiling if viewed looking east.

In 1929 the remaining ceilings were painted (Vesey chapel, nave and tower), and the details are as follows:

Fig. 41: *Vesey chapel ceiling – detail (BHD)*

Vesey chapel ceiling

The Vesey chapel ceiling has eight panels depicting the biblical passage known as the Beatitudes (Matthew 5: 3–11) at the east end. These were designed to be over the new altar placed in the chapel at the same time. The remainder of the ceiling has a design of thistles and Tudor roses, and the whole is surrounded by birds, oak leaves and squirrels, representing Sutton Park.

W. Hobart Bird, in his brief guide to Holy Trinity, makes the following observation about this ceiling: 'Note the gorgeous panelled gilded roof of the north chancel chapel – it is probably unique in ecclesiastical art.' (Bird, 1940, p. 104)

Nave ceiling

The nave ceiling has five sections, with the Tudor Rose much in evidence. Each beam has an angel at the end bearing a shield containing symbols of particular saints, now known to be the twelve apostles. These are in place along the nave as follows, starting from the east end:

East

North side	Symbol	South side	Symbol
St Peter	Keys	St Matthew	Sword (upside down)
St James the Great	Shell	St John	Chalice and dragon
St Andrew	Saltire	St Matthias	Scimitar
St Bartholomew	Three knives	St Simon (the Zealot)	Saw
St Jude	Ship	St James the Less	Halberd
St Thomas	Spear	St Philip	Cross

West

Table 5: *Apostles and their symbols depicted in the nave ceiling (Source: NADFAS, 2001, Woodwork, 397b, adapted)*

The NADFAS survey has queries against some names and also includes St Paul in the list. It is clear from further research that the saints are the twelve apostles, and these have been matched as accurately as possible to their known symbols as placed in the nave ceiling at Holy Trinity.

Tower ceiling

The tower ceiling (hidden between 1950 and 2018) is a pattern of squares, the principal colours being green, black and gold on a light grey background. It was cleaned in 2018 following the opening up of this part of the tower.

Fig. 42: *Tower ceiling (HTSC)*

Chapter 5 gives information recently uncovered about the names of those who designed and created the ceilings in 1929.

JOINT STOOLS

There are two stools used regularly at Holy Trinity as stands for flower arrangements which Roger Lea describes as worthy of note. In a reference to the will of one Thomas Clifton of 1684, he says that there was 'one item of furniture which seems to have been in every house – there were six in Clifton's bedroom. [This] was the "joint stool"; two seventeenth century oak joined stools are still in use in Sutton Parish Church.' (Lea, Thomas Clifton 2, HS 71, 18 Sept 2007)

8

MEMORIALS

BY MARIAN BAXTER

Memorials, hatchments and gravestones of all shapes, designs and sizes are an integral part of many churches, whether they are inside the church or outside in the graveyard, and Holy Trinity Church is no exception.

Evidence shows that the church was built in the thirteenth century and, as the church guide of 2018 states, 'since the first building much has changed, with nearly every century bringing some alteration'. With extensions, the raising of the roof, the lowering then raising of the floor and other changes, it is not surprising that not all of the memorials inside the church have survived. The churchyard has seen even more changes over the years.

A visit by members of the Sutton Coldfield Local History Research Group in 2017 to see the changes of the re-ordering led to some members asking about some of the people named on the brass plaques, marble and stone memorials and hatchments. It was noted that one or two memorials related to people who were not even buried at the church.

A small team from the research group, consisting of Marian Baxter, Eileen Donohoe, Ann Geraghty, Janet Lillywhite and Don McCollam, offered to research the stories behind these memorials, perhaps 'putting some flesh on the bones' of local people from earlier centuries, whether buried inside the church or outside, or with a large or small memorial. It was felt strongly that all these people have had a part to play in Sutton Coldfield's community.

With the help of Susie Walker, who carried out extensive research into the lives of the individuals, and a member of the Holy Trinity Heritage Project team, the researchers systematically worked their way around the inside and outside of the church to record on spreadsheets all of the memorials and then to commence the detailed searches to find out who all of these people were. The project did not include the windows but dedicated itself to all the other memorial types.

The research commenced, making use of relevant websites, parish and church records, newspapers, census returns, the *Dictionary of National Biography*, local biographies and histories, archaeological reports, the local history section of Sutton Coldfield Library, war records, shipping records, and many more.

Included in this chapter is a taste of the results. At some time in the future, a booklet will be published detailing more of the stories, and it is hoped that the stories of each individual will be made available online or at least on request for those wanting detailed information, for example for family history research.

With so many alterations to the internal structure of the church it is no surprise that not all of the memorials have survived, but a few of the early memorials are still to be found.

In 1985 the Federation of Family History Societies began a long-term project to record the monumental inscriptions in all churches and churchyards throughout the country. The Birmingham and Midland Society for Genealogy and Heraldry, as a member of the federation, encouraged its members to record the local churches. The monuments in Holy Trinity Church were recorded by Ethel Pritchard who was also a member of the Sutton Coldfield Local History Society. Interestingly some memorials recorded in this survey were no longer to be found in 2000 when a survey was undertaken by The National Association of Decorative and Fine Arts Societies, which recorded and described in full some fifty-nine memorials. This list is the definitive record of what can be found inside the church today. (NADFAS, 2000).

Fig. 43: *Gravestones round perimeter of Holy Trinity today (HTSC)*

In 2016 Archaeology Warwickshire was commissioned to conduct a dig prior to the re-ordering of the church. Two burials found were thought to be of a mediaeval date. A number of other burials, with the remains in poor condition, were uncovered in two large vaults, and a number of coffin burials were excavated. Other finds included fragments of mediaeval and post-mediaeval pottery, animal bone, clay pipes, glass bottles and mediaeval floor tiles (see Coutts, 2019).

Note: in this chapter, the names of individuals or families where fuller information is included are shown in bold, to make the many names more easily retrievable.

MEMORIALS IN THE CHANCEL, VESEY AISLE AND TOWER

Much is already written and available about Bishop Vesey, the Sacheverell family, the Pudsey family and the more well-known families of Sutton Coldfield, but this research has led to some fascinating information about lesser-known individuals whose memorials are in and around the church. The earliest monument in the church is that of Bishop Vesey, and Chapter 2 of this book gives full details of his life and of his tomb in the Vesey chapel. The story of the Pudsey and Jesson families (whose memorials are in the Vesey chapel) is in Chapter 13 about various noteworthy parishioners.

On the chancel north wall near the east end are two brass plaques; the upper is shaped as a woman with hands together in an Elizabethan costume of hood and short cape, ruff and farthingale. She is standing between two smaller figures depicting her son, Raphael, and daughter, Elizabeth. The lower brass has a Latin inscription and confirms both plaques as being for **Barbara Eliot**. The inscription reads, 'Here lies Barbara Eliot, daughter of Raphael Simonds, Gentleman, the wife of Roger Eliot, Master and Rector of this church. She died September 1606 in the 24th year of her age. She gave birth to Raphael Eliot and Elizabeth Eliot.' This is the brass plaque which was originally on the floor of the chancel over her grave but was moved to its present position when the chancel floor was raised in 1857. (For further information about the Eliot family, see Chapter 11).

Another of the early wall brasses is that of **Josias Bull** which is in the chancel on the opposite south wall. In his book *An Investigation of Holy Trinity Parish Church*, Norman Evans states that:

The brasses were originally over the grave in the Chancel and were moved to their present position when the floor was raised. They are four parts; the upper brass displays his Coat of Arms which is of 'three annulets in fees between three bull's heads, erased at neck, a crescent for differences (Bull) impaling a chevron between three covered cups, an annulet for difference (Butler) for his wife.' The inscription on the brasses below his effigy reads:- 'Here lies resteth ye body of Josias Bull late of this Town, Gent. He tooke to wife Katherine Walshe widdoe daughter of Willm Botelier of Tyes in Essex Esqr by whom he had issue 4 sonnes and 1 daughter: Josias, Henry, George, John and Ann. He deceased the 29th of March Ano 1621. About ye age of 50 years.' (Evans, 1987, p. 21)

On the lower brass the boys are shown grouped together with Ann standing near them.

A monuments researcher, Jon Bayliss, has provided information (by email to the editor in 2019) about the manufacture of the brass plates as follows:

I have previously photographed the brasses myself and believe they both belong to the same style, designed in the Cure workshop in Southwark and made in Southwark or the city. As you can tell from your photographs, the figures are engraved on different coloured metal from the inscriptions, which is suggestive of the latter being replaced. The Bull date of death is too late for the style of figure, so I would be interested to learn if there were payments for new plates at the time of restoration. [There is no mention of this in vestry minutes or press reports]. I am also particularly interested in the Harman indent at the east end of the north aisle, which is Coventry work.

Although the figures of Barbara Elliott and Josias Bull are both later than the brasses I covered in my article 'The Southwark Workshops, 1585-1605' in the *Transactions of the Monumental Brass Society* in 2015, they both belong to the group I identified there as designed by the Cure family of Southwark. Brasses from this group can be found all over England. They were presumably both once set in slabs of black Belgium marble. The inscription plates of both are replacements and are on different coloured metal.

'LOST' MEMORIALS

Both Evans and Gardner have written about the others buried in the chancel whose memorial tablets were moved or lost when the floor was raised and the slabs hidden. These include:

Catherine, daughter of **Samuel Leigh** (d. 1695). Memorial on pillar on south side of sanctuary.

Fig. 44: *Brasses of Barbara Elyot and Josias Bull on chancel wall (HTSC)*

Walter Peyton, warden of Sutton Coldfield in 1623. (d. 1639, buried in chancel vault with his wife, Dorothy, who had predeceased him. Family lived at Marlpit Hall, near Worcester Lane).

John Barnes – memorial on the south wall just before the choir vestry entrance.

Thomas Willoughby JP (d. 1661 – more information in Chapter 14)

Samuel Stevenson, High Sheriff of Warwickshire and JP. (d. 1709 aged 82. Licensed to conduct Presbyterian marriages in his house in Sutton, the banns being previously read at Holy Trinity).

Henry Stibbs, warden in 1731, died that year aged 39.

Charles, son of **Edward Biddulph** Esq. (d. 1747 aged 17)

Both Stibbs and Biddulph's names are recorded by Agnes Bracken in her history of 1860.

Other memorials in the chancel record most of the Rectors from the Riland and Riland Bedford families.

A slab in the floor of the Vesey chapel, near the tomb, is thought to be of members of Bishop Vesey's (the **Harman**) family. It is noteworthy for the loss of the covering brass plate recorded by Dugdale (see Chapter 2) and also the fact that all the figures are in shrouds. Parish archivist Margaret Gardner summarised the known facts about the likelihood of the burials relating to members of John Vesey's family, but this is not as clear-cut as might be supposed, as some of those supposedly buried there would have died some time before the north aisle extension Vesey had built c1530. This has led to conjecture by Margaret that there might have been an existing churchyard on the original north side of the church and that the aisle extension simply brought some burials within the church (Gardner, 2000, pp. 18–19).

Jon Bayliss writes about this as follows:

> The slab near the entrance to the Vesey chapel that once held brasses I find particularly interesting and presumably commemorated members of Vesey's family. It was made in Coventry and showed them in shrouds. The one surviving Coventry brass showing such a shrouded figure is at Edgmond, Shropshire. The slab in Holy Trinity was quarried at Vaudey Abbey in Lincolnshire, a source used by this Coventry workshop only in the 1520s and 30s. (Jon Bayliss, by email, 2019)

This newer information suggests that the slab is co-eval with the aisle extension.

On the floor in the Vesey aisle of the church can be found two floor slabs. Research carried out by Ann Geraghty and Roger Lea shows that several families named **Honeyborne** lived in Sutton Coldfield in the seventh century. There is some evidence that skilled weavers from the village of Honeybourne (near Evesham in Worcestershire) came to Sutton in the 1530s as part of Bishop Vesey's plan to establish a weaving industry here. Over the centuries there have been many different spellings for Honeybourne: Honiborn, Honnyborn, Hunnyborn, Huniborn and Hunyburne. The incised stone slabs on the floor of the aisle are two of six which have been replaced in their old position in the new floor of the church and, although difficult to read, one is inscribed 'in memory of Mr Thomas Hunnyborn died August 1728'. The second slab reads 'in memory of Jane wife of Thomas Hunnyborn, died August 1732' aged 71. Thomas was elected warden of Sutton Coldfield in 1720 and 1721. During his term he was embroiled in a dispute with 'squatters' in cottages which were deemed illegal and unfit for habitation. Thomas tried to evict the cottagers but found they were able to prove their rights to live there, and his attempts failed.

In the tower, on the north wall, is the marble tablet for Joseph **Mendham**. His story is recounted in Chapter 11 in the section entitled 'Other clergy of Holy Trinity'.

Early in 1795 he accepted the curacy of Sutton Coldfield and on 15 December married Maria Riland, the second daughter of the Revd John Riland, Rector of Sutton Coldfield. They had two children: Robert, born 1798, and Ann Marie, born 1799.

He died on 1 November 1856 aged 87. He is remembered as 'a tall sad looking clergyman of eminent personal piety, impeccable manners and cultivated taste'. His wife Maria had died on 27 May 1841, some fifteen years earlier. Colville's

Warwickshire Worthies (qv), records that the son, Revd Robert Riland Mendham, of Wadham College, Oxford, was the literary companion of the father's declining years and he assisted his father in his constant efforts to relieve distress. Robert died on 15 June 1857, aged 59, a bachelor, within a few months of his father, having left a legacy to Boldmere Church for the building of a spire. In the 1871 census Joseph's daughter Ann Marie was living with Dr George Bodington and his wife in Maney. She is described as a 'boarder' and a 'lunatic' on her own means. She died on 23 September 1871.

On the central pillar on the north side of the chancel is a memorial to **Ann Ash,** who died in 1789 aged 31. She was the older unmarried sister of Mary, the wife of Rector the Revd Richard Bisse Riland, and she spent much of her time with them at the rectory. The memorial tablets to the **Riland** and Riland Bedford families are on the east end wall of the chancel as well as on the wall under the lychgate off Coleshill Street. Further information about the Riland and Riland Bedford clergy and family is in Chapter 12.

A marble rectangular wall tablet on the north wall of the tower commemorates John and Mary **Oughton**. John ran one of the seventeen water and windmills which could be found working in Sutton Coldfield over the decades. John Oughton took over the gun barrel mill from Joseph Oughton in 1772. John had a gun barrel business in Birmingham in 1780. The house, watermill and dam were on the site near to the current Plantsbrook School in Upper Holland Road. Its three millpools, bordered by evergreens, extended along the line of the present South Parade, and, fed by the Ebrook, covered an area of over 8 acres. Here in the second half of the eighteenth century and early part of the nineteenth century, bayonets were forged and gun barrels bored and ground by power of the waterwheel for the gunsmiths of Birmingham. Holland gun barrel mill played its part through its owner in setting up the Birmingham Proof House. John Oughton was a prominent figure in Sutton Coldfield and became warden in 1813. He died in April 1849, aged 74. His widow Mary, who continued to live at Holland House, died on 9 January 1859 aged 79. In Richard Holbeche's diary (1892) he recalls the 1850s when Mrs Oughton lived at Holland House as 'a very old lady in her lace bonnet'.

MEMORIALS IN THE CHURCH TO SOLDIERS AND OTHER YOUNGER MEN

Two brass plaques caught the attention of Eileen Donohoe whose research showed that neither Bernard Winder nor Gilbert Rippingille is interred at the church. The memorial to **Bernard Winder** (Fig. 45) can be found on

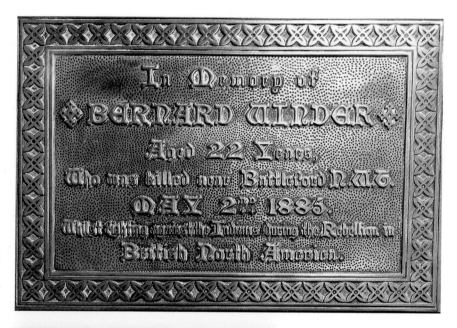

Above, Fig. 45: *Memorial to Bernard Winder (ED)*

Left, Fig. 46: *Memorial to Gilbert Rippingille (ED)*

the nave west wall behind the serving area of the café in Holy Trinity. It is a simple brass plaque which is both sad and intriguing. A young man lost his life after travelling to a new country full of hope and with a sense of adventure. His mother died when Bernard was only 7 years old and by the time he was 18 in 1881, his father Walter was a wealthy businessman with a thriving saddlery and ironworks in Birmingham, and employed by the Manor House in Sutton Coldfield as saddler, ironmonger and whip maker. According to the census of that year, Bernard, a former pupil of Bishop Vesey School, was employed at the Manor House as a farmer, his main interest being with the horses. He worked alongside his father and elder brother, Walter A, who was a currier. For reasons unknown, Bernard and his brother set off for Canada. They left Liverpool for Quebec on the *Sardinian*, arriving in May 1881. It appears that Bernard joined with forces fighting ongoing battles over land with native Americans. He worked as a teamster, looking after the horses which were used to pull the 'chuck wagons' carrying food and firearms, as well as the Gatling gun carriages. On May 2 1885, during the battle of Cut Knife, Battlefield, Saskatchewan, only four men were killed. Sadly, Bernard was one of those to be caught in crossfire and die.

The memorial to Gilbert **Rippingille** (Fig. 46) is a large, elaborately carved marble plaque clearly paying tribute to a dearly loved son who died at the age of 20. It can be found on the nave east end north side wall, next to the clergy vestry. Gilbert was born in Middlesex, the third son of Edward and Ellen. The family moved to Station Road, Boldmere in Sutton Coldfield, and in 1881, Gilbert was 8 years old. His father owned the thriving Albion Lamp Company in Aston Road North in Birmingham, and was a well-respected Suttonian. Gilbert was a good, popular student who went on to study Fine Art, following in the footsteps of his renowned uncle, the successful painter Edward Villiers Rippingille, who has oil paintings and watercolours in many galleries. In the spring of 1893, on 17 April, he accompanied his elder brother Harry on a voyage. Harry was the superintendent engineer for a fleet of Chinese boats and Gilbert was going along as companion or as a working artist. A passenger list on that date names the boat as *Ben Lawers*, which was making a fifty-day voyage to Penang, Singapore, China and Japan. After arriving in Penang, Harry had a bad attack of typhoid fever. Gilbert helped to nurse him back to health but shortly after, he contracted the fever himself and did not recover. He rapidly weakened and tragically lost his life on 4 July 1893, in his 21st year. He was a popular young man in Sutton Coldfield and an obituary, which appeared in *The Sutton Coldfield News* on 5 August of that year, expressed the family's sadness.

In the nave on the south wall (near the underside of the south gallery stairs) is the brass wall plaque dedicated to **Henry Charles Hill**, who was born in Sutton Coldfield on 2 February 1852, the eldest child of John and Ann Hill. The family lived in Coleshill Street and in the 1861 census his father is listed as a builder employing twenty-one men. Henry attended Bishop Vesey's school and by 1870 he was living in India, employed by the Indian Forest Service, which was established by the British government in 1864 in order to conserve valuable timber, especially teak, for the British Navy. He went on to become Inspector General of Indian Forests. He was a member of the Freemasons in Shimla from 12 August 1870 until his death in 1902. He came home to Sutton Coldfield on leave in May 1902, intending to return, but died while on holiday at Hessle in Yorkshire on 7 November 1902. Hill is also noteworthy for his donation to the church in 1892 of a misericord, which remained in the church until 2008 when it was sold. (A misericord is a hinged seat which can be tipped up to allow monks some support when standing during their long services. This one was thought to be c1490 and its carving showed a man picking grapes.)

A brass plaque at the east end and on the south side of the nave commemorates **Percival Allen Grove**. The obituary states:

> Second Lieutenant Percival Allen Grove, Royal Warwickshire Regiment, died on Wednesday from wounds received in action, was the elder son of Mr Allen Grove of Messrs Grove and Son, Birmingham, of The Cedars, Sutton. Lieutenant Grove, who was 27 years of age, was a chartered accountant, was educated at Bishop Vesey Grammar School. He joined the Birmingham City Battalion on their formation and was granted a commission in a Warwickshire Territorial in September last.

The rectangular brass plaque tells us that Grove died on 5 July 1916 and is interred at Saint Sever cemetery, Rouen, France.

THE REAY-NADIN WROUGHT IRON MEMORIAL

One of the unusual memorials is to be found on the Victorian pew end in the nave at the west end of the south aisle. (When these pews were in place in the church, this memorial was on the central nave side of the front pew.) This is an enamelled wrought iron shield and framework in dark green, which is enhanced with gilded leaves to the sides and top. The concave shield contains the coat of arms of Sutton Coldfield granted in 1935 (see Fig. 47).

Fig. 47: *The Reay-Nadin memorial (MB)*

It is the memorial to Robert Armstrong Reay-Nadin. He was born in 1867 in Newport, Monmouthshire, and his parents were Elizabeth and Robert Reay. On 28 July 1870, when he was 2 years old, his widowed mother married Walter Nadin in Manchester. His stepfather, whose surname he adopted, was a solicitor, and this is the profession that Robert followed. In 1900 he married Edith Daniel and moved to Yardley, becoming assistant solicitor to Birmingham Council.

In May 1904 he became town clerk of Sutton Coldfield and was also clerk to the Municipal Trustees. During the Second World War he helped the recruiting campaign and made arrangements for the Birmingham City battalions to train in Sutton Park, in addition to raising the local Defence Force, enrolling special constables and being Food Control Officer for the borough. On behalf of Sutton Coldfield he conducted the case when Sutton obtained a strip of land (in opposition to Birmingham) from the old Perry Barr district, ensuring that Sutton Park on the Birmingham side was surrounded by borough land. He campaigned for better housing and was a member of the government advisory committee on town planning. He promoted the development of the first town planning scheme along the Garden City lines in 1911 and 1929. In 1934 he was made an honorary freeman of the borough. In July 1937, only a few weeks before his death, he was made a Justice of the Peace. A memorial service was held at the parish church on 18 August. The Rector, Revd G. L. Harvey, described him as 'A great public servant, and one who had a genius for friendship'. Robert is buried in the Sutton Coldfield cemetery.

THE GRAVEYARD

The date for the building of Holy Trinity Church is uncertain. It is generally thought to have been founded in 1250, with the earliest record for the church itself being 1291. It is likely that the early section of the burial yard is contemporary with the beginnings of the church, with burials taking place inside and outside the building. With the expansion of the church building, some external burials came to be within the walls of the church.

As was the case in many churchyards, later burials were sometimes made over the top of earlier ones in succeeding centuries.

In his investigation of the church, Norman Evans recorded the comment of Thomas Bonell, a Sutton solicitor writing in 1762, who stated that the churchyard was:

> taken notice of for consuming the bodies deposited therein very quickly: in two vaults lately opened the corpses have been found to have been reduced to mere dust, together with the coffins of wood which enclosed them, the interment of which has been within the memory of man. (Evans, 1987, p. 85)

Evans surmises that this phenomenon was due to the nature of the sandstone.

With the population of Sutton Coldfield increasing, it became very apparent that the old churchyard would have to be enlarged. In May 1817 the Archdeacon of Lichfield, on his inspection of Holy Trinity, reported that 'a new burial ground is wanted', noting at the same time that he was not satisfied with the way the churchyard was being maintained. 'Pigs, horses and cows are to be kept out of the churchyard', he ordered, 'and it is to be grazed only by sheep'.

In 1832, the burial ground was enlarged by adding land on which the former garden and schoolhouse of the Bishop Vesey School, put up by Bishop Vesey in 1541, had been located.

An extract from Richard Holbeche's diary describes the churchyard in the 1860s as badly kept and unenclosed, with sheep grazing there.

By 1876 the number of remaining spaces for graves was steadily diminishing and consideration was being given to locations in Sutton for a new burial ground. Sites were inspected on Maney Hill, Tudor Hill, on the Four Oaks Estate, on Tamworth Road, in the Royal Road and Ebrook Road area, and on land to the east of Coleshill Street.

Eventually, 4 acres of land adjoining Rectory Road were purchased, and the Bishop of Worcester consecrated the new burial ground on 4 May 1880 'for use of members of the established church'. The first interment was on 1 November 1880.

The churchyard was closed in the same year as the cemetery was opened, and thereafter churchyard burials could only be in existing family graves. By the end of the 1940s, the churchyard had become an overgrown wilderness as there were in most cases no longer families to tend their forebears' graves.

There have been twenty-four burials in the churchyard since 1911, and the last was in 1928. 'The church has a record of burials by law as required, but there is no graveyard plan showing where the individual graves were.' (Information from a preliminary report for the building of the Trinity Centre, 1992)

The churchyard was cleared of the majority of headstones in 1950 and, according to Margaret Gardner (2000), the responsibility for maintenance of the churchyard was taken over by the Sutton Coldfield Borough Council. Many of the headstones were placed against the west wall, overlooking Trinity Hill and the old town school (now the Baptist church). Fig. 48 shows the south path and churchyard with railings taken before these were removed, presumably for needs in the Second World War.

Fig. 48: *Churchyard with railings – early twentieth century (NGE)*

149

In 1992 an archaeological survey was conducted by Birmingham University Field Archaeology Unit to assess the character and survival of any possible archaeological remains in view of proposals for the construction of a church hall and car parking within the churchyard. The report stated:

> some of the tombstones and grave surrounds were broken up at the time of the clearance. Parts of two substantial pits … revealed at the east end of the excavation contained numerous fragments of broken memorial stones, grave surrounds and bricks, evidently reburied after the graveyard had been cleared. (Leach and Sterenberg, 1992, p. 4)

In the 1990s, with the building of the Trinity Centre, graves which were still in place were deconsecrated and the remains re-interred where they would not be disturbed. The gravestones were relocated along the west wall overlooking Sutton Coldfield. Many memorials remain in place around the church.

The parish registers of Holy Trinity Parish Church commence in 1603 and can be found in Warwickshire County Record Office. However, a copy of an earlier part of the register – baptisms, marriages and burials covering the years 1565–99 – is to be found in the Bishop's transcripts at Lichfield Record Office (now based in Stafford). The first page of the vellum document is headed: 'The register Book of all weddings christenings and burieges in Sutton Coldfield in the County of Warwick in the tyme of Roger Eliot, gent, parson there from the years of our Lord god 1565.'

As the existing parish registers commence in 1603, it seems that the church authorities failed to make a further vellum copy of the paper register, and the paper copy has been lost. Transcripts of 1565–99 entries by N. T. Tidesley can be found in Sutton Coldfield Library. Microfilm copies of the 1603–1710 registers can also be found in Sutton Coldfield Library, along with transcriptions, with a names index, compiled by members of the Sutton Coldfield Local History Research Group.

In the time of Charles II, legislation was introduced to help the wool trade of the Cotswolds. In 1667, and further implemented in 1678, the legislation stated:

> No corpse of any person (except those who shall die of the plague) shall be buried in any shift, sheet or shroud, or anything whatsoever made or mingled with flax, hemp, silk, hair, gold, or silver, or in any stuff or thing, other than what is made of sheep's wool only; or be put in any coffin lined or faced with any sort of cloth or fluff or anything whatsoever, that is made of any other material but sheep's wool only, on pain of forfeiting £5.

All had to comply. This can be seen in the parish registers of Holy Trinity: an entry for 31 August 1678 states 'Thomas Bennian, in woollen, according to the Act of Parliament, being the first sole buried here.' A burial on 14 March 1684 is recorded as being of 'Ann Lynes, wife of Thomas Lynes, the last that was buried in Wolen.'

There is no trace as to the position of these burials in the churchyard today.

Although there are references to the early burials in the church registers, it has been extremely difficult to research the site or personal information of the individuals and families of these people interred in the churchyard, because of the lack of records and the fact that the majority of the gravestones have been moved, in some cases several times. Also no maps or plans showing the layout of the churchyard have been found, and extensive research has concluded that no plan was deemed necessary when the headstones were moved. There are very few Victorian photographs of the actual churchyard and those found have not been detailed enough to help identify the standard gravestones, although the position of the larger ones can be plotted.

The members of the Sutton Coldfield Local History Research Group decided to work with what was in the churchyard now rather than what had been there in the past.

GRAVESTONES

Using the websites of A. K. Lander 'A History of Gravestones' and the International Southern Cemetery Gravestone Association's *A History of Gravestones*, along with Richard Taylor's *How to Read a Church* and Peter Watkins and Eric Hughes's *Here's the Church*, we looked at the history of gravestones.

Grave markers, headstones and tombstones are known today collectively as gravestones, and have long served as memorials. They come in all sizes and shapes. It is believed that they date back as far as 3000 BCE. In earlier times the graves would be marked with wood, rocks or stones, possibly as a way to keep the dead from rising. Cemeteries evolved in the nineteenth century; until then, people used to have burial plots near their family home. Once churchyard burials started to become popular in the 1650s, gravestones began to become more widespread. Tombstones and monuments made from slate were put up to commemorate the deceased, and from this point inscriptions were carved on them. Large stone monuments would be used to mark an entire burial chamber rather than a single grave. The early tombstones and monuments were usually marked with the name, age and year of death of the deceased. Once cemeteries developed, it became more popular to engrave the headstones with small epitaphs about the deceased.

The eighteenth century saw a short-lived burial practice of covering the graves with iron cages. During the Victorian period, the most popular materials were marble, granite, iron and wood. In the nineteenth century the importance of gravestones to honour the dead increased and inscriptions became more widespread, often including a few words about the deceased, as well as the name, and dates of birth and death. It was also in the Victorian period that poorer people began to commemorate the dead with memorials, as in the past it had only been the upper classes who could afford to do this.

With no site plans for the early burials, the team, Don McCollam, Marian Baxter and Janet Lillywhite, decided to look at the evidence, which can be seen today in the churchyard. It has been much more difficult to find personal information about the people in the churchyard than about those who have memorials inside the church.

The majority of the headstones in the churchyard date from the late 1700s and 1800s. It is not known how many of them either survived or were damaged or lost when the graveyard was cleared in 1950/51, nor to whom they belonged.

We do know that memorials to some of Sutton Coldfield's more eminent residents, which the team would have expected to find, could not be traced, including Agnes Bracken. The story of Mary Ashford, whose gravestone is still in the churchyard, is covered as a footnote to Chapter 4 of this book. Although there are memorials in the church and some large tombstones to eminent members of Sutton Coldfield's population, the researchers for this chapter concentrated on the lesser-known stories of the ordinary folk who were remembered at the church, confident that those of more well-to-do families are covered elsewhere.

Information on George **Bodington** can be found on the Bodington Family Histories, George Bodington MD 1799 to 1882, and works written by Andrew MacFarlane are in Sutton Coldfield Library, as are several substantial articles on the Holbeche family by Janet Jordan.

Some of the stones laid flat on the north side of the church are almost impossible to read. However, one of the early stones that can be read is for the **Scott** family. The gravestone is that of:

Rugeley Scott youngest daughter of Richard Scott of Ashfurlong in this Parish by Mary, his wife. She died 10 March 1764 aged 70. Maria Scott born 24 February 1762---- died 1781? Aged 91---------- and another for Wilthard (?), Scott, son of Richard Scott of Ashfurlong in this Parish, Gent: by Mary, his wife. Who departed this life February 24th, aged 59.

On the south side of the church another early stone reads, sadly:

near this place lie the bodies of Mary, Mary, William and Edward sons and daughters of Abraham and Mary **Oulton**. Mary died on 28th March 1754 aged 5½; Mary died on 3rd April 1757, aged 4; William died 19th February 1759, aged 4; Edward died 21st February 1759, aged 10 and John died 14th March 1759, aged 14 months.

On the south side again another stone is for Thomas **Brockas,** born 2 November 1780, died aged 5, and Elizabeth Brockas, born 1746 and died 29 March 1803. It is not certain if this Brockas family is related to Charles Brockas, whose memorial stone can be found on the west wall of the church. Charles Brockas, a tailor by trade, was born in 1774 and died on 7 September 1846, aged 72. He married Mary Sneyd who was born in 1781 and died aged 78 in 1859. They had five children, the oldest of whom, Eliza Caroline, was born in 1801 and died on 19 April 1842. She married Thomas Whitworth, a builder, and they lived in Coleshill Street. Harriet was born in 1813 and William, born 1815, worked as a draper and tailor in the High Street in Sutton Coldfield, employing seven men. Louisa Brockas was born 10 January 1818 and married Samuel Smith on 17 February 1846 at Holy Trinity Church. Her husband was a victualler at the Dolphin Inn, Coventry Street, Birmingham, with his father Joseph.

Another licensed victualler was Isaac **Aulton,** who was born in Sutton Coldfield in 1813 and died 23 January 1883 aged 70. His wife, Mary Ann Hunt, was born in 1814 in Wednesbury and she died, aged 58, in 1872. They were married on 10 March 1834 at St Peter and St Paul's Church, Aston. According to the census and probate records, Isaac ran the Woolpack Inn at Castle Street, Dudley, from 1851 until his death in 1883. Both were buried in the Holy Trinity churchyard, but it is not known what their connection was to Sutton Coldfield.

Running a pub and a farm was the occupation of William **Davis**, the son of Jonas and Mary, who was baptised at Holy Trinity Church on 28 December 1774. He married Elizabeth Kesterton on 10 October 1799 and they had four children. Charles was born 26 August 1801 and died 2 November 1823, aged 22. Richard was born on 3 February 1811 and died on 31 January 1863, aged 51. Stephen was born on 10 January 1812. He died 30 October 1897, aged 85, and Septimus was born 3 August 1816 and died 13 July, aged 6.

In the 1841 census William and Elizabeth are living at Maney near the Cup Inn and William is described as a 'farmer and Publican'. William died 20 November and was buried in Holy Trinity Churchyard. The family continued to live in Maney and after Elizabeth died on 9 March 1868, Richard, the eldest son, took over the running of the farm. In 1861 he is described as a 'farmer occupying 90 acres, employing four men and one boy'. He died on 31 January 1863 and was buried on 6 February. Stephen became a steel engraver; he married Thirza Bradbury at St Martin's Birmingham in 1868. They had one daughter, Mary, born 21 June 1871. The family lived at The Driffold (Maney) and Stephen died on 30 October 1897 aged 85.

Another farmer born in 1831 was James **Reynolds**. He was a farmer of 110 acres called School Farm.

Another connected to farming is James **Thorley** of Sutton Coldfield, born 1803 and died 13 March 1863. He is described as an agricultural labourer. His wife Elizabeth, also of Sutton Coldfield, was born in 1803 and died on 30 June 1886, aged 83. They lived in Belwell Lane with their four children. John was born in 1835, Thomas 1837, Charles 1840, and Henry 1842.

Moving away from farming, Emma **Goldingay** was born in 1844 in Sutton Coldfield and died 28 June 1900. She married John Goldingay, who was born in Marston Green. In the 1871 census, John is described as a labourer and Emma did not work. They were living in Brittles Buildings, Water Works Street, at the time of the 1881 census, and Emma was a laundress and John a plate layer. By the 1891 census they had moved to Sutton Coldfield to live in Church Hill and John was now an excavator.

Henry **Stephenson**, born in Middleton, was a 'carpenter with 2 men' and married to Harriet, who was born in Birmingham. They lived in High Street with their two children, Ann and Henry, until Henry's death on 15 November 1878.

Ann **Smith**, born in Shropshire and died in 1878 aged 60, was wife to Frederick Smith, who was born in 1821 in Boston, Lincolnshire. Their first son, Alfred Broom Smith, was 19 when he died on 24 May 1867. Frederick was a cabinet maker and they and their children Alfred, Harry, George and Maria, lived near the rectory in 1861. After the death of Ann, who is buried in the churchyard, along with her son Alfred, Frederick moved his family to 97 Duke Road, Chiswick (London).

Plumber was the trade of another person who moved to Sutton Coldfield from Shropshire. George **Haynes** was baptised on 13 February 1814 in Kinley, and he married Ann Grinley on 24 March 1840 in Bridgnorth. At the time of the 1841 census, George, Ann and their eldest son, William, who was 4 months old, were living at Knockin near Oswestry, and George was employed as a painter. By 1845 they had moved to Sutton Coldfield and were living at Doe Bank. George was employed as a painter and glazier. Sadly, their eldest daughter Ann, born in 1843, died and was buried on 17 February 1845. However, by this time they had a second daughter, Mary Ann, and then four sons were born: George in 1849, Arthur in 1851, Thomas in 1853 and James in 1855. Unfortunately, Arthur and Thomas died, Arthur in 1869, aged 17, and Thomas in 1873, aged 20. By 1871, the family had moved to High Street and George's business had expanded. He is now described in the census as a master plumber, employing six men and one youth. His eldest son, William, is also working in the family business and the younger sons, George and James, are working as a house decorator and a gas fitter's apprentice. George died on 4 November 1875 aged 61. His wife Ann remained living in the High Street with her eldest son William and his family until her death on 11 June 1874, aged 74.

Joseph **Handy,** born in Walsall, Staffordshire, died 24 April 1894 in Sutton Coldfield. He was a retired barber. His wife was called Georgina Johanna Sidley, born 1804 in Burton-on-Trent. They were married on 25 March 1835 at Saint Philip's Church in Birmingham (now Birmingham Cathedral). In 1851 they lived in Coleshill Street. From the 1861 census we find he lived in High Street, his occupation was a hairdresser and he was a widower. He had a daughter named Sarah, who was a housekeeper. She was born in Birmingham in 1840 and died on 3 July 1862, aged 22. Joseph continued to live in the High Street as a hair-dresser-cum-barber until he moved into the alms houses in Sutton where he died.

James **Bourne** was born 24 April 1775 in Dalby, Lincolnshire. He became a licensed independent minister. He lived with his wife in Maney and died on 11 June 1854.

Watkin **Maddy** was an astronomer and a native of Herefordshire. Educated at Hereford Grammar School, he graduated as a second wrangler in 1820 from St John's College, Cambridge. An MA followed in 1823, and in the same year he took orders, and in 1830 a degree of BD. He was elected to a fellowship on 18 March 1823 and received the office of moderator. In 1826 he published *The Elements of the Theory of Plane Astronomy*. Around 1837 Maddy resigned his fellowship for reasons of conscience. He supported himself by teaching mathematics in London until his death in Sutton Coldfield on 13 August 1857. The *Dictionary of National Biography* says 'his character was of the highest stamp'.

William **Lowe** was born in 1807 in Middleton and died aged 54 on 31 March 1861. His wife, Ann Slater, was born in Lichfield and was buried in the grave on her death on 5 October, aged 70. William's occupation was a carpenter.

Frank **Lucas** was born 28 October 1817 and baptised in Sutton Coldfield on 25 December 1817. He lived in Langley and was a wire cutter, possibly at Penns Mill. His wife, Mary Ann Lucas of Birmingham, was a dress maker. Sadly, their daughter Ann died at the age of 5 on 25 January 1853 and their son Frederick died aged just 9 months. Thomas Lucas was born in 1845. He was a scholar on the 1851 census and was in the workhouse by the 1861 census. Edward Lucas, Frank's father, was born in 1770 and a carpenter by trade. He became a Chelsea Pensioner.

One of the larger memorials in the churchyard is surrounded by an iron fence, and covers the vault in which Joseph **Webster**, his wife and some of their twelve children are buried. Apart from the eighteenth-century fashion of covering the graves with iron cages, as can also be seen with the Smith monument on the north side of the graveyard, the iron railings were also an indication of the trade of the Websters, who had acquired Mr Penn's watermill in 1752, where they manufactured bars and rods from iron. The family lived in the house overlooking the mill pool at Penn's Mill. They were pioneers in producing a steel suitable for drawing into wire, particularly piano wire, for which they became known throughout Europe. At their other mill in Hay Mills, they produced the wire for the first successful transatlantic telephone cable, which was laid by the S.S. *Great Eastern* from Valentia in Ireland to Trinity Bay in Newfoundland. Joseph Webster was the third Joseph to have owned the mill, and he was very active in local affairs, a Justice of the Peace and warden of Sutton Coldfield in 1808 and 1810. He was also the principal founder of St John's Church in Walmley in 1845.

Now lost to us is the grave of Thomas **Dawney** (see Fig. 49). Norman Evans described this grave as follows:

It was marked in a very distinguishing manner by a massive, roughly cut stone slab forming a solid gabled roof supported along each side by equally massive vertical stone slabs. This stood in the churchyard for some 300 years until it was removed along with most of the tombstones to enable the graveyard to be kept tidy by regular mowing. (Evans, 1987, p. 81)

The entry of 9 September 1671 sites the grave of that gentleman:

There was Buryed the ixth Day of September Mr. Thomas Dawney in the Churchyard in a grave on the north syde the Dyall Post about ix feet deep. Att th [what] time the Towne Hall floore fell downe by the presse of people there.

This refers to the old Moot Hall, which stood at the top of Mill Street now occupied by the traffic island, the crowd having assembled for the purpose of receiving a dole which was being distributed in accordance with Mr Dawney's will. (Ibid.)

The last story connected with a memorial in the graveyard is that of William **Twamley**, who was born in 1763. By the end of the eighteenth century he was the tenant miller at New Hall Mill and New Shipton where, with his sons, he improved both properties. According to Roger Lea's 'History Spot' in the *Sutton Coldfield Observer*, Twamley and others used to put horses into Sutton Park to graze, paying the Warden and Society ten pence (10*d*) a quarter. In 1787, the warden put

Fig. 49: *The Dawney tomb c1895 (SCL)*

the charges up to 18*d* a quarter. Twamley and others went to the courts to appeal, stating that the 10*d* charge was enshrined in the 1528 town charter and could not be altered. They won their case. More can be found about this (and the subsequent case put before the Court of Chancery suggesting the Warden and Society were not managing their affairs correctly) in Agnes Bracken's *History of the Forest and Chase of Sutton Coldfield* (Bracken, 1860) and in W. K. R. Bedford's *The Manor of Sutton* (Riland Bedford). Zachariah Twamley, William's son, says 'Sir John Scott told his father no man could have taken a more honourable matter in hand,' as Twamley took an active interest in the case. (Lea, Twamley jug, HS 56, 5 June 2009) The Chancery case was finally resolved in 1824, with the Warden and Society agreeing to a scheme for better governance of the town, but unfortunately William died on 5 January 1825 before the new scheme was put into effect. Zachariah wrote a history of Sutton Coldfield (see References).

9

STAINED GLASS

With many of Holy Trinity's windows now filled with stained glass it is hard to imagine it without. Yet, as Richard Holbeche describes in his memoirs of life in the 1860s, for most of its life this was the case: 'There was no coloured glass in the whole church with the exception of a glass door which opened to the Vestry under the Four Oaks Gallery.' (Holbeche, 1893)

The information here gives detail of the images in just those of the windows which tell a story.

Patterned stained glass is evident in the windows along the north wall next to the north gallery, as well as in the high windows in the nave, known as the clerestory. There is also a rather attractive piece of patterned glass now visible above the interior entrance of the church which, until 2016, was obscured from view from the floor of the church by the north gallery extension along the west wall.

EAST WINDOW

The main focus of the church as one looks from the west end main doors is the large window at the east end of the chancel, which was given in memory of William Riland Bedford, Rector from 1822–43.

The centre shows Christ on the cross and is the key image. It forms the centre of a panel of five 'lights' or windows depicting scenes from Christ's life. The three lights at the very top show two angels standing either side of 'Christ in majesty'.

The frame is of fifteenth-century origin and it is thought to have had stained glass until the late seventeenth century showing the arms of the Beauchamp family (Earls of Warwick). Certainly this had been removed before the second edition of Dugdale's *Antiquities of Warwickshire* in 1730. The glass would have been filled with plain glass rectangular leaded lights after this until the current window was installed by Gibbs of London in 1863.

Norman Evans gives the following full description:

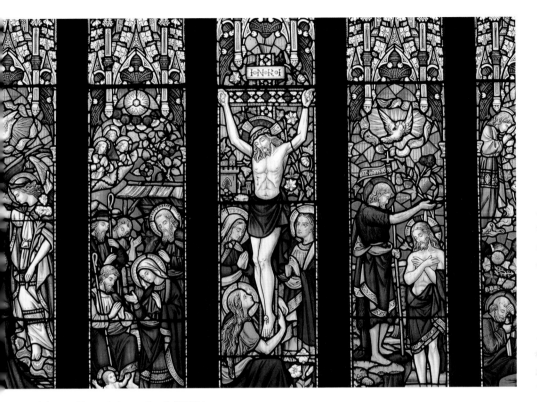

Fig. 50: *East window – detail (BHD)*

At the head of the window is a figure of our Lord in Glory attended by angels holding emblems of the Trinity and the Holy Ghost. He is adored by four figures: a prophet (St John the Baptist); an apostle (St Peter); a Martyr (St Paul); (Exeter Cathedral is dedicated to St Peter and St Paul) and a Bishop (Vesey) representing the Church on earth. The five lights below refer to the Annunciation, the Adoration of the Shepherds, the Crucifixion, the Baptism and the Agony in the Garden. Below are angelic figures holding appropriate texts. (Evans, 1987, p. 22)

VESEY CHAPEL WINDOWS

The Bishops' Window

The east end window depicts bible stories commemorating Bishops associated with Holy Trinity as follows (L to R):

Bible story and reference	Bishop	Dedication
Isaiah receiving a gift of figs to heal King Hezekiah. 2 Kings 20:1–11	John Arundel, physician to Henry IV, Rector 1431–1437, subsequently Bishop of Chichester	Richard Sadler, churchwarden, and his wife Sarah
Joseph asking Pharaoh for the land of Goshen Genesis 47:4	Bishop Vesey	James Packwood, curate, d.1869
Joshua, Zerubbabel and Haggai rebuilding the temple of Jerusalem Haggai 2:1–23	John Hacket, Bishop of Lichfield. Kinsfolk lived at Moor Hall. Restored Lichfield Cathedral after Civil War	Thomas Colmore, d. 1870
Elisha teaching in the schools of the Prophets 2 Kings 2:3	James Fleetwood, Bishop of Worcester (1675–83). Teacher at Oxford University	Members of the Smith family who lived at Ivy House, High St

Table 6: *Description of the stained glass in the east end window in the Vesey chapel.*

The so-called Bishops' window commemorates all Bishops associated with Holy Trinity up to that point, though a twenty-first century Rector subsequently left Holy Trinity in 2004 to become a Bishop (James Langstaff who became Bishop of Lynn), the first ever to do so directly from his post at Sutton Coldfield.

Fig. 51: *The Bishops' window in the Vesey chapel (BHD)*

The table gives detail of the Bible story that is being depicted, the name of the Bishop it commemorates, suggesting why that particular story was chosen, and the name of the dedicatee of each light.

The Holbeche Window

This is on the north wall of the chapel and shows the coats of arms of Bishop Vesey on the left, Exeter (where he was Bishop) in the centre, and of Dr Richard Williamson on the right, in whose memory it was installed by Sarah Holbeche. Historian Roger Lea notes that 'Sarah Holbeche thought so well of Williamson, who left in 1851, that she commissioned a stained glass window for the church; on April 10th 1865'. Sarah herself commented in her diary: 'My window hoisted, disappointed at first view but not dissatisfied – merit or demerit is with Hardman [the famous Birmingham craftsman who made the window]. I have done well for the church, and gratified myself in doing honour to Dr. Williamson.'

It may be remembered that Richard Williamson was a member of the Riland family from the female line, and that he was replaced as Rector by William Kirkpatrick Riland Bedford when the latter came of age.

CHOIR VESTRY (SOUTH CHAPEL)

The Barnes Window

The window on the south wall on the left-hand side is dedicated to Ernest William Barnes, Bishop of Birmingham (1924–53), and depicts places associated with his life including educational institutions and churches associated with his previous posts as a priest. All the places are named on the window. A cutting from the *Birmingham Daily Gazette* of 6 January 1956 notes:

> A stained glass window in memory of the former Bishop of Birmingham, Dr EW Barnes, is to be dedicated by the present Bishop, Dr JL Wilson, at Sutton Coldfield Parish Church on February 16th. An anonymous donor gave £300 for the memorial.

The donor has remained anonymous.

The Colmore Window

The window on the south wall on the right-hand side is dedicated to members of the Colmore family. It depicts the newly risen Christ supping with fellow travellers on the road to Emmaus (Luke 24: 30–31). It was given in 1907 in memory of

Quintus Charles Colmore (1851–1904) and also of his son, Guy Blayney, born in 1887, who had died aged 11. (Evans, 1987, p. 46)

The Mary Boggon Window

The window at the east end of this space depicts 'The Marys of the New Testament' and was given by the Rector John Boggon in memory of his wife Phyllis Mary Boggon (Fig. 52). The window was made by Miss Nora Yoxall and Miss Elsie Whitford, whose studio was in Blockley, Gloucestershire, and was dedicated on 10 January 1965 by the Bishop of Birmingham, Dr John Leonard Wilson.

The images are described in the table below as they appear in the four lights of the window frame:

A lighted candle			
Items used in daily life: plate with bread, bottles of wine and oil, fruit in a basket, corn, a broom, a harp, a shepherd's crook, a lighted oil lamp	Nativity, with Joseph, Mary and Jesus	Moon and darkened sun dimly illuminating the crucifixion of Christ with Mary and John at his side	A tree of life rising through suffering (a crown of thorns) towards celestial light
Jesus in the house of Mary and Martha	Virgin Mary as a joyful mother	Virgin Mary as a saddened mother	A chalice Jesus appearing first to Mary Magdalen 'Touch me not, for I am not yet ascended.'
Alabaster vase	Annunciation 'Behold the handmaid of the Lord'	The meeting of Mary and Elizabeth (mother of John the Baptist) 'Blessed art thou among women.'	The Resurrection – Mary Magdalen and Mary the mother of James with the angel at the tomb. 'He is not here, He is risen.'
Mary Magdalen washing Christ's feet 'She hath wrought a good work upon me.'			

Table 7: *Description of the Boggon memorial window in the choir vestry (east wall).* *(Information taken from Evans, 1987, pp. 43–4)*

Above left, Fig. 52: *The 'Mary Boggon' window (HTSC)*

Above right, Fig. 53: *The west window in the tower (HTSC)*

Tower

The clear glass of the west window of the tower was filled with stained glass in 1869 (Fig. 53). Mr W. Blews Robotham of Boulton, Derby, commissioned the depiction of 'Faith, Hope and Charity' in memory of the Misses Blews of Maney. The makers were Ward and Hughes of Soho, London. The window was obscured from 1950 to 2018. (Evans, 1987, p. 64)

South-west corner

The window on the west wall is a memorial by Revd W. K. Riland Bedford to his mother and to his sixth child, who died in 1865 at the age of 4. The light on the left (Christ holding a child) commemorates Arthur Edward Riland Bedford. The right-hand image of the resurrection commemorates Grace Campbell Bedford (d. 1875). The window is by Ballantine of Edinburgh.

On the south wall are two stained glass lights to the memory of Charles Edward Chevasse, a churchwarden and a member of a well-known Midlands family. It was erected by his widow and children and shows two lights, the left-hand one of Jesus as the Good Shepherd, and Jesus as the light of the world on the right.

Above left, Fig. 54: *The Chevasse window – detail (BHD)*

Above right, Fig. 55: *The 'Eric Walker' window (HTSC)*

North wall

The window in the north-west corner of the church is to the memory of Eric Walker, a former chorister at Holy Trinity who died in France in the First World War (in 1915). The two lights of the window show the patron saints of England and France, St George on the left and St Dionysus on the right. The latter carries a head in his left hand, which was apparently to symbolise the martyrdom of Dionysus (or St Denis as he is sometimes called in France), a third-century saint who allegedly walked some miles after the event, preaching with his head in his hand.

The only other stained glass in the church is the modern patterned glass in the inner doors to the south porch of 1983.

10

WOODWORK

BY CAROL HOARE

For nearly 150 years, Holy Trinity Church, Sutton Coldfield, has been the custodian of some very rare ecclesiastical woodwork, dating from the reign of Mary Tudor who was Queen of England from 1553 to 1558. It was obtained in 1875 from Worcester Cathedral, and until the recent re-ordering of the church, formed the screens and stalls in the chancel. However, its historical significance was not fully understood, and for many years it was described as being Jacobean, and therefore not particularly unusual, but this view has changed. Recent investigations by experts (particularly by Dr Nicholas Riall, to whom I am deeply indebted for his detailed information) have now assigned a mid-sixteenth-century date to some of it, which makes it almost unique in English church architecture. In 2011, Dr Charles Tracy, an expert in church furniture, was commissioned to write a report on the woodwork before re-ordering started, and at that time he was uncertain of its exact age, but he is now in agreement with Dr Riall and acknowledges its significance and importance. Revd Professor Diarmaid MacCulloch, Professor of the History of the Church at Oxford University, also agrees with the earlier date, and, in a letter sent to Holy Trinity in support of the heritage project funding bid of 2016, describes it as 'precious and unparalleled' and has this to say:

> What is so important about this woodwork? Put simply, it is the only surviving substantial material from a major programme of Catholic Counter-Reformation refurnishing, after Reformation destruction, which is left in the British Isles. It is precisely dateable to 1556, and it was the gift of Queen Mary Tudor, in honour no doubt of the burial in Worcester Cathedral of her mother's first husband, Prince Arthur.

So how did Holy Trinity Church come to have this rare survival from the sixteenth century?

Fig. 56: *The chancel in 2011 showing woodwork from Worcester Cathedral (CT)*

In 1834, the Coventry archdeaconry (which at that time included Sutton Coldfield) was taken from the Lichfield diocese and attached to that of Worcester. Between 1857 and 1874 Worcester Cathedral underwent a massive restoration – partly overseen by Sir Gilbert Scott – during which the choir stalls with pillars and columns were removed. A quantity of this discarded carved oak was acquired by Holy Trinity Church for use in its own programme of alteration in 1875 to meet the needs of Sutton's growing population, and to accommodate changing forms of worship. A photograph of the interior of Holy Trinity taken by William M. Grundy in 1852 shows the nave filled with box pews, and a very different chancel: no stained glass in the east window and no choir stalls, a very small plain altar, the pulpit on the right-hand side, and most interestingly of all, box pews extending to within 5ft of the altar rail.

However, in 1875, all this changed. The box pews in the body of the church were removed and replaced by open ones; the floor of the chancel was raised, and the choir, which had previously been accommodated elsewhere in the church, was given a prominent position in the chancel, with choir stalls and fittings in the side chapels being constructed from the woodwork obtained from Worcester

Cathedral. There is an inscription on the screen dado rail in the Vesey chapel, which informs us both of the origin of this material, and when it was installed in the church: 'This carved work part of the choir and organ cas(e) [letter and word/s cut off to make way for a later doorway] Worcester [interrupted here by a pillar] Cathedral was removed AD 1864 and placed here AD 1875'.

None of this, however, explains why the woodwork is quite so special, and to appreciate this we need briefly to consider the religious changes of the sixteenth and seventeenth centuries.

It was a time of great religious and political unrest. After Henry VIII broke with Rome in order to obtain his divorce from Katherine of Aragon, though he proclaimed himself head of the English Church, he remained Catholic in religious practices, and little was altered in the way services were conducted and church buildings arranged. However, the Reformation was gathering momentum, and Henry's young heir, Edward (son of Henry's third wife) was greatly influenced by the new ideas. When he ascended the throne in January 1547, at the age of 9, he and his council began to impose Protestantism throughout his kingdom. This included a compulsory change from Latin to English as the language of the Mass. Along with his advisors he was anxious that all signs of mediaeval Catholicism – which Protestants considered superstitious – should be obliterated from church buildings, so statues were defaced, paintings and stained glass windows smashed, and other signs and symbols of the old faith destroyed.

When Edward died in 1553 at just 15 years of age, he was succeeded by his half-sister, Mary. But she was the daughter of Henry's first wife, Katherine of Aragon, and still a devout Catholic. She had struggled to maintain her faith at some risk to herself throughout her young brother's reign, and once on the throne was determined to restore England to the 'True Faith'. Catholic priests were reinstated and church services returned as far as possible to the old forms. Mary was also determined to make church buildings, once again, fitting places for 'true' worship and to re-equip them for Catholic services, and this is where our woodwork fits in. Worcester Cathedral was chosen by Mary in 1555–56 as the recipient of substantial funding for new choir stalls, a Bishop's throne and an organ. It is believed that some of this Marian woodwork can now be found in Holy Trinity Church, along with some later panelling, also from Worcester.

But Mary's reign was even shorter than Edward's, lasting only five years. She had also made herself deeply unpopular and feared by ordering the burning of heretics, and when she died in 1588, her reforms died with her. England under Elizabeth I once more became Protestant, and though Mary was certainly not the only monarch to execute those she disagreed with, she became remembered in history as 'Bloody Mary'.

THE CHOIR, LOOKING WEST, BEFORE RESTORATION.
(From Wild.)

Fig. 57: *Aquatint by Charles Wild 1823 of choir at Worcester Cathedral (Strange)*

From then on, English churches adopted a simpler style in their worship arrangements, and though added to during the Jacobean period, they continued to avoid anything that could be considered 'idolatrous' or recalled Catholic ideas. Not even cathedrals were immune, so by 1563 Mary's organ at Worcester had been destroyed, the pipes being melted down to make dishes that were given to the canons' wives, while the organ case was made into bedsteads. However, the organ was replaced in 1612, complete with a new Jacobean-style casing which features in an aquatint of the Worcester cathedral choir in 1823 by Charles Wild (see Fig. 57). It is this engraving, along with a later one from 1861, that particularly helps us identify the woodwork now held in Holy Trinity Church.

The Wild aquatint offers a view of Worcester choir taken from the east and shows the communion rail, the choir stalls and the organ. Though some details have been omitted, we can see that the east side of the organ case is closely similar to panels in the Vesey chapel in Holy Trinity. Other identifiable similarities can be seen between the Worcester woodwork and that now to be found in Holy Trinity. For example, the lion's paw feet that are just visible under the forms set in front of the choir stalls in the Worcester engraving are the same as those on the bench legs that are used to support the choir benches in Holy Trinity. The Worcester choir stalls also incorporated colonnades of pillars set around the three sides of the choir, supporting galleries and placed in front of the upper stalls. Many of these colonnades were transposed in their entirety to Holy Trinity, and specific details of swags, frieze and cornice can also be identified in Wilde's engraving.

It is clear, therefore, that the oak furnishings placed in Holy Trinity Church represent a large element of those that once formed the choir stalls of Worcester cathedral. Nicholas Riall estimates that between about one third and a half of the original choir furniture at Worcester was brought to Sutton Coldfield. Some is now stored in other parts of the church, including the Jacobean communion rail that features in the foreground of Wilde's aquatint.

The later engraving of the Worcester choir in 1861 allows us to see the shape and style of the stall frontals, which match those found in Holy Trinity, and this supports the date carved on the Vesey chapel rail. The year 1864 was quite probably the date at which the remainder of the Worcester choir stalls were dismantled.

The collection of pieces from the Worcester choir stalls was purchased for £100 by the Reverend W. K. Riland Bedford, who was Rector of the parish from 1850 to 1892. It is likely that he was acquainted with the then Bishop of Worcester, Henry Philpott (Bishop 1860–90), whose armorial was later to be painted on one of the shields in the panelling of the reredos, at the east end of the chancel. At much the same time as the chancel and aisle chapels were furnished with Worcester material, a new north gallery was designed and installed by the Birmingham architect Henry Richard Yeoville Thomason, which features panels that are copies of those from Worcester.

We are still, however, left with the difficulty of accurately dating the woodwork. Some is clearly Jacobean, and there are records in Worcester Cathedral showing that work was carried out in the choir after the Restoration in 1660, but other documentary evidence suggests that some can still be identified with the gift of Queen Mary, and made in 1556–57, thus suggesting they are Marian. If this is the case, then the woodwork in Holy Trinity Church is incredibly rare. Nicholas Riall has this to say: 'A central difficulty with this set of work is that it truly is unique, it is absolutely one of a kind that is without a direct parallel …' He continues:

> The brief, five-year long reign of Mary is not characterised by a coherent style that can be attributed to her or her reign, but rather it is characterised by a group of pieces each of which is to an extent different, one from the next. There are not many of them.

He then mentions examples in other churches, some identified by Eamon Duffy as having possible links with the work obtained from Worcester, but concludes that though there are similarities, none offers a complete parallel.

AREAS OF PARTICULAR INTEREST

THE WORCESTER WOODWORK IN THE CHANCEL

The Reredos

Immediately under the east window is a finely carved festoon, another rare survival, and possibly part of the organ case of 1612, and below it, a series of decorated panels create a reredos, though these originally formed the fronts of the choir stalls at Worcester. Pairs of panels are divided by short, fluted classical columns and framed by decorative carving taken from classical architecture and usually described as *all'antica* or 'antique'. Above these can be seen strings of candelabra featuring different Renaissance motifs, such as a snail, a drum, a skull, and a lion's head with a ring in its mouth.

On some of the panels are shields containing carved symbols of the Passion, (images associated with the suffering and death of Jesus).

The most notable of these shows a cross and scourges, and another depicts a representation of the five wounds of Christ (Fig. 59). Both of these shields are supported by open-mouthed fish whose tails curve into the shape of lilies. In these carvings we see clearly Roman Catholic iconography recalling the Passion and death of Christ as well as reminding worshippers of ancient Christian symbolism: the fish symbolising the Church and the Resurrection, and lilies, which are the emblem of the Virgin Mary. There is also a panel carved with a motif of St Catherine, set against the wheel on which she was martyred. Riall

suggests this may well have been an image created in Worcester Cathedral in honour of the Queen's mother, Katherine of Aragon. The strongly Roman Catholic imagery on these panels is highly unlikely to have been created after the reign of Mary I, and is not found in Jacobean work.

Fig.58: *The chancel c.1970 showing the Worcester Cathedral woodwork (R&C)*

OTHER WOODWORK IN THE CHANCEL

Riall's arguments for a Marian dating of the woodwork do not depend solely on the iconography of the carving, for he also considers joinery techniques and looks at stylistic features in some detail. He examines the columns brought from Worcester, explaining that their shape and style is characteristic of Tudor royal palaces from about the 1530s.

He recognises that no actual examples have survived, but says they can be seen in paintings of the royal family, e.g. *The Family of Henry VIII*, c1545 (artist unknown) and in a design sketch for a fireplace attributed to Holbein and dated c1540.

The technique used in the panel carving also indicates an earlier date, with the openwork carving seeming to 'flow' onto the backing panel, and the edges of the carvings being smoothed and rounded to provide what appears to be a seamless work. This was a style long practised by Gothic joiners, which continued to be used well into the sixteenth century. If we compare the panels in the lower sections of the Vesey chapel, we can see a difference in skills between the makers of the two sets of work: the Vesey chapel panels overlie the panel behind but are solid, not carved through. The extent of the classical architectural grammar used in the chancel panels, and the elegant combination in which this was applied, is also not found in Jacobean work.

Often unnoticed, but also interesting in helping to date the woodwork, are the lion's paw clawed feet on the bench legs (see Fig. 60).

Above left, Fig. 59: *'Wounds of Christ' on reredos (CT)*

Above right, Fig. 60: *Lion's paw clawed foot on bench leg (woodwork from Worcester Cathedral) (CT)*

This design was based on classical Roman originals and developed by an Italian architect, Sebastiano Serlio, in a series of books from 1537. They were very popular until the mid-1570s, but were no longer fashionable in Jacobean times. As has already been mentioned, the feet are visible in front of the choir stalls in Wilde's aquatint.

Yet another indication of a sixteenth-century date is the strapwork that can be seen in the colonnade friezes. Acanthus leaves are surmounted by flowers with large floppy leaves. Each leaf has a rounded nick in its edge, a feature which is only found between 1540 and 1575:

> Taking all these strands together we can conclude that most of the Worcester woodwork in Holy Trinity Church can only date to the Marian refitting of the cathedral choir in 1556-7. It is a wonderful survival, and is the sole remnant of a set of English choir stalls from the middle of the sixteenth century. (Riall, 2018)

However, it should be noted that the recent re-ordering of the church, beginning in 2016, made big changes to the Victorian layout of the chancel. Both priests' desks and all the choir stalls were removed and replaced by modern chairs, but the reredos and the colonnaded screens on either side were left in place. The priests' desks and some of the old choir stalls have been placed in front of the reredos, while desk frontals, and panels from the sides of the priests' desks have been fastened to the wall in the south aisle. Here, two shields can be seen on the panelling, the escutcheon on the left being that of James Fleetwood, who became Bishop of Worcester in 1675, and the one on the right that of Bishop Philpott of Worcester, in whose time the woodwork was dismantled from the cathedral and brought to Sutton. A number of other pieces are stored in the north gallery.

THE VESEY CHAPEL

In style, it is clear that the panelling in the Vesey chapel is Jacobean, and this is reinforced by the presence of a crowned thistle among the carving. This symbol, associated with Scotland, points to James VI, monarch of that country from his birth, but also reigning as James I of England from March 1603. In addition, because the panelling can be connected to the new organ built at Worcester by Robert Kettle in 1612–13, this allows us to place the panels into a specific context and, unusually for this style of work, a precise date.

The parclose, or screen, between the chancel and the Vesey chapel is also interesting. The dado panels (i.e. the panels underneath the columns) are formed from the woodwork which originally constituted the organ case at Worcester. The semi-circular headed panels, formerly high up on the organ screen, are now at floor level, and the slender columns which were originally below them are now above them. They can be seen in the Wilde aquatint.

As mentioned earlier, a carving in the oak of the parclose reads: 'This carved work part of the choir and organ cas[e] … Worcester [Cathedral] was removed AD 1864 and placed here AD 1875.'

A small section of this has since been removed to make a doorway from the chancel to the chapel. The escutcheon on the parclose facing the north door of the chapel is of Prebendary Barkesdale, one of the donors of the cathedral organ.

OTHER WOODWORK IN THE CHURCH

The focus of this article so far has been the east end of the church, and the highly significant woodwork obtained from Worcester Cathedral. It is, of necessity, quite brief, and for those who would like more specific information, I recommend the detailed and scholarly account by Dr Nicholas Riall, published in *The Antiquaries Journal, 2019*. However, unique though it is, this is not the only woodwork of interest that Holy Trinity Church has to offer.

THE COMMUNION TABLE

The present Italianate communion table, created by C.E. Bateman, was given in memory of Amy, wife of the Rector (Revd W. K. Riland Bedford) who died in 1890. Both Norman Evans and Margaret Gardner say that part of the old sixteenth-century communion table, installed during the reforms of Edward's reign, was incorporated into an oak screen at the west end of the south chapel until this was removed completely during the recent re-ordering. The screen which now divides the south chapel from the south aisle is Marian (see Fig. 59).

THE PULPIT

The pulpit dates from 1760 and was designed by William Hiorn. It has a wine glass stem, an elaborately carved tester surmounted by a gilded dove, elegant columns, and a sunburst ceiling inlaid with mahogany and other exotic woods. It was elevated up seven steps so that the preacher could see over the top of the box pews which filled the nave at that time and first stood on the south side of the chancel, with its tester (sounding board) above it, possibly suspended from the chancel arches. However, in 1829 the tester was removed and stored in the Vesey chapel, but during the re-ordering of the church in 1875 it was replaced with new supports in the form of slender columns from Worcester Cathedral. The whole thing was moved into the nave, and the wooden staircase placed on its east side, leading directly from the chancel. Though all the elements of the pulpit date from different periods, together they form a very attractive whole (Fig. 61).

Over the centuries, sermons preached here have sometimes led to controversy (see Chapters 11 and 14), and occasionally to somnolence. Local historian Roger Lea writes:

> The pulpit was the scene of less edifying events. On one occasion when Rector John Riland was in the pulpit he leaned too close to the candles and his wig caught fire. [See Fig. 69 in Chapter 12 for a picture of John Riland]. Mr. Packwood was Curate in the mid-nineteenth century – 'he had a monotonous soothing voice' wrote Richard Holbeche, 'we frequently got into trouble for sleeping.' His aunt Sarah Holbeche noted that Lady Hartopp of Four Oaks Hall provided a special cushion for the pulpit, and commented in September 1866 'Lady Hartopp's good fat pulpit cushion has been supplanted by an antependium – to sit softly on it will we hope mollify the hard words of our preacher the Rev. J.P.'

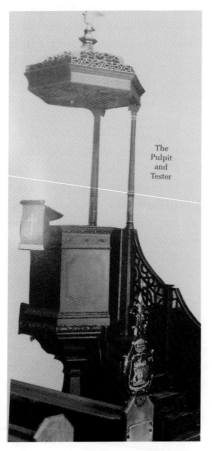

The
Pulpit
and
Tester

See the section in Chapter 13 about the Hartopp family for more information on Lady Hartopp's gift of 1856.

Fig. 61: *Pulpit of 1760 (prior to 2016) (HTSC)*

THE GALLERIES

The present south gallery is eighteenth century, being built as part of the alterations carried out in 1760 under the supervision of William Hiorn, the architect–builder. It still contains the original woodwork and pews from that period, and offers a good idea of the seating accommodation offered in churches at that time. Further information about this can be found in Chapter 3 of this book.

In 1879 the church was extended on the north side by the building of the present Vesey aisle. This necessitated the removal of the old gallery (corresponding to the present south gallery) and the raising of the Vesey aisle roof to accommodate it.

In 1828 the 1760 galleries were extended to the east in order to accommodate pupils from the new town school at services (see Chapter 4). Rush matting was put down on the boys' side to deaden the sound of their boots. However, both children's galleries and their staircases were removed in 1868, and the children then seated on benches in the side chapels. (Evans and Gardner, 1987). The top of the girls' doorway can be seen behind the Jesson memorial in the Vesey chapel.

In Richard Holbeche's reminiscences of the church in the 1860s, he comments that he 'found it a great diversion during the long service to listen to the master in charge of the boys in the nearby children's gallery administering "knocks to their heads".' (Holbeche, 1893)

During the 1760 alterations, a further gallery was built across the west end of the nave. This held a special area designated for the use of Simon Luttrell and his family from Four Oaks Hall (see Chapter 13), and also accommodated the choir and the new organ given by John Riland. Changes to the tower area are noted in Chapter 7. The fine carved beam which formed the front of the organ floor is part of the Worcester Cathedral oak and has now been repositioned underneath the north gallery.

THE WEST DOORWAY

In 1828 the west door was closed and the tower used as a vestry, but during the alterations of 1884, it was re-opened and a new vestibule was built. This was constructed using four columns from Worcester Cathedral and carved panels, including a set of royal arms, from another church, St Michael's in Coventry (a mediaeval church at that time in the Worcester Diocese, but elevated to cathedral status in 1918 and destroyed in the Second World War bombing of 1940. The ruins now form part of the new Coventry Cathedral.) We do not know the precise age

Above, Fig. 62: *'Fox and goose'
decoration on woodwork from St
Michael's, Coventry (CT)*

Left, Fig. 63: *Oak door in South
porch (HTSC)*

of the St Michael's woodwork, but its style dates it to the Jacobean period, and the impressive carving portrays examples of mediaeval imagery: there are dragons and a representation of the legend of the fox and the goose (see Fig. 62).

Above the north door is what appears to be a carving of a griffon, clearly male, and over the south door, a female equivalent. To quote Dr Riall again, 'In the centre, facing E, are the lion (left) and unicorn (right) supporters used for the Royal arms in this period. Note too that both are rampant male, as was the norm, thus indicating a strong and virile monarchy.'

The magnificent brass door handles in the shape of dolphins came from Valetta, Malta, where the Rector's daughter Ethel Frances Riland Bedford, went to live after her wedding in Holy Trinity. (Evans, 1987, p. 70)

THE OLD OAK DOOR

The south porch was for many years the regular point of access to the church. The door which closes the stone archway is exceptionally solid, being constructed of two thicknesses of wide oak planks: horizontal on the inside and vertical on the outside. There are no strengthening battens, but the whole door is held together by heavy round-headed studs and supported by two wrought iron hinges 4ft 2in (127cm) long. Some of the studs have been arranged on the outside into a date, 1704, and the initials 'TA TM', indicating that Thomas Abell and Thomas Martin were churchwardens at that time (see Fig. 63).

CONCLUSION

As has been discussed earlier, the Marian woodwork obtained from Worcester Cathedral is of national significance, being a very rare survival from the mid sixteenth century. It is a unique heritage and this building is fortunate enough to be its home. But the reign of Mary Tudor forms only a small part of the history of the Christian church, and despite a number of re-orderings over the centuries, the woodwork in Holy Trinity offers other interesting examples of the way church furnishings developed and changed in response to local needs and contemporary attitudes, both religious and social. Together they remind us that Holy Trinity church has always been, and still is, an active part of the community, linking past, present and future in a living and ongoing worship tradition.

11

RECTORS AND OTHER CLERGY

The long line of incumbents at Holy Trinity, usually designated 'Rector', starts with Simon de Daventry in 1250.

There is a Rectors' Board in the Vesey entrance of the church which displays every name to the present day (Fig. 64).

While we know the names, we know varying amounts about each of the people who served the church in this capacity, i.e. as the nominated priest in charge of the church and parish.

A hugely influential line of clergy hailed from the Riland and Riland Bedford families, and these deserve a section of their own, which duly follows in the next chapter.

THE CHANGING ROLE OF CLERGY

It may be helpful to set in context the Rectors of Holy Trinity against the background of the role of clergy in general over the centuries.

In the mediaeval period, when the first stone church known as Holy Trinity was built in Sutton Coldfield, most churches were erected at the behest of a rich patron who also appointed a priest to pray for his soul and possibly the family too, in order to effect the best possible chance of a place in Heaven at the end of their lives. Such churches were called 'chantries', and Dugdale records the chantry being established in Sutton Coldfield as described in Chapter 1 on the early history of the church.

By the beginning of the fifteenth century there were vicars-general in place in most dioceses who were effectively deputising for the Bishop in his absence in matters which did not specifically require a Bishop (such excluded duties might have been ordinations of clergy or consecrations of new churches or chapels). To begin with this was a temporary appointment for the specified absence, but the posts gradually became permanent, being confirmed at the start of a new Bishop's tenure and then removed at his discretion. A book on the subject of ecclesiastical institutions in the

Fig. 64: *The Rectors' Board in the Vesey entrance (HTSC)*

fifteenth century is helpful in describing the different elements of church administration, from the role of Bishops, through monasteries and diocesan administration to the role of priests and other clergy in churches and chantries. (Thompson, 1947)

The detail helps to set in context the kind of church Holy Trinity would have been as a chantry and then a church with an incumbent known as a Rector. In the present day, we no longer have 'vicars-general'; nor do we have the post of diocesan 'official' as such, but the latter would equate in some parts to the role of the modern diocesan registrar. We do still have suffragan Bishops who share all duties with the Bishop – for example in the Diocese of Birmingham there is a suffragan Bishop of Aston.

Thompson makes two interesting observations which have a bearing on the early life of Holy Trinity. In the first he refers to the system of several separate endowments of priests to chantries being lodged together 'in a common dwelling house'. He says later, 'the process of founding collegiate bodies of chantry priests in parish churches on this system became a marked feature of the church life of the fourteenth and fifteenth centuries'. (Thompson, 1947, p. 146)

He goes on to state:

> in the early part of the fourteenth century, owners of castles and manor-houses began with some frequency to endow chantries of several priests in their chapels. .... Guy Beauchamp, Earl of Warwick, endowed a chantry of eight chaplains at Elmley Castle. (Ibid., p. 148)

This information could give us a link with the earlier chapel in Sutton Coldfield which was built at the manor house in Sutton Coldfield and the first building of Holy Trinity (*see* Chapter 1 on the early history of the church).

The term 'vicar' today is interchangeable with the term 'Rector', the latter specifically denoting a living where tithes accrue to that incumbent. In churches established in much later centuries, the term vicar was used for the incumbent and equally implied conferment of the living on that incumbent until he chose to move on or retire. The word 'vicar' is related to 'vicarious' and just means a substitute, stemming from the earlier 'vicar-general' role.

Another use of the word vicar was in the term 'vicars choral'. These were substitutions by cathedral clergy who were expected to sing in the choir, but would instead appoint a substitute (possibly a better or more enthusiastic singer) to undertake this role. In Lichfield Cathedral the adult singers are still called 'vicars choral' – unlike other cathedrals where they tend to be termed 'lay clerks'. Amongst early references to corporate groups of vicars choral is that at Lichfield in 1240. (Thompson, 1947, p. 78)

Another feature of church and town life pertaining particularly to the Rectors was the system of tithing – a biblical-based form of taxation whereby the Rector received a sum of money from landowners and cottagers. There is more detail about this in the chapter concerning the church history from the end of Bishop Vesey's time until 1800 (Chapter 3).

RECTORS AT HOLY TRINITY

William Kirkpatrick Riland Bedford in his history of the town (Riland Bedford, 1891) has a list of the Rectors, with the patrons listed in a column to the left. He in turn has taken the first part, including the list of patrons, from William Dugdale's *Antiquities of Warwickshire (Dugdale,* 2nd ed, 1730, pp. 914–5). This is extremely useful in showing the changes not only in personnel, but in the owner of the patronage, that is, the person who appointed a new Rector. Various synonymous terms are used to refer to the patronage, others being 'advowson' and 'living'.

While the list is on the Rectors' Board and also on the website where it can be updated, it is worth replicating Riland Bedford's list here and including his own son, who was the last of that line and under whom the patronage was transferred to the new diocese of Birmingham in 1909, where it is likely to remain the case for the foreseeable future. Variants and additional descriptions in Dugdale's list are noted here too.

Patron	Incumbent / Rector	Date appointed	Additional Dugdale notes
	Simon de Daventry	1250	
	Richard de Bello	1294	
Earl of Warwick	Gregory Harold	1305	
	Richard de Bello	1308	
King Edward of England this time Patron The Crown in minority of Patron	Robert Hilary	1317 (*1318*)	
	William Shepragg (*Shepraff*)	1326	
Thomas de bellocampo Count (Earl) of Warwick Earl of Warwick	John de Buckingham	1345	*[v.p.m.]*
	William de Shaneburne (*Cap*)	1348	*[v.p.cessionem]*

	Simon Basset de Sapcote (*Cler*)	1349	[*v.p.m.*]
	William de Barton (*Cler*)	1361	
	Ralph de Friseby (*Pbr*)	1361	
	Roger de Tangley (*Pbr*)	1382	[*v.p.m.*]
	Nicholas Stokes	1389	[Victe Laudabilis & conversationis honeste in ordine psalmistat. constitutes, nec alibi beneficiatus]
	Ralph Bromley (*Cler*)	1391	[*v.p.r.*]
	Thomas Henster (*Pbr*)	1391	[*v.p.r.*]
	Richard Penne	1397	
Thomas "Dux Surr. Co, Cantii" Thomas Holland, Duke of Surrey	John de Malverne (*Pbr*)	1397	
Henry King of England in the minority of Richard Earl of Warwick The Crown in minority of Patron	Richard Penne (*Cap*)	1401	[*v.p.r.*]
Earl of Warwick	Lewis Beelte	1412	[*Rr. De Kynwarton Wig. Dioc. Dat. Per Episc. Cov. Apud Heywode, 7 apud Bredonb per Episc. Wigorn*] [*permut cum R. Penne*]
John Verney et al, Richard Earl of Warwick being across the sea John Verney etc for patron beyond seas	John Arundel	1431	[*v.p.m. L. Boult*]
Richard de Bellocampo Earl of Warwick	John Adams (*Pbr*)	1433	
	Thomas Hill (*Cler*)	1436	[*v.p.r.*]
	John Stones (*Pbr*)	1463	[*v.p.m. Joh. Tihy*]
	Richard Brackenbergh	1469	

Henry 7	Edward Scott LLD	1499	*[v.p.m. R. Brakynborgh]*
Crown	John Taylor DD	1504	
Henry 8	George Heneage LLD (*John*)	1516	*[v.p.r.]*
	John Burges STB	1521	*[v.p.r.]*
	Ralph Wendon	1527	*[v.p.r.]*
Thomas Gybons	John Fodon (*Cler*)	1563	*[Rogerus Ellyot … 1564. v.p.r. Joh. Ffodon]*
Queen Elizabeth Crown	Peter Sankye	1583	
Elizabeth Elyot, widow	Roger Elyot (*Cler*)	1595	
Robert Shilton	John Burges MD	1617	
	Anthony Burges DD	1635	*[Jacobus Fleetwood S.T.P … 1642*
John Shilton	William Watson	1662	*v.p. amotionem A. Burgess propter Nonconformitatem]*
	John Riland MA	1689	
Richard Riland	Richard Riland (*Cl*) MA	1720	*[v.p.m. J Riland]* **Dugdale's list ends here**
Richard Bisse Riland	Richard Bisse Riland MA	1758	
John Riland	John Riland MA	1790	
William Riland Bedford	William Riland Bedford MA	1822	
William Kirkpatrick Riland Bedford	Richard Williamson DD	1843	
	William Kirkpatrick Riland Bedford MA	1850	
William Campbell Riland Bedford	William Campbell Riland Bedford MA	1892	
Diocese of Birmingham	Charles William Barnard MA	1909	

Table 8: *Incumbents (Rectors) of Holy Trinity from 1250 until 1909.*

Note: Incumbent's names in italics are on the Rectors' Board, but not the other sources. Others are listed by Riland Bedford (1891, p. 74) with the exception (not surprisingly) of the last to share his family name (his own son). Patrons in italics are in Dugdale's list and in the reprint of Riland Bedford's book of 1968, p. 80. Dugdale's variations from the other sources or additions are in italics. The first four named Rectors are NOT in Dugdale.

LATIN TERMS

Latin abbreviations after some of the names in Table 8 above (e.g. *pbr*) are explained below.

Accal or Accol	might refer to a Rectors being a local inhabitant rather than being an absentee
Cal/Non	Calends/Nones days of the Roman calendar. (People are most familiar with the term 'Ides' because of Julius Caesar's death on the Ides of March.)
Cap	capellanus chaplain
Cler	clericus clergyman
Pbr	presbyter priest
STB	Sacrae Theologiae Baccalaureas = Bachelor of Sacred Theology (see John Burges 1521)
v.p.m.	vacante per mortem - vacancy through/by death
v.p.r	vacante per renunciationem - vacancy through/by resignation

In reference to the vacancies (p.m. and p.r.), the death is made clear by the naming of the previous incumbent, except in the case of John Stones in 1463 replacing a previously unrecorded name – John Tihy. As there is a long span under the previous name at this point it might be assumed (though not proved) that this other Rector was in post at some point towards the end of the period and that he then died in office.

It is interesting to note 'Rogerus Ellyot' appearing in this guise some years before the name reappears. Also this first mention of Roger Elyot is not on the church Rectors' Board. Some further investigation has revealed two priests named Roger Eliot, the first being listed as Rector in 1564 in the Church of England clergy database (entry number 25935) and the second (the one on our board) to be his son serving from 1595. In the same database this Roger (entry number 25937) graduated BA from Magdalen Hall, Oxford, in 1589. It would appear that Elizabeth Eliot named as the patron and also the widow would be of the older Elyot, and so 'our' Roger's mother. More information follows chronologically below.

The other interesting annotation relates to Anthony Burgess, whose incumbency is described more fully below.

EARLY INCUMBENTS

It has not proved possible to trace any information to date about Simon de Daventry. Richard de Bello is mentioned in the history of the Hereford Mappa Mundi as follows:

The map is attributed to one "Richard of Haldringham or Lafford" (Holdingham and Sleaford in Lincolnshire) who was also known as Richard de Bello. Whilst the map was drawn in Lincoln, it was almost certainly in Hereford by 1330.' (www.historic-uk.com/HistoryUK/HistoryofEngland/The-Hereford-Mappa-Mundi)

Another source suggests the map was drawn c1290.

This would fit with our two dates of incumbency of Holy Trinity of 1294–1305 and 1308–16, though whether this was actual incumbency or as patron is not known. The latter seems more likely.

Elizabeth Allison, a current resident of Sutton Coldfield and member of the Local History Research Group, has researched the life of one of the early Rectors of Holy Trinity, Robert Hillary. She writes as follows about his life and place at Holy Trinity, setting it usefully in the context of a mediaeval priest's career:

ROBERT HILLARY – ELIZABETH ALLISON

The Hillary family (also spelt hilary or illari) originated in the Normandy town of St Hilaire and came to England during the Norman Conquest. Over time, branches of the family established themselves as prominent landowners with connections to the de Greys of Codnor castle. The Hillarys of Bescot (nowadays part of Walsall) owned land at Aldridge, Fisherwick, Bloxwich, Walsall, Prestwood and Tamworth. Very faint traces of ditches connected with their manor house can still be traced in Bescot Park, near Hillary School. Nowadays a busy motorway soars on a flyover above the site and it is hard to imagine the scene when some enemies of the family besieged the house in the thirteenth century .

A career in the Church would be considered a suitable life for a younger son who otherwise had no great 'prospects' (and it seems possible that Robert was one of at least five sons). He could have been as young as 14 – the youngest age for any ordination – when he became an acolyte, which was then the first stage in a clerical career. On 17 June 1318 he was ordained as a sub-deacon in Penn parish church (Bishops at that time followed an itinerary for performing ordinations). In December of that year he was raised to the rank of deacon.

On 9 March 1318 he had been 'instituted to the vacant church of Sutton in Colefeld. Patron the King'. This meant that he was now the Rector of Holy Trinity but he was not (yet) a priest. The term 'patron' referred to the person who had put Robert's name forward (presented) to the Bishop for his approval. Usually the patron for Sutton Coldfield's appointment would be the current head of the Beauchamp family of Warwick but in 1318 this person was still a boy (as noted by Dugdale, *see Table 8*). In these cases the king, Edward ll (or his advisors) took over the role. The Hillaries of Bescot had family connections to the Berefords of Langley, one of whom was a high-ranking judge, so it seems likely that he had put in a good word for Robert – or more likely with some influential person in the royal entourage rather than the King, who was himself still a child.

On 13 January 1319, Robert was given permission to study for one year. The pope at the time, Boniface VIII, had become very concerned with the number of clergy who were uneducated and unable to instruct their parishioners in their faith. He decreed that permission could be granted to clerics to leave their parishes for a year and study at university. It is not known which university Robert attended but it was probably Oxford. The other possibility, Cambridge, was a much less frequent choice. While he was away his parish still had to support him financially and as part of his licence to study he was required to become an ordained priest.

When he was named the Rector of Holy Trinity Church he became legally entitled to receive the tithes which his parishioners owed to the church. He was responsible for the upkeep of the chancel but the parish had to maintain the rest of the building. He was entitled to accommodation, which could have been a house in the area now called Rectory Park, near to the church's glebe land. Following his ordination as a priest, his duties would include officiating at weddings, hearing confessions, administering the last rites (Extreme Unction) and above all celebrating mass, as only a priest could perform the communion rituals. If the church was sanctioned to perform baptisms (and receive the associated fees) the font would be an important symbol of that right. Weddings in those days involved a simple ceremony performed at the church door: the couples exchanged vows and the priest gave them a blessing. There was little privacy about making a confession, as the priest and penitent simply sat side by side on a bench.

The area now taken up by the Vesey Gardens in front of the church would have been especially busy on Tuesdays. In 1320, Earl Guy of Warwick had been granted the right for a weekly market – a useful money-maker for the Earl as Sutton was on a route to Lichfield and its cathedral, attracting passers-by. Permission had also been granted for an annual fair on the eve and parochial feast day of Holy Trinity. Perhaps Robert took the opportunity of mixing with his parishioners in a cheerful atmosphere. [End of text by Elizabeth Allison]

THE BLACK DEATH AND THE FIFTEENTH CENTURY

Margaret Gardner, one-time Parish Archivist at Holy Trinity, mused on the period of the Black Death in an article for the parish magazine (Gardner, 2000, p. 5), noting that there were five Rectors in post from 1345 to 1361 (the plague apparently arrived in Sutton in 1348). The list in Table 8 above shows two appointments in 1361 and again in 1391, both potentially attributable to the resignation of the first-named. (The term v.p.r. ascribed to the names in 1391 confirms this – see note on page 184 about Latin abbreviations).

However, in the case of Richard Penne, who appears briefly in 1397, there seems to be a change in patron allowing for a short-term replacement until 1401, when Penne appears again, serving until 1412.

The fifteenth century records a number of changes of incumbent and one that bears particular remark – John Arundel. The statement from Riland Bedford about the patronage is interesting here, though no further information is known as to why the patron at this point was 'beyond seas'. This implies our modern term 'overseas', so incommunicado, and in fact Dugdale's description in Latin makes this clearer.

Arundel is recorded as the only Rector of Holy Trinity to become a Bishop later in his career (as Bishop of Chichester in 1452) until the twenty-first century. James Langstaff was consecrated Bishop of Lynn (King's Lynn), a suffragan post in Norfolk Diocese, in 2004, immediately after serving four years as Rector at Holy Trinity. He became Bishop of Rochester in 2010.

Not only did Arundel achieve this promotion, he was commemorated in the nineteenth-century stained glass window in the east end of the Vesey chapel at Holy Trinity, as one of four Bishops associated with the church. There is more information about this window in Chapter 9.

The other observation to make is the introduction of letters after the Rectors' names at the end of this century. While Oxford and later Cambridge universities had been established much earlier, many clergy were now routinely academically trained, usually Oxford graduates, probably reflecting its closer location to Sutton and the fact that it was the older university, as Elizabeth Allison has also noted above in relation to Robert Hilary. Some of the degrees conferred were in other disciplines such as law and medicine, but we see DD occasionally (Doctor of Divinity) and MA most frequently, which in the case of Oxford and Cambridge has always been a degree conferred a year after graduation as Bachelor of Arts, rather than as a result of a graduate's undergoing a further academic programme.

SIXTEENTH CENTURY

The first incumbent in the new century was John Taylor, who served from 1504 to 1516. His story is both unusual and heart-warming. He was the oldest of triplet boys, born in good health to William and Joan Taylor who lived in a cottage in Barton-under-Needwood in Staffordshire to the north-east of the church there.

The other boys were named Rowland and Nathaniel, and their birth was c1480. It is said that John and his brothers were presented to Henry VII in their childhood as something of an attraction, after the King had been hunting nearby. According to one source (Holland, 1923) the king was lost and appealed, incognito, at the door of a cottage for the way to Tutbury, where William, described in this source as a poor man, gladly gave him directions. It was in return for this that, in being somewhat taken with these three boys, Henry afforded them royal patronage and promised to pay for their education if they survived to adulthood. (further information is online at: https://www.geni.com/people/John-Taylor-triplet-1/6000000000357893092)

All three did survive and were educated to the level of doctor and secured preferment. John secured a doctorate in canon law from the University of Ferrara in Italy in 1500. He was made a 'confrater of the English hospital in Rome', ordained priest in 1503 and presented by King Henry VII to the living of Sutton Coldfield in 1504. He subsequently served not only in this role but as a member of the court, joining ambassadorial missions and subsequently accompanying the new king to the Field of Cloth of Gold (as John Vesey did). He also secured numerous other church appointments (as was the custom), so it is unclear how much time he would have spent in Sutton Coldfield. (Cooper, 1999, pp. 51-2).

In the early 1500s we see the period in which changes to the church were brought about by a clergyman native to Sutton but not a Rector – John Vesey, Bishop of Exeter. At this point in Holy Trinity, Ralph Wendon was appointed Rector (in 1527), just as Vesey was founding the grammar school and about to secure the charter for Sutton Coldfield from Henry VIII (1528).

Wendon is not widely known, yet he survived the changes in religious allegiance of his sovereigns, remaining as Rector until 1563, a period of thirty-six years. This makes him the longest-serving Rector after William Kirkpatick Riland Bedford (forty-two years), discounting the supposed tenure of the first incumbent Simon de Daventry of forty-four years. It seems more likely in de Daventry's case that there are one or two names missing until we have Richard de Bello listed (himself probably Earl of Warwick or of that family).

Wendon, like Taylor, is mentioned in Tim Cooper's interesting book about the last generation of Catholic clergy in the diocese of Lichfield and Coventry.

The other Rector of this period in Cooper's account is George Heneage, listed on the church board as Rector from 1516 to 1521 (In Dugdale he is referred to as John, but Cooper uses George).

Roger Elyot (served 1595-1617), who is mentioned above, gave a silver communion cup, cover and paten in memory of his wife, Barbara, who had died in 1606 aged just 24. She had given birth to a son, Raphael, in 1605, and he went on to become a priest. Raphael is described in the annals of Oxford University already as a priest (the Latin term *sacerdos*) when he entered Oriel College in 1624 aged 18. However, Barbara died having borne a daughter, called Elizabeth, who also did not survive. A brass plaque to the memory of Barbara was moved from the chancel floor above her grave to the north-east corner of the chancel wall when the floor was raised in the nineteenth century. The plaque depicts Barbara in Elizabethan dress with Raphael and Elizabeth beside her.

In 1516 a John Burges is recorded in the lists of Rectors and then another man of that name in 1617. The second one was immediately followed by an Anthony Burges, though these were not apparently related.

However, they shared fame (and notoriety) for their preaching. John Burges, whose tenure as Rector was from 1617 to 1635, was imprisoned (possibly in the Fleet Prison) for a sermon which apparently was too Puritan in tone, and perhaps was unwisely delivered to a congregation that included King James I. Anthony Burgess (Rector from 1635 to 1662) apparently preached to Parliament in the 1640s and was a chaplain in Cromwell's New Model Army.

Both clergy wrote lengthy sermons outlining their differing views on tenets of the Roman Catholic faith compared with those of the Protestant. Chapter 14 reflects on changes and controversies affecting Holy Trinity including some contentious preaching.

A previously unrecorded name comes to light at this point and this is Edward Chetwynd, described as living at Ingestrie in Staffordshire in 1577 then attending Exeter College, Oxford, from 1592. He secured his DD in 1616, and, according to the Atheneae Oxioniensis (records of Oxford University) he declined to take up the post at Holy Trinity, preferring to remain amongst his former parishioners in Bristol: 'whereas he was a little before presented to the rich rectory of Sutton Colfield in Warwickshire, (twice the value of his dean[e]ry) he thereupon gave it up, purposely because he would live among, and so consequently please, the inhabitants of Bristol'. It is interesting to muse on Chetwynd's refreshing reason for turning down a rich living.

The Chetwynd entry in Atheneae Oxioniensis goes on to confirm that John Burges took up this post as: 'an eminent scholar … and doct. of physic, whose memory is fresh in those parts among the godly.' Burges is recorded also in these annals as being buried in the chancel at Holy Trinity in the same vault as his wife Dorothy when he died aged 72 in 1635.

At this point in the sequence of clergy, it is important to note the changes of patron. Dugdale's additional notes (not given in Riland Bedford's list) do not include the detail given by Norman Evans in his history of the church (1987) and also vary slightly in the dates given. Evans says in his timeline for the year 1559: '30th December. Queen Elizabeth I sold the advowson of Sutton Coldfield to Glascock and Blunt who on the same day sold it to John Gibbons, LLD.'

The following entry for 1660 says, 'The advowson was sold to Thomas Gibbons of New Hall.' (Evans, 1987, p. 89)

Given that the first of these is for the very end of December, it might be supposed that all these transactions happened very close together. Evans does not mention Roger Eliot's widow as being patron at any stage, and this does seem an unusual practice. We do know that Thomas Gibbons sold the advowson to John Shilton (senior) and it then passed down.

James Fleetwood, DD, is recorded as having been put forward for the post in 1642 by the Crown (Charles I), but he did not take up the post, presumably sensing that his royalist allegiance would not be welcomed in the Puritan stronghold of Sutton Coldfield (Riland Bedford, 1891, p. 80; Evans, 1987, p. 28). Evans notes that he eventually became chaplain to Prince Charles and was sworn in as his 'chaplain in ordinary' when Charles became king (Ibid.). Fleetwood subsequently became Bishop of Worcester (1675–83) and is now celebrated in the Bishops' window in the Vesey chapel (see Chapter 9).

According to Evans, Anthony Burges 'fled' his post in 1642, being an avowed Puritan who must have sensed danger in remaining in a post under the patronage of the Crown. However, once the commonwealth (the period under the Lord Protector) was over and the monarchy restored, Burgess returned. During the period of the commonwealth there was no incumbent at Holy Trinity, as appears to have been the case across the land. Chapter 14 deals in more detail with the registers and administration of baptisms, marriages and deaths during this time, providing a fascinating insight into the very different situation that pertained for this short period.

Interestingly, Burges resigned in 1662 because he could not accept the distinctly Protestant tenets of the new Book of Common Prayer.

William Watson, the Rector from 1662 to 1689 was presented to the living by the then patron, John Shilton (II). Watson seems an unlikely candidate for this living as he hailed from Worcestershire, but the move was clearly made to ensure that a priest was appointed who would use the new liturgy. Watson was born in Evesham in 1613 and went to Lincoln College, Oxford, where he gained his MA. A descendant of this Rector has given Holy Trinity further information, by email, as follows: 'My direct ancestor, always referred to as Doctor William Watson, the Rector, was buried at Sutton Coldfield on 5th May 1689.'

The Church of England Database gives Watson as MA but no mention of a doctorate. This concurs with the wording on Holy Trinity's Rectors' Board and the other lists. The Sutton Coldfield parish records note that his son William married Katherine Biddulph at Holy Trinity on 8 November 1683, and they had two children baptised in the church – Elizabeth and Katherine.

There is no record in the church of this Rector's burial but it is still probable that he was buried in the church. Maybe any memorial has disappeared or, more likely, was not commissioned. Watson's wife retired to Stoke Prior, where there is a memorial to her in the local church.

John Shilton presented John Riland to the living, and there followed a succession of Rectors from the same family until the start of the twentieth century. This is described in a separate chapter which follows this.

TWENTIETH CENTURY

At the beginning of the twentieth century, the last in the line of Riland Bedfords (William Campbell, son of William Kirkpatrick) was Rector. According to the memoirs of a parishioner at the time, Harold Osborne, his decision to hand over the patronage to the newly formed Diocese of Birmingham was influenced by a number of factors, not least the number of additional churches in Sutton Coldfield, with the concomitant shrinking of the parish of Holy Trinity. The newest church (at that point), St Peter's in the newly created adjacent parish of Maney, was consecrated in June 1905, with capacity for 400 worshippers, and subsequently extended to accommodate 600. While this was partly to deal with the explosion of population following the coming of the railway (a temporary 'iron hut' had been built as early as 1877 in Maney), there must have been the realisation that it would be odd to have the patronage of the historic parish church still in the hands of one family when all the new churches were under the wing of the Bishop of Birmingham.

Osborne questioned why William Campbell Riland Bedford had given up the living and retired early (in his 40s) when he 'was above the average both in preaching and organising ability and was popular with all classes and creeds. I rather fancy he saw a big job looming in the distance which he had not the energy to tackle.' (Osborne, ed. Howell, 2017, p. 41)

There had also been an Act of Parliament in 1898 reverting livings to the Ecclesiastical Commissioners and it is probable that William Campbell Riland Bedford expected the new diocese would now take over the appointment of clergy and the properties and endowments attached to that living in line with this act.

A press cutting of the time explains the implications of the change of the living, requiring an Act of Parliament in 1907, allowing for the Rector to remain in post with a stipend for two more years (until 1909), then to receive a comfortable pension. This is reproduced here in full:

Rectorate of Sutton: Finances adjusted under Act of Parliament

An Act of Parliament which received the Royal Assent on July 4, but which has escaped general notice is what is known as the Sutton Coldfield Rectory Act 1907. This measure was framed for the purpose of dealing with the endowments in connection with the rectory, and the transference of each endowment to the Ecclesiastical Commissioners. This could not be done without the sanction of Parliament, and the desirability of the step was by the formation of four ecclesiastical districts. These four districts are St James (Hill), St Michael (Boldmere), St John (Walmley), and St Peter (Maney). It was necessary to apportion corn rents, tithe rent charges, etc., for the benefit of the incumbents of those districts.

The living of Sutton Coldfield is in the gift of the Bishop of Birmingham, and the population of the parish is over 4,000. It is contended that this number of people is too large for one church, hence the formation of the four districts referred to. The Rev. W. C. R. Bedford, the present Rector, contemplates resigning the rectory within the next two years, and under the new Act the tithes, investments, endowments, and glebe lands will pass into the hands of the Commissioners, but as long as Mr. Bedford remains Rector, he will be paid £2,000 per annum, while on his retirement, if such retirement takes place within the next two years, he will receive a pension of £500 per annum. The right of nominating the minister or incumbent of every district formed out of the parish of Sutton Coldfield will be vested in the Bishop of Birmingham. In the event of the resignation of the Rev. W. C. R. Bedford, the new incumbent of the parish of Sutton Coldfield is to receive £600 per annum during the time any pension is being paid, and on the latter payment ceasing, he will be paid £700, and an additional £50 per annum pending the provision of a new rectory house.

(*Birmingham Daily Gazette*, 5 September 1907)

A later article in the *Birmingham Gazette and Express* (4 September 1908) stated that it was now felt that 'the spiritual needs of the district and diocese would be better served if the rectory, the property attached to it and the endowments were transferred to the Ecclesiastical Commissioners'. The act promised to improve and develop the glebe lands, constructing roads, improving sewerage systems, and increasing the value of properties and spending moneys 'for the cure of souls' in the parish of Sutton Coldfield.

The paper further declared that: 'This object has the full approval of the present Rector, who has assisted materially in its furtherance.'

In the Diocese of Birmingham

Canon Charles William Barnard, appointed by the Bishop of Birmingham, was Rector from 1909 to 1926. According to a cutting in the *Tamworth Herald* of 21 November 1925 (announcing his retirement) he was born in Lancashire, studied at Oriel College, Oxford, and served his first curacy in Barrow-in-Furness. From there he went to a parish in Beverley, then via Rowley Regis to Kings Norton, arriving there as vicar in 1893 to a population of 8,000, which increased in size to 20,000. His tenure there saw the building of two churches nearby (The Ascension in Stirchley and St Agnes in Cotteridge) as well as a mission church in West Heath. He was made an honorary canon of Worcester in 1904 and then of Birmingham when the new diocese came into being and encompassed his parish, as it does today.

In 1911 there were substantial celebrations for the coronation of George V, with the church playing a major part through bell-ringing and a service in the morning with a parade by the local regiment. Barnard's tenure encompassed the First World War, and he began what would become the most dramatic decorative change to the interior of the church, and the major work at Holy Trinity of the twentieth century, barring the creation of the Trinity Centre at the end of that century. This began with the decorative painting of the barrel-vaulted chancel ceiling in 1914. The war, understandably, halted this work, and it was under the rectorship of the next incumbent, Canon William Lyon, that the work could recommence, reaching completion in 1929, with the decorative painting of the ceilings in the nave, Vesey chapel and the tower. A screen was erected to the memory of Charles Barnard and his wife, paid for by their daughter. Charles had retired in 1926 to Leamington Spa where he died in August 1928. He was buried with his wife Agnes (who had died in 1913) in the cemetery in Rectory Road. The new screen served to turn the aisle extension housing Bishop Vesey's tomb into a separate space by dividing it from the nave. This new space then became known as the Vesey chapel.

Lyon also reintroduced the parish magazine, publication of which had halted at the start of the First World War, and oversaw the processes which would lead to the building of a new church, St Chad's on Hollyfield Road, where the congregation had previously been served by a temporary 'tin hut'. The Holy Trinity magazines of the year 1927 give a full account of the building progress and the joyous consecration service at the end of the year. One senses in Lyon the qualities of an innovator and a very capable organiser, and he achieved a great deal in just five years at Holy Trinity, during a time of economic depression too. It is no surprise that he later progressed to a post as archdeacon (of Loughborough).

George Harvey served from 1931–45, overseeing both the celebrations for the silver jubilee of George V in 1935 and the creation in 1939 of the Vesey Gardens and external memorial to Bishop Vesey on Church Hill just beyond the church north side. The Second World War followed close on the heels of this and there would have been great responsibility for church leaders attending to the spiritual needs of civilians and of families losing loved ones.

Canon John Boggon succeeded Canon Harvey at the end of the war and served for twenty years, a period of great change again for church and society. In his tenure he oversaw the modest changes to a small part of the building, the south chapel, which was refurbished in light oak in 1960 to form a library area with memorials to recent church wardens. New stained glass appeared – one window being dedicated in 1956 in memory of the Bishop of Birmingham, EW Barnes (Bishop from 1924 to 1953), who had presided over a service at Holy Trinity in 1950 to dedicate the new pipe organ installed in the tower. The other new glass was given by John Boggon himself in memory of his wife Mary. This window (on the east wall of this chapel) depicts the three Marys of the bible and is considered rather beautiful partly because of its design, but also because of its use of subtle colours. More detail about the window is in Chapter 9.

Canon Alaric Rose was Rector from 1965 to 1983, followed by Canon Edward G (Ted) Longman (1984–1996). The fiftieth Rector was Dan Connolly (1997–8), and James Langstaff served from 2000–04. John Routh became Rector in 2006.

The name of each new Rector is added to the board in the porch. A gallery of photographs of the incumbents from the early twentieth century is now in place in the church, and information is also on the website, where updates are regularly made.

OTHER CLERGY OF HOLY TRINITY

It would be impossible to compile a full list of the many priests who must have served as curates at Holy Trinity, even in more recent times.

In earlier centuries many of the Rectors would have been absent for large parts of the year, covering a number of other appointments, not necessarily in the church, but possibly also as part of the Court or roles in other professions like the law or medicine.

A curate would be appointed to do the day-to-day work, inevitably on a much lower rate of pay, as attested in works of fiction from writers like Jane Austen and Anthony Trollope. The tradition amongst the landed gentry was for younger sons who would not inherit family wealth to enter either a military career or the church, and this did not really change until the twentieth century, when there was a move towards vocational ministry and a more equitable system of remuneration in line both with employment law and parity across diverse parishes regardless of their individual wealth or ability to pay stipends. Livings gradually changed to reflect the need for clergy to be able to retire and receive a pension.

However, this was not the case in earlier times, and the curates are in some cases documented for their long or noteworthy service. Three names stand out in particular, and these actually followed one another in the post of curate: Francis Blick, Joseph Mendham and James Packwood.

The Revd Francis Blick became a curate at Holy Trinity in 1779. When the Rector, Richard Bisse Riland, died suddenly in his 50s, his younger brother John took over this post, holding both this and his previous post at St Mary's Birmingham for a while. However, he had differing views on theology, and when Blick preached a sermon in January 1791 (on John 7: 17) with which Riland did not agree, a series of acrimonious letters was written between the two, and subsequently published by Blick together with the sermon, when he resigned his post (a copy is in the church records). Blick moved to a parish in Tamworth and died in 1842. Fig. 65 shows the title and dedication pages of a contentious sermon.

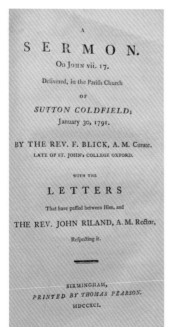
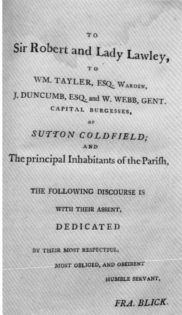

Fig. 65: *Title page of sermon by Revd F Blick (HTSC)*

Joseph Mendham, curate for thirty-two years and a distinguished scholar, died aged 87 in 1856. His memorial is on the north-west wall of the tower and commemorates all the members of his family (see Chapter 8 for more information on the wider family). He was born in London on 14 February 1769 and christened at St Stephen's Walbrook on 10 March. He was educated at St Edmund Hall, Oxford, and appears to have been given his post as curate at Holy Trinity by the then Rector, John Riland, following his marriage to Riland's second daughter Maria, in 1795. This may also have been precipitated by the debacle with Blick.

The Mendhams lived in a house on the Lichfield Road near the grammar school, and here Joseph started to acquire books and pamphlets on Catholic and Anglican doctrine at a time when the Roman Catholic Emancipation Bill of 1829 was in process. He learnt both Spanish and Italian to enable him to study original sources and subsequently wrote two books: *The memoirs of the Council of Trent* and *The literary policy of the Church of Rome*, which Evans describes as 'standard works of reference'. (Evans, 1987, pp. 58–9).

Mendham was inducted as vicar at the new church of St James Hill in 1835 but retired on health grounds after a few years. His wife pre-deceased him, and his son died a few months after his father, himself a priest and apparently leaving a legacy to St Michael's, Boldmere for the construction of the church spire. Neither his son nor his daughter married, and his daughter died aged 72 in 1871. Information about the memorial in the church to the Mendhams is in Chapter 8.

James Packwood, curate at Holy Trinity for forty years, died on 14 March 1869 aged 75. He is commemorated as a dedicatee of one of the parts of the Vesey chapel east window, and more information about this is in Chapter 9.

As curate to the Rector William Kirkpatrick Riland Bedford, he would have undertaken all the duties required when the Rector was absent, which appears to have been for numerous lengthy periods during his equally long tenure. This is confirmed by Richard Holbeche in his account of life in the 1850s: 'The Rector was absent a good deal, and old Mr Packwood the senior curate did most of the work. He had a rather monotonous and rather soothing voice, so that we frequently got into trouble for sleeping.'

Packwood was also very active in affairs of the town, being a member of the Society (Council), and warden in 1829 and 1830. According to Norman Evans, he was called upon to assist with the translation of Henry VIII's charter from Latin, which the town initiated in 1849. In that same year he was elected one of the two 'Capital Burgesses', the previous holders both having died – Sir William Cradock Hartopp and John Oughton (both of whom also have memorials in Holy Trinity). (Evans, 1987, p. 83).

12

THE RILAND AND RILAND BEDFORD CLERGY

BY SUE INGLEY

It is incredible to think that for more than 200 years the clergy line of Holy Trinity Church in Sutton Coldfield was dominated by one family, the Rilands, later intertwined through marriage with the Bedfords.

In English law, the patronage or 'advowson' enabled a patron or 'avowee' to present to the diocesan Bishop a nominee for appointment to a vacant ecclesiastical benefice. Traditionally most avowees were the lords of the manor, as had been the situation at Holy Trinity under the earls of Warwick in earlier centuries. Sometimes the patron was the Crown, as was the case at Holy Trinity through the Tudor period to the reign of Elizabeth I.

In 1559, Thomas Gibbons of New Hall bought the advowson of Sutton Coldfield from the Crown. Much later, this came down through Robert Shilton to John Shilton of Birmingham in 1662, a transaction that ultimately led to the Rilands beginning a clerical dynasty at Holy Trinity. Shilton's daughter, Katherine, married John Riland (1657–1720), who became the first Rector from this family in 1689. From then on, the post of Rector was handed down through generations of Rilands and eventually Bedfords through the female Riland line, mainly through sons, but occasionally a brother or son-in-law took the living. The 'dynasty' ended with the decision of William Campbell Riland Bedford to pass the advowson to the recently formed diocese of Birmingham. This was enshrined in law by the Rectory Act of 1907, with William Campbell Riland Bedford retiring as Rector in 1909.

William Kirkpatrick Riland Bedford, the penultimate Rector in the family line, served as Rector for 40 years. During that time he published a history of Sutton Coldfield, a useful source for much of this volume, and also a history of his family's line of Rectors entitled *Three Hundred Years of a Family Living, being a history of the Rilands of Sutton Coldfield*, published in 1889 by Cornish Brothers. Much of the information for this chapter comes from that book and so, after the first reference, the page number(s) only are given for references to this text. The author is referenced in the text just by his surname 'Riland Bedford' to distinguish him from other members of the family. Other sources are referenced in the usual format.

JOHN RILAND (1657-1720)

John Riland, the first member of the family to become Rector of Sutton Coldfield, was born in 1657. His father, also a John 'Ryland' (Riland Bedford, 1889, p. 12) was descended from yeoman stock in Over Quinton, Gloucestershire. John was a clever child, attending Stratford Grammar School and entering Magdalen College, Oxford, at the age of only 14 (see Fig. 67). Described as being 'very learned, humble, peaceable and heavenly minded' (p. 32), he became Rector of Exhall near Alcester in 1647, Rector of Bilton near Rugby, also in Warwickshire, in 1660, and Archdeacon of Coventry in 1661. In 1665 he gained his final post as Rector of St Martin's in Birmingham, where he continued until his death in 1672. His monument still exists in the chancel of St Martin's today.

John Riland's mother, Cecilia Stanley, was the daughter of William Stanley of West Bromwich and a cousin of the Shilton family. John and Cecilia had two children, John and Maria. Maria unfortunately died before her brother, but John thrived and went on to attend Magdalen College at Oxford University in 1673 and ultimately to become a priest, just as his father had done.

In his student days, however, he was more militantly opposed to the monarchy than his father, heavily aligning himself with the Puritan Shiltons and opposing Dr Farmer and later Dr Sacheverell of New Hall, who were both sympathisers of James II and the Jacobite cause (p. 21). Indeed, Riland Bedford intimates that treasonable notes added in the margin of a book in the rectory, Bishop Prideaux's *Compendium of History,* were probably added by John Riland. In this book, the author quotes how Henry I thought 'an unlearned king was a crowned asse'. The inscribed marginal adds, 'If so, what is our K George?'. This could well have rebounded on John, had the book fallen into the wrong hands. Despite this, for the most part John Riland was generally thought of as being a 'High Churchman' going about his duties in a peaceable way, with 'not much to record'. (p. 20)

John and his wife Katherine (née Shilton) had seven children: John (1690–1765), William (1691–1692), Catherine (1692–1779), Charles (1694–1715), Richard (1695–1757), Thomas (1696–1704) and Elizabeth (b. and d. 1698). Unfortunately, only three of these children outlived John Riland. Catherine married a William Sadler of Castle Bromwich in 1717, but died without issue. John, the eldest, went to Magdalen College, Oxford, but failed to graduate and, declining to take up the

Rectors of Sutton Coldfield from the Riland and Riland Bedford families

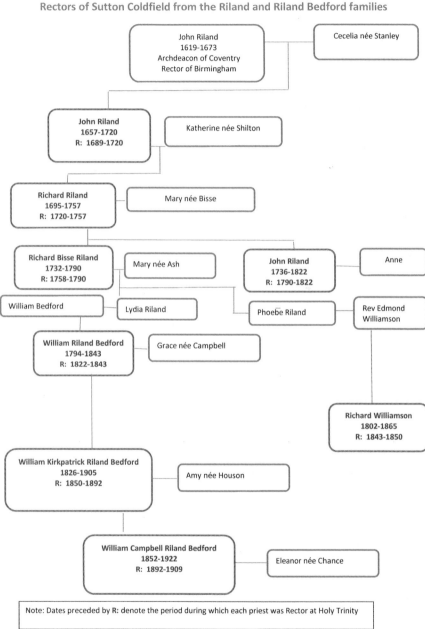

Fig. 66: *Rectors from Riland and Riland Bedford families (a tree) (ST from NGE)*

post of Rector due to his anti-royalist views, became instead an active member of the corporation and in 1728 warden of Sutton. It was therefore Richard, the fourth surviving son, who ended up becoming the next Rector of Sutton Coldfield when their father died.

John Riland's other most notable claim to fame was the building of a new rectory. This is recorded in Chapter 3 about developments at Holy Trinity in the eighteenth century. John was also active in movements resisting rises in land tax in 1705 and co-initiating the construction of a pool at Longmoor Brook in Sutton Park. This pool eventually became the property of the corporation and was invaluable in supplying power to a corn mill, built some years later.

In 1708, his first wife Katherine died, which perhaps spared her the tragedy of seeing her father fall into financial difficulties. By 1696 John Shilton had already started to build up debts (possibly not even paying a portion of his daughter's dowry) and by 1706 he was forced to mortgage the advowson. In 1710 John Riland paid off the mortgage and bought it. On 23 May 1717, John married Elizabeth Sedgwick, the daughter of a local gentleman. Sadly, this marriage was brief as John died in 1720 and Elizabeth shortly after in 1724.

Fig. 67: John Riland I in boyhood 1665 (WKRB)

However, his purchase of the advowson ten years before his death at least meant that he could leave an enduring legacy. This ensured that the Rectorship of Sutton Coldfield could remain within the Riland family for the foreseeable future.

RICHARD RILAND (1695–1757)

Richard Riland was born in 1695, the fourth son of John and Katherine Riland, and was the first Rector of Sutton Coldfield to have been born in the parish. Portraits of him as a child represent him as being of 'a fresh chubby, regular countenance, without any very striking characteristic of feature or expression' (p. 24).

However, he proved himself extremely intelligent and was educated at Magdalen College, Oxford, taking his BA degree in 1715 and being awarded his MA on 1 February 1716–17. The fact that he gave ten guineas to the New Building Fund at Magdalen demonstrates his affection for the time he spent there studying, unlike his elder brother John, who left without graduating.

In 1720, on the death of his father, he succeeded as Rector of Sutton Coldfield at the age of 25 years. He continued in the living for another thirty-seven years, with 'uneventful' significance (p. 25), and appears to have enjoyed a happy marriage and a contented domestic life. In 1729 he married Mary Bisse, a 'woman of cultivated understanding and noble qualities' (p. 28). Mary was the daughter of Mr George Bisse Esquire from White Lackington in Somerset. Many polite letters of courtship were exchanged between the couple, with Richard ultimately professing, 'I intimated to you in my last (letter) that I had an offer of some considerable importance to make … it is that of a Husband; if you are not better provided, I am at your service.' (Jones, 1984, p. 105)

Mary accepted and they went on to have two sons, Richard Bisse, born 1732, and John, born four years later. They now became a close-knit family unit, and one only has to read the letters sent to their children whilst they were away at university to see how close and affectionate they were towards each other. Both parents address them endearingly as 'Dear Dear Dick' and 'Jack', Richard concludes with 'Yr ever loving Pap' (p. 28) and Mary with, 'I hope you are well and do well, which I pray for continually' (p. 28). Both sons did indeed do well, both attending Queen's College, Oxford, and eventually becoming Rectors of Sutton Coldfield.

We also learn from Mary and Richard's correspondence that they were very interested in culture and the arts, attending operas, musical performances and

plays. Richard boasts to his eldest son how 'Yr Mother & I have been two successive nights at the Playhouse' (p. 31) and how they enjoyed the 'Harlequin Sorceror'
and heard the oratorio 'Jephtha', which 'perform'd by near 100 hands' was 'so
grand' (p. 32). In other letters he mentions trips to Cupers' Gardens, Drury Lane
and Sadler's Wells, in which 'the performances were astonishing' and admits they
can attend these as 'We have too much leisure on our hands, which has giv'n us
time to go to some places of diversion' (p. 35).

One may perhaps also speculate that Richard Riland had an interest in nature,
for, according to Riland Bedford, he should be remembered for his planting of an
avenue of lime trees from the rectory door westwards into Sutton. Few, if any, still
remain today, but in their time they must have provided a beautiful and impressive
link from the rectory to the town.

By 1757, Richard's health was in decline and during that April he travelled to
London, partly on business but mostly to seek medical advice. On 19 May a Dr
Heberden was consulted but sadly, as the summer progressed, Richard deterio-
rated, dying on 2 August.

RICHARD BISSE RILAND (1732–90)

Richard Bisse Riland became the third Rector of Sutton Coldfield in 1758, the
year after the death of his father. Fig. 68 shows him just before he took up his
appointment at Holy Trinity.

His time as Rector makes for interesting reading, for though in general he was
described as zealous, orthodox and charitable and 'an ornament and an honour
to the clerical profession' (MacFarlane, 1989, p. 13), in many other instances he
became embroiled in controversial issues within the town. For this reason, he
could therefore be said to be one of the most intriguing characters of the Riland
dynasty.

Educated at Queen's College Oxford, he was soon admitted to deacon's orders
by the Bishop of Lichfield and Coventry on 19 September 1756 and in the following year acted as curate in Sutton while his father was absent in London.
On 15 January 1758 he received priest's orders from Bishop Cornwallis and on
4 February was inducted into his living in Sutton Coldfield.

Richard's tenure as Rector coincided with the momentous work of 1760 to
add new pews to the church, and the subsequent challenge by parishioners to the
allocation of pews to individuals by the corporation. This is documented more
fully in Chapter 3 on developments at Holy Trinity in the eighteenth century.

The Rector, though, also found himself in court over another issue, this time concerning the payment of tithes on the land owned by Simon Luttrell, Lord Irnham of Four Oaks Hall. These were required to be paid according to an Act of Parliament of 1756, but the notoriously high-minded Lord Irnham declined to pay. The case was taken to court and a resolution concluded in the Rector's favour. While a positive result for Richard, this may not have enhanced his relations with the local gentry.

Furthermore, it is recorded that Richard Bisse Riland held very strong opinions on many issues in which he 'often found himself in the minority' (p. 41). His views on public improvements proved controversial and surprising when, in 1777, he played an active part in stopping a theatre being built in Birmingham – surprising because his parents clearly loved music and dramatic arts. In addition, having seen the benefits of the convenient travel routes in London during his student days, he failed to understand any objection to a turnpike road being constructed in Sutton. Understandably this did not endear him to local residents.

Fig. 68: *Richard Bisse Riland aged 25 (WKRB)*

His most controversial view, though, was his support for land enclosures. In 1777, the corporation drew up plans to 'enclose the Park and other common lands' in Sutton. Richard and Sir Joseph Scott of Great Barr both spearheaded the project which, if successful, would have guaranteed the Rector alone a seventh of the park. Not surprisingly, this aroused great opposition and resentment, and one opponent was even moved to write a poem expressing his disdain. This was entitled 'Bishop Vesey's Ghost To The Rector of Sutton' (18) (p. 60) and aimed to express the dead Bishop's warning to him for allowing such an unjust scheme to occur:

Cease, cold-hearted cruel Rector,
Give Inclosing projects o'er,
Hear for once a midnight lecture,
Never strive to rob the poor.

Fortunately for the people of Sutton, the proposed enclosure never passed into law, but it probably did little to endear Richard to his parishioners.

Despite all this, however, Richard Bisse Riland was perceived as a caring and benevolent person in both his personal and professional life. On 29 May 1759 he married Mary Ash, one of the daughters and heirs of William Ash Esq of Paston in Northamptonshire, and remained married for thirty-one years. That this was a happy marriage can be inferred from a letter he wrote from Scotland in 1783 where he states that 'no home, place or wife hath the same charms for me that my own has' (p. 96).

They had three children: Lydia (b. 1761), George (b. January 1763) and Phoebe (b. 1767). Sadly their son only lived for a year, dying in April 1764 (p. 73). Their daughters, on the other hand, thrived to carry on the dynasty and traditional family profession of entering the church. Phoebe married Edmond Williamson, Rector of Campton in 1793, producing eight children, two of whom, Edmond and Richard, became vicars, the latter becoming headmaster of Westminster School and Rector of Sutton Coldfield from 1843 to 1850 (see below).

Lydia, their eldest daughter, married a William Bedford of Elmhurst on 30 September 1784, a move which brought the Bedford name to the dynasty. They had four children, Emma, Sophia, Maria and finally William Riland Bedford, who eventually became Rector of Sutton Coldfield in 1822.

Richard Bisse Riland did show care for his parishioners. According to Riland Bedford, in a handwritten document entitled 'Houses and Inhabitants in The Parish of Sutton Coldfield' dated autumn 1784, he showed a detailed and sensitive knowledge of 'every soul in his cure'. He could name the number of houses, cottages, freehold homes, numbers in each denomination, widows, married couples, children, inmates and servants, and he took an interest in town life.

As a magistrate, he took time to listen, respond and follow up many cases, including dealing with apprentices and their 'harsh masters', helping poor farming families with disputes on the road and dealing with stage coach robberies, which were becoming more frequent. His concern for a little girl injured by the coach of a Miss Winn, daughter of Sir Rowland Winn, indeed shows his benevolence, where he states writing to her, 'I am happy to hear she is perfectly recovered and suffered so little.' (p. 66)

He also contributed £100 towards the General Fund and in December 1778 persuaded the corporation to grant £30 to establish a school for the poor. In 1780 he became chair of Birmingham General Hospital and sought ways to benefit his parish.

His career was further enriched by becoming chaplain to Dr Porteous, Bishop of Chester in 1777, curate of Water Orton for two years in 1782, and prebendary of Dornford (Lichfield) in 1784. By the end of the decade, however, his health rapidly declined and he died early in 1790, leaving his brother John to take up the post as Rector of Sutton Coldfield.

JOHN RILAND (1736–1822)

As Richard Bisse Riland died leaving no male heir, the advowson of Sutton Parish passed to his brother John in 1790. Referred to affectionately in the family as 'Little Jack', John was a likeable character. Ordained into the curacy of Sutton Coldfield in 1759, he was described as of an 'amiable character', 'genial disposition' and showing 'goodness of heart'. Contemporary newspaper cuttings refer to him as 'a finer type of man than his predecessor of 1778' (newspaper cuttings 1885–1975 Vol, p. 121) and past accounts show him as having more time for his parishioners. He was known to also hold strong libertarian views not only on religion, but also social issues such as enclosures, slavery, evangelism, the role of women, pollution and agriculture.

Like his brother Richard, John went to Queen's College, Oxford, and was reported as having an intelligent, enquiring mind and enjoying a good debate. Whilst at university, he wrote a reply on the Anti-Calvinistic side in response to a sermon by Reverend Richard Elliot, and continued to question issues and theories throughout his life. In 1781, there was a letter evidencing his involvement in a controversy with the non-conformists in Birmingham, specifically the new Baptist movement, which encouraged adult baptism by full immersion.

John took an active interest in town affairs, becoming a member of the Corporation around 1760 and warden in 1762. In terms of his faith, Riland Bedford notes a moment in 1761 when he recorded that 'God opened my eyes to behold the wondrous things out of his law and he then gave me to experience John iv 45'. (p. 122)

By 1762, he had accepted the assistant post of curate at St Mary's Church in Huddersfield, from a renowned evangelical leader Henry Venn (1796–1873). Venn was an Anglican clergyman and often lobbied Parliament on social issues of the day, such as the abolition of the Atlantic slave trade. In this post John soon gained the esteem of Venn and his followers, and continued to reflect his values of mission and the championing of the oppressed when he returned to Sutton Coldfield as Rector.

In Huddersfield he married a member of the congregation, Ann Hudson, in 1768. Their marriage lasted fifty-one years, and they had four children: Priscilla (1770–1837), Maria (1772–1841), Lucy (1775–1869) and a son, John (1778–1863). Priscilla and Lucy never married but carried on their father's charitable works. Lucy was a major contributor to the building of the new St John's Church in Walmley in 1845, donating £1,000. There is a brass memorial tablet to her in the chancel at Holy Trinity.

Fig. 69: John Riland II aged 60 (WKRB)

Maria and John both married. In 1795 Maria married John's assistant curate Joseph Mendham, MA of St Edmund Hall, Oxford, a man of similar religious views, whilst in 1820 John married Maria Wolesley. John, like his father, held radical religious views and though he did not become Rector of Sutton, he did obtain a curacy in Yoxall, Staffordshire. He later also gained the chaplaincy of Magdalen Asylum in Birmingham. He contributed to the building and maintenance of the asylum, and an engraved portrait by Radcliffe was presented there on his death in 1863.

John Riland Senior is described as 'a fine old gentleman ever mindful of the interests of his poor parishioners'(Midgley, 1904, p. 89) and 'in touch with concerns of the townspeople', (MacFarlane, 1989, p. 14). Dressed in his bushy wig, flapped hat and long black cassock coat, he was said to give sweets to the children and comfort to the poor, sick and elderly. (Midgley, 1904, p. 90). Fig. 69 shows John aged 60 in his fine wig.

His enthusiasm for his ministry must surely be seen in the account of one of his elderly parishioners who said that he always asked him to report his news quickly, 'for I have much to do and little time' (p. 123).

He also passionately opposed the enclosure of the park and common land in Sutton, in complete contrast to his brother, who had supported its implementation. John, however, saw it as detrimental to the interests of the cottagers in the parish and its unpopularity can certainly be summed up in a contemporary verse in *The Vesey Papers:*

If 'tis a crime in man or woman
To steal a goose from off a common,
Then surely he has less excuse
Who steals the common from the goose. (Riland Bedford, *Vesey Papers)*

In addition to distributing 'comfits' to children in the parish, John was also concerned to guide them spiritually and in education. His diligence in teaching the catechism (p. 125) was renowned, and he was instrumental in opening Sunday schools for girls in 1806 and boys in 1811. He also strongly urged the use of local funds to establish elementary schools, and this will have had a bearing on the schools which were set up in Sutton in 1825 (see Chapter 4).

He also took an interest in agriculture and gave sermons in 1796 on tithe corn, and in 1805 on farmers, showing respect for the work of farm labourers. (Riland, John, 1805, p. 2). Simultaneously, at a time when there had been food shortages due to a poor harvest and the French wars, he went on to advocate that farmers should not be tempted to charge higher prices for their produce, warning 'consider and beware; and do not yield to evil'. (Riland, John, 1805, p. 9). This was an interesting benevolent gesture, when some ten years later the controversial Corn Laws were to be passed, which caused much hardship during the thirty-one years they lasted. John's sermon appears ahead of its time.

Equally revealing is his 'Sermon To Servants – With A Dedication to Masters and Mistresses'. Here he aligns his sympathies with the working classes, calling himself a fellow 'Servant of God' (Riland, John, date, p. 7). Throughout his life, John campaigned for social good causes on subjects as diverse as 'The scriptural preservation of women from ruin' and his aversion to noise and smoke pollution (pp. 127–8).

By 1819 John had lost his wife, and reports of accidents and mishaps indicate a decline in his health, as when he was said to be oblivious 'that his cauliflower wig had caught fire from the pulpit candles' (p. 144). In 1822, just a fortnight after his 85th birthday, he apparently sank down just before ascending the stairs and 'in a few moments had entered into eternal rest' (p. 144). John Riland was no doubt one of the Rectors of Sutton whose loss was lamented by his parishioners.

WILLIAM RILAND BEDFORD (1794–1843)

On the death of John Riland in 1822, his son (also John), declined to take up the post of Rector of Sutton. The vacancy therefore passed back to his nieces Lydia and Phoebe Riland, who had been given the advowson anyway by Richard Bisse Riland, their father.

In 1784, Lydia, the elder daughter, had married William Bedford of Elmhurst. They had four children: Emma, Sophia, Maria and William. In 1793 Phoebe, the younger daughter, had married Edmond Williamson, himself a Rector (of Campton in Bedfordshire). They had eight children, the second being Richard. Both William Bedford and Richard Williamson would in turn be part of the Riland Bedford line.

Lydia's husband, William Bedford, decided to buy his brother-in-law's share of the advowson and make his only son, William Riland Bedford, Rector of Sutton. This may have served his plan to promote the enclosure of land in Sutton. Certainly this marks the point where the Bedford name was combined with that of Riland.

William Riland Bedford was born in 1794 and started his education in Tamworth, under the tuition of Mr Blick (curate at Holy Trinity). In 1804, he was sent to Rugby School, where he was apparently popular, 'heading a successful revolt against certain fagging regulations which the juniors considered unjust' (p. 152). [Note: 'fagging' was a name for duties inflicted by older pupils on younger ones at public schools].

In 1813 he went to University College, Oxford, where fellow students included Sir Thomas Phillips and Percy Bysshe Shelley. William appears to have enjoyed poetry, writing essays, literature and translating. In 1816 he graduated with his BA and was awarded his MA in 1820. In 1817 he was ordained curate of Water Orton by the Bishop of Worcester, and in 1819 transferred to the curacy of Broadway and Buckland in Worcestershire, where he remained for three years. In 1822, on the death of his great uncle, he became Rector of Sutton Coldfield.

During his time in the post, many changes were to occur in Sutton. Despite all the lobbying and protesting from John Riland before, the Enclosure Act was finally passed in 1824. William was to gain an allotment of land in lieu of tithes, and a corn rent was fixed for the old enclosures. The Corporation, now deemed as 'Lords of the Manor', gained large areas of wasteland and became proprietors of many cottages. Fortunately, Sutton Park was not included in this act and remained a public property administered by the Corporation for the benefit and recreation of the local neighbourhood.

Improvements were made to the park entrances. Previously the only entry had been through the Driffold, where cattle rangers assembled their cattle to be marked, before leading them down the narrow road to Wyndley Pool. This was three-quarters of a mile from the town. Details of the arrangement made with Simon Luttrell to exchange land are in Chapter 4.

The residents of Sutton benefited from charitable schemes such as the supplying of ten alms-houses, blankets for the poor, free medical advice and vaccinations for children, as well as aid for apprentices and school leavers. A certain amount of assistance was also granted to pregnant women, 'poor maidens' needing dowries, and widows, provided by the Lord's Meadow Charity.

William Riland Bedford therefore enjoyed a time as Rector when Sutton was prospering. In 1823 he became domestic chaplain to the Marquis of Lothian and later married Grace Campbell, youngest daughter of Charles Sharpe of Hoddom Castle in Dumfriesshire. Grace was descended from the great historical family of Kirkpatrick and had a grandfather and brother who had been and were Members of Parliament for Dumfries.

The marriage was happy and lasted for twenty years, producing five children: William Kirkpatrick, Charles John, Richard Bisse, and twins, Francis and Campbell, but it was the eldest of these who would carry forward the name of his distinguished forebears and become Rector of Sutton.

William Riland Bedford is described as 'a country gentleman' and active in not only his parish duties but as an 'energetic magistrate' (p. 153). He was also an enthusiastic horticulturist, planting and cultivating many ornamental and timber trees. This proved advantageous to Sutton Coldfield when enclosures were being implemented. In 1829, to demonstrate his expertise, he even published a short book entitled *The Midland Forester by a woodman of Arden*. This contained much valuable information for those with a similar passion for trees.

During his time as Rector, he personally funded improvements to the rectory too. In 1833, a new wing was added and the front was modernised by taking down the old courtyard wall and tithe barn. In addition, the pond, where the 'meat fish' had been kept in his grandfather's time, was filled in, and new stables and offices were erected.

He was visionary in his realisation that it would be timely to consider building churches in areas of the wider parish where the population was growing. More detail about this is in Chapter 4. It is thought that the work this entailed, particularly with protracted arrangements for the building of St John's, Walmley, may have contributed to his last period of illness. The shock of the sudden death of his friend Charles Barker (the headmaster of Bishop Vesey Grammar School) in 1842 may also have led to a decline in William's health, and on 6 July 1843 he collapsed with a stroke in Temple Row Birmingham, and sadly died.

The onset of the final stroke appears to have been exacerbated by the circumstances of his journey to Birmingham. This is recorded in a long account of the post-mortem in the *Birmingham Journal* of 8 July 1843.

It appears that there was a complaint by the owner of a pony that William's carriage had hit the animal on the journey from Sutton and that the owner was demanding that William seek the advice of a vet and perhaps pay compensation. The witness statements confirmed that there was no blow struck and that another man had assured the owner of the pony that he had the Rector's address and his word that he admitted the act and would pay compensation. In the next moment William fell to the ground, clearly as the result of a stroke, and was officially recorded as having died of apoplexy. The long press report ends rather poignantly as follows:

> Deceased was forty-eight years of age and in possession of a very valuable hereditary living. He was a magistrate of the county and had generally taken an active part in magisterial business. He has left a widow and five children, to one of whom, who is at Eton College, it appears he had written a letter on the morning of his death, before he left home. The lady of deceased, whose grief may be conceived, but not described, remained by his side until his death.

When William died, the post would normally have passed to his eldest son, William Kirkpatrick, but due to his youth (he was not yet 17), temporary ill-health and delays in his higher education, he was not ready to take over at this point. Instead, the post went temporarily to his father's cousin, Richard Williamson.

A legacy of William Riland Bedford's time as Rector is the stained glass in the window in the east end of the church given in his memory, which remains a focal point for worshippers and visitors (see Chapter 9 for full details of the window).

RICHARD WILLIAMSON (1802-65)

Richard was a cousin of the late Rector on his maternal side and headmaster of Westminster School, maintaining his headship of the school for the first three years of his term as Rector (1843 to 1850). He was born in Campton, Bedfordshire, on 25 November 1802, second son to Phoebe Riland, younger daughter of Richard Bisse Riland, and the Reverend Edmond Williamson.

Richard was himself educated at Westminster and went up to Trinity College, Cambridge, in 1821, gaining his BA and MA by 1825. In 1827, he was made a fellow of Trinity and following entry to the Inner Temple was ordained deacon in 1828 and priest in 1829. He was created a Doctor of Divinity in 1835.

Richard showed equal passion for education as he did for the church. His successor, William Kirkpatrick Riland Bedford, was later to write of his 'zealous conscientious work' (p. 156) during this time, and how one of his greatest contributions to the artistic world was his designing of classical costumes for the annual Latin plays at Westminster. Indeed, he produced a booklet, entitled *Eunuchus Palliatus*, explaining these designs in 1839.

In addition, Richard was to produce a 'School Classics Notebook'. This, together with a list of boys admitted to Westminster School from 1811–28, was a book divided into three sections covering 'Geography and Places', 'Philosophy and Persons' and 'Antiques and Things'. It is now housed in the archives of Cambridge University.

On 4 January 1833 he married Anne Gray in Godmanchester, Huntingdon. Anne was the sixth of fourteen children, whose parents were Elizabeth and Robert Gray (Bishop of Bristol).

Richard and Anne were married for thirty-two years, though they remained childless. Richard continued to combine his work as headmaster and as Rector of Sutton Coldfield for three years, from 1843, but by the end of this period, his devotion to his parochial duties induced him to resign his post at Westminster School in 1846.

It was therefore in 1843 that Richard Williamson took up the post of Rector of Sutton Coldfield and 'was to devote himself unremittingly to the duties of a parish priest' in which, according to his successor William Kirkpatrick, 'his scholarship and high personal conscientiousness combined to cause him to excel' and probably be the 'best pastor who ever presided in Sutton' (pp. 156–7).

There can be no doubt that Richard took his clerical duties seriously and he continued to oversee the varied plans for church extension that had been proposed in his predecessor's time. In addition, he encouraged the building, in 1845, of the daughter church in Walmley and, with the interest and experience as a former headmaster, sought to improve education facilities throughout Sutton. This included the establishment of an infant school and the founding of a permanent library (see Chapter 6 for further information), which to this day can be regarded as part of his legacy.

However, Richard's career as Rector of Sutton Coldfield ended when William Kirkpatrick was in a position to take over, and, with the attractive offer of a vicarage in Pershore, Worcestershire, he decided to resign in the autumn of 1850. There is no doubt that his departure was of great sadness to the people of Sutton, for as Sir William Hartopp quoted in the *Birmingham Journal* (17 August 1850): 'We shall ever think with pleasure of the social intercourse which you and Mrs Williamson have promoted amongst us … and the great attention you have given to our schools … the improvements … and the wants of the poorer classes.' The paper reports how the couple were also presented with 'plate' as a gift and a 'tea pot set'.

Richard Williamson was to reside as a vicar and rural dean in Pershore for fifteen years. In 1851, he was made honorary canon of Worcester Cathedral and during his curacy he did much to restore the Abbey Church of Pershore 'to a state of magnificence', most of which was from his own funding. He also set up an infant school and sought to support local churches.

It is, however, in testimonies to him after his death, that we learn the most about the man and his legacy. The local paper in Worcester makes reference to his 927 letters, written for personal applications for subscriptions, his hard work restoring the church, his charitable works and his devotion to the sick of the parish when there was a cholera outbreak. (*Worcester Chronicle*, 6 December 1865, p. 9)

Richard Williamson died on 11 September 1865, aged 62 years, in Datchworth, Hertfordshire. He left a widow and a personal estate worth £11,282 7s 6d.

After his death he was not forgotten in Sutton when diarist Sarah Holbeche (1802–82), one of his great admirers, was moved to commission a window in the north wall of the Vesey chapel to his memory. This was made by Hardman, the famous Birmingham craftsman, though it seems at first she was not too pleased with his handiwork. However, she ultimately accepted the window and wrote, 'I have done well for the church and gratified myself in doing honour to Dr Williamson'.

WILLIAM KIRKPATRICK RILAND BEDFORD
(1826–1905)

William Kirkpatrick is now perhaps the most famous of the Riland Bedford dynasty, because of his writing both about the history of the town and also about the long line of Rectors from his family. It would appear that, like many of the Rectors, he did not spend much time in Sutton Coldfield, but his ministry, social, judicial, sporting and historical interests all contributed to making him one of the town's most famed sons.

He was born on 12 July 1826 at the rectory, and was educated at at Bishop Vesey's Grammar School under Charles Barker. From there he went on to study at Westminster School, gaining a Queen's scholarship in 1840. Although he took his examinations in 1843, an outbreak of typhoid fever in the winter prevented his completion of his studies. His illness was to return later in his life, but on recovery at this point he went to Brasenose College, Oxford, where he became secretary of the Oxford Union and appeared to enjoy his studies and debating. Fellow students, such as William Alexander, who became Bishop of Armagh (and was the husband of the celebrated hymn writer Mrs C. F. Alexander), and Arthur Purey-Cust, later Dean of York, became life-long friends. In 1847 he took his degree and later gained a Master of Arts in 1852.

In 1849 he was ordained at Lichfield Cathedral and took up a brief curacy in Southwell in Nottinghamshire. Two years later, in October 1850, he succeeded Richard Williamson and became Rector of Sutton Coldfield, remaining in the position for forty-two years.

In the early part of his new post, he lived with his widowed mother in Wylde Green House (on the junction of Birmingham Road and Wylde Green Road), but in September 1851 he married Amy Maria Houson, youngest daughter of Joseph Houson of Southwell. They had eleven children: seven sons and four daughters (p. 165). Fortunately, all survived into adulthood, with the exception of the sixth child, Arthur, who died at the age of 4 in 1865. William subsequently commissioned stained glass windows in Holy Trinity to the memory of Arthur and also his mother (see Chapter 9).

William Kirkpatrick was involved in a great deal of activity in the church and town. This involved fundraising through bazaars for the building of new churches and developments to Holy Trinity.

He also became a member of the Corporation of Sutton Coldfield, warden from 1850 to 1854, chairman of the Aston Board, founder and president of the Benefit Society, and president of the Sutton Coldfield Institute, where he gave lectures on topics such as 'Parody' (1860) and 'The Luttrells of Four Oaks' (1895).

In 1848, having qualified as a magistrate, he took up duties in Warwickshire and Aston. Indeed his 'Peeps Into The Curious Past: Reminiscences of an Aston Magistrate', make for fascinating reading. His stories of hysterical women in carriages being afraid of being robbed and hiding their jewels in their shoes, and

Fig. 70: *Revd William Kirkpatrick Riland Bedford (SCL)*

the antics of the eccentric Judge Maule, demonstrate his gift for humorous reporting. On a more serious note, however, some reports show his benevolent nature as a guardian of the poor, as in the case of an old soldier who he found ten years later to be entitled to a large sum of money.

He also took an interest in transport and became a director of the Birmingham, Erdington and Sutton Coldfield Railway Company, which opened the first railway line to Sutton in 1862.

Politically, he was sympathetic to the Tory party of the time. He was also a Freemason, becoming Master of the Apollo University Lodge in Oxford. Then in 1855 he presided over the Lodge of Light in Birmingham and in 1860 the Warden Lodge in Sutton Coldfield. He was Provincial Grand Master of Warwickshire and Staffordshire for six years, and in 1861 became Grand Chaplain of England.

For six years after his appointment to the post of Rector, William worked fervently to perform his clerical duties, but from 1856, ill health for him and his wife resulted in lengthy leaves of absence. Records indicate that he made several trips to London, Edinburgh and abroad to Malta, Gibraltar and southern France, seeking medical treatment and convalescing. This resulted in his virtually taking a thirteen-year sabbatical. Little is known about these illnesses, but during this time he did accept further official positions, such as chaplain to the Bishop of Gibraltar. In addition, he continued his writing, publishing books and articles focused on local and ecclesiastical history.

In 1858, his *The Blaze of Episcopacy* was published, which according to the *London Evening Standard* (30 July 1897) was a 'handsome and learned' catalogue of the arms of English Bishops. This was followed by *The Regulations of the Old Hospital of The Knights of St John at Valetta,* which he wrote in 1882. Others included *Three Hundred Years of A Family Living* about the Riland Bedfords written in 1889, his *History of Sutton Coldfield* in 1891, *Malta and The Knights Hospitallers* in 1894, which was inspired by his stay in Malta, and *Outcomes of Old Oxford,* about his fellow students, in 1899. He wrote books on the Manor of Sutton, Bishop Vesey *(The Real Vesey)*, the Vesey buildings, Holy Trinity Parish Church and the Luttrells of Four Oaks.

In addition, he was a regular contributor to the monthly *The Gentleman's Magazine*, which specialised in antiquarian topics. He also wrote for *Woman's World*, and from 1866 to 1869 he edited *The Atlas*, a weekly newspaper that had been founded in 1826. This was particularly known for its music, theatre and literary reviews, and promoted temperance. It re-emerged as the *Public Schools Chronicle*, which William continued for a time to edit. At the same time, he also published a memorial volume to his artist uncle Charles Kirkpatrick Sharpe, who had died in 1851, called *Etchings, with Photographs from Original Drawings, Poetical and Prose Fragments*. He was also party to the founding of the original *Sutton Coldfield News*.

William also pursued sporting interests. From his days at Oxford, cricket had long been of great interest to him and in July 1847 he founded the Sutton Coldfield Cricket Club, which often played in Sutton Park. Later, his eldest son William Campbell was to play for Warwickshire. In addition, he took up archery, practised in past generations of his family in the rectory, and he declared it 'a very healthy and agreeable amusement', to the *Aris's Birmingham Gazette* (19 December 1853). This led to his founding the Toxophilite Society (for lovers of archery) and in 1885 writing *The Woodmen of Arden from 1785*, describing the development of the group. In July 1856, he combined his love of the two sports by forming the Free Foresters, a group of cricket and archery enthusiasts, whose story he was to write in 1895 with W. E. W. Collins, entitled *The Annals of The Free Foresters 1856-1894*.

In the 1880s, however, despite all these extra interests, William Kirkpatrick continued to care for the needs of his large family and parish. In the case of the latter, it was clear that by 1879 the burial grounds of Holy Trinity Church were full, and so William sought to use some of the glebe lands on the opposite side of the rectory and park to provide for a new cemetery. This was finally consecrated in 1880 by the Bishop of Worcester.

At the same time, he turned his attention to the extra 4 acres of glebe land to the side of the cemetery and, as his family was becoming too large for the rectory, he decided to build a house for his eldest son on this site. The land was leased to a Birmingham builder, Thomas Barnsley, on the condition that he would build a house that would be leased back to Riland Bedford for ten years, costing at least £3,000. William negotiated this transaction to his own advantage, finding a legal clause that would ensure the house would legally belong to the Rector, rather than the parish. The result was the construction of a large typically Victorian house named 'Broomieclose', which was completed on 1 September 1882 and, in a rate book of 1885, names his son William Campbell Riland Bedford as the occupier. This house was later to become the forerunner of what is now Good Hope Hospital.

By the end of his life, William was able to reflect on a full life. In the final section of his *Reminiscences of an Aston Magistrate*, he lists that he has seen so many changes – new buildings, transport, water supply and improved medicine, the development of steam, electricity, the penny post, improved law and order – that 'I sometimes wonder what the old century has left the new century to do'. (Riland Bedford, c1900, p. 37). This attitude appears to relate both to his many interests and to his clerical duties, as his sermon on the Jubilee of 1887 professes. Here, in a reflection of his own deep faith, he states that even royalty must be holy and that the greatness of England can only be refreshed through religion. In a patriotic finale he concludes: 'Make your nation holy and you make it magnanimous, make it magnanimous and you make it mighty till the end of time.' (Riland Bedford, 1887, p. 8)

In 1890, his wife Amy died, and two years later, William retired from the post of Rector of Sutton Coldfield, his eldest son William Campbell Riland Bedford succeeding him. For the next few years he went to London, but in 1898 he returned, taking up the post of vicar at St John's, Walmley. He was now in his early 70s and for three years he stayed in this post, preaching twice every Sunday. In late 1900 he married Margaret Browne and they eventually moved permanently to Earl's Court in London. On 23 January 1905, he died at his house in Fordwych Road, Cricklewood, leaving an estate valued at £18,281 13s 6d (£1,429,118.75p in today's terms). His second wife received £500 and gained the income from a trust fund worth £1,500, the other beneficiaries being his children.

In the *Sutton Times* (29 January 1905), his obituary was four columns long. He was cremated at Golders Green, West London. The service was conducted by a Reverend H. E. Wilson (MA), who had in fact been a former curate at Sutton Coldfield. The following Monday, his ashes were interred in the family vault at Holy Trinity Church.

An interesting testament to the character of William Kirkpatrick comes from Bernard McEvoy, who wrote a series of articles, which were then published as a book called *Wandering in the Aisles*, about the different churches of Sutton Coldfield and Erdington for the local paper, including one on Holy Trinity (McEvoy, 1878, pp. 34–40). In it he describes the best qualities of a parish priest, being able to relate to people from every walk of life and different classes equally well. He goes on to say of William Kirkpatrick Riland Bedford: 'He is a man of strong common sense and no affectation … there is a good deal of firmness and decision about him … he has considerable insight into men … and is not above using it.' (Ibid., p. 35)

WILLIAM CAMPBELL RILAND BEDFORD (1852–1922)

When William Kirkpatrick Riland Bedford retired in 1892, it was expected that his eldest son would succeed him as the next Rector of Sutton Coldfield. Born on 29 May 1852, William Campbell was that eldest child and son of William Kirkpatrick and Amy Maria Houson. On 29 June he was baptised in Holy Trinity and went on to enjoy a privileged childhood with ten siblings.

In 1868, he was admitted to Clare College, Cambridge, and gained his BA in 1871, and subsequently his MA. As with his forebears, it was inevitable that he would train for the ministry, and in 1875 he was ordained. In the same year he became Curate of St Michael's in Coventry and held this post for two years. From 1877-8, he moved to All Saints in Leamington and it was whilst he was here that he married Miss Eleanor Phoebe Timmins Chance, whose father James, owned Four Oaks Hall.

The marriage by all accounts was very grand, taking place in Holy Trinity on 5 December 1877. The service was certainly a family affair, conducted by William's father and the bride's uncle, Reverend T. P. Ferguson of Shenfield. Reports from the *John Bull* magazine of 15 December 1877 describe the occasion in detail, with the bride's 'white brocaded silk dress trimmed with Brussels point lace and sprays of orange blossoms' and 'tulle veil headdress with a wreath of flowers'. Other facts mentioned were the eight bridesmaids 'in white, trimmed with ruby velvet and lace', who wore mob caps and pendants bearing the bride and groom's monogram.' In addition, Sutton Town was 'decorated with flags and evergreens, and a triumphal arch was erected by the gateway of the churchyard.' The wedding breakfast for sixty was held at Four Oaks Hall, with 130 attending a ball in the evening. In addition, the press noted that tenants were 'regaled at a dinner at the Royal Hotel' and that the wedding presents the couple received were 'very numerous and handsome' (*Leamington Spa Courier*, 15 December 1877).

William Campbell and Eleanor enjoyed a 45-year marriage. Their four children were Eleanora Campbell (b. 1881), Edith Esme (b. 1883), Phoebe Stella (b. 1884) and finally a son, William James (b. 1898). In 1878, William Campbell became incumbent of Little Aston in Staffordshire (a relatively new church), where he stayed until 1881. The following year, he became curate at Holy Trinity. However, it was not until 1889 that he secured his first appointment as an incumbent, as vicar of Knowle, Warwickshire. He was to remain in this post for three years, until taking up his position as Rector in Sutton. Contemporary accounts in local papers describe how, on his leaving Knowle, grateful parishioners presented him with much magnificent silverware and paid tribute to his constant kindness and zealous ministering.

By 1892, with failing health, William Kirkpatrick decided to retire as Rector of Sutton Coldfield, and it was at this stage that William Campbell took over the post, securing the living which was now worth £3,000 a year. In the same year as his appointment, he sold his home, Broomieclose, which his father had built for him by the new cemetery in Rectory Road, to a Colonel S. D. Williams, and moved back to the rectory in Rectory Park.

William Campbell's tenure saw various changes to the church, notably the fundraising and subsequent building of the new choir vestry, the installation of electricity, and a new organ at the turn of the century, all described more fully elsewhere.

William, like his father, was also a keen sportsman, and throughout his life excelled at cricket, golf and archery. In his youth he played cricket for Warwickshire, became president of the Leamington Cricket Club and, whilst he lived in Knowle, became captain of their club too. Indeed, when he left there, the members must have thought highly of him, as the *Leamington Spa Courier* (1 October 1892) reported that they presented him with a complete set of *The Badminton Library*, a well-respected sporting publication of seventeen volumes of sporting books, which claimed to cover all major sports and pastimes.

He also emulated his father in being an active Freemason, serving for upwards of a quarter century. In 1861 he was appointed a Grand Chaplain and went on to be a senior surviving Past Grand Chaplain of England. It was in this capacity that he was no doubt reported to be present at the laying down of the foundation stone ceremony at the newly built St Peter's Church at Maney in 1905, (he had played a leading role in the planning and construction of the neighbouring parish church). This was a very elaborate Masonic ceremony which involved Lord Leigh, Provincial Grand Master of Warwickshire and Lord Lieutenant of the county. He was to officiate using the very trowel that Sir Christopher Wren had used to lay the foundation stone of St Paul's Cathedral. In 1875 William was initiated into the Sutton Coldfield Warden Lodge (number 794), and six years later was installed as its Worshipful Master. In 1884, he was appointed Provincial Senior Grand Warden of Warwickshire and belonged throughout his life to numerous other lodges.

By the end of his career, it was fitting that William had achieved the office of an Honorary Canon, but by 1907, things were beginning to change. In 1898 an Act of Parliament had been passed which reverted advowsons from individuals to the Ecclesiastical Commissioners. It was therefore clear that changes might be proposed once William retired. The developments of this time are described in the previous chapter.

William Campbell retired in 1909, moving to Leamington Spa in Warwickshire, where he had lived previously. He died, aged 70, on 15 August 1922, leaving to his wife a property with the gross value of £580 3s 1d. With him, the Riland and Riland Bedford line of Rectors at Holy Trinity ended, though the family's legacy still lives on in memorials and changes to the town and church.

A FOOTNOTE TO THE RILAND BEDFORD FAMILY

William James Riland Bedford, William Campbell's son, did not become a priest, but after attending Winchester College pursued a military career on leaving the school in 1915. The website of Winchester College includes details of war service of its alumni and records the following about the life of William James, who survived the First World War and later military action, dying in 1943 in the Second World War:

> Bill Bedford was born on 16th April 1898, the only son of Canon William Campbell Riland Bedford and Eleanor (daughter of Sir James Timmins Chance, 1st Baronet), Rector of Sutton Coldfield. He entered [the school] in 1911. Although not particularly prominent in School life, either academically or as a sportsman, he did manage to be on Dress for XVs.

On leaving Winchester in 1915 he went to RMA Woolwich and was commissioned as a second lieutenant into the Royal Field Artillery. He served in France and Belgium from 1917–18, being wounded and ending the war with 10 Reserve Brigade.

He pursued a military career after the end of the war and found himself in continuous action from 1942 in the Second World War. In late April 1944 his division was fighting in Tunis. The Winchester College website continues:

> Heavy shell-fire was falling on the advancing British forces, and at an awkward moment one of the vehicles shed a track. As Bedford's group stopped, the Germans took advantage of its immobility, as one of Bedford's officers, Captain Box, later recalled:
>
> 'I heard a high-pitched whistle and flung myself flat on the corn. A 105mm shell had dropped on the track about twenty yards away on my left, and as I scrambled to my feet I saw the Colonel of the King's Own Yorkshire Light Infantry emerge from the smoke with a look of extreme agony on his face and half of his left arm missing. I dashed forward and found the Battery Commander on the spot too. He said, "The Colonel has been hit," and I thought for a moment he meant the CO of the KOYLI, but a glance behind our Colonel's carrier showed me that he was mortally wounded and could not live for more than a few minutes. He died without regaining consciousness. Three of his carrier crew were also killed outright, and the CO of the Lincolnshire Regiment was also killed. Truly a disastrous shell.' Bill Bedford lies in Grave 16.F.20 of the Medjez-el-Bab War Cemetery, Tunisia. (From Winchester College at war website: www.winchestercollegeatwar.com/ archive/bedford-william-james-riland/ Downloaded 18/3/18)

13

PARISHIONERS OF NOTE

While some parishioners are referred to in other chapters in relation to a memorial in stone or glass, and the clergy of Holy Trinity are detailed in Chapters 11 and 12, this chapter focuses on a few of the families whose members were notable in some other way in the church, and often also in the town. In some cases two or more generations are described.

The families are described in chronological order where possible, as some are linked down the generations either through marriages or their houses.

PUDSEY AND JESSON

While Bishop Vesey had no wife or children, his brother Hugo (Harman) had six children by two wives. One daughter from the first marriage, Elizabeth, married Roland Pudsey of Yorkshire, and Eleanor, from the second marriage, married Robert Pudsey. The rather magnificent memorial monument in the Vesey chapel, near the Bishop's tomb, was made in the following century at the request of Jane, widow of Henry Pudsey, when her husband died on Good Friday in 1678. Henry was the great-great-grandson of Robert and Eleanor. His parents were George and Anne, and his sister was Susannah, who is recorded in Chapter 14 as being married at Langley Hall during the period of the Commonwealth.

The Pudsey family home, Langley Hall, stood to the east of the present Falcon Lodge Estate. Their land stretched from Four Oaks and Little Sutton across to Lea Marston and Kingsbury. Henry and Jane had five children, of whom only two daughters, Elizabeth and Anne, survived childhood.

When Henry died, his two daughters inherited. Elizabeth, the elder daughter, married Henry, Lord Ffolliott (3rd Baron Ffolliott) in 1696. Henry had Four Oaks Hall built on their land in 1700. It was designed by William Wilson (see below for more information on Wilson, and Chapter 6 for an account of the hall).

Fig. 71: *The Pudsey monument in the Vesey chapel (SCL)*

Subsequently he had a private gallery constructed across the north-west end of the nave in Holy Trinity for himself and his wife in 1708.

Henry Ffolliott died on 17 October 1716, and is in the burial records for Holy Trinity as having been buried on 23 October 1716, but there is no memorial to him nor any evidence for or against his being in the Pudsey tomb. His daughter pre-deceased him (aged 13) and he died without a son, so the Barony of Ballyshannon became extinct on his death and his estate passed to a relative. Elizabeth was buried in the Pudsey vault beneath the chapel floor in 1742.

The younger daughter of Henry and Jane, Anne, inherited Langley Hall and lived there with her husband, William Jesson, a glovemaker from Coventry, after their marriage. They had ten children, though not all survived. They are also buried in the vault, but their memorial is known as the Jesson memorial, and stands in the south-east corner of the Vesey chapel. They are commemorated in the top half of the monument, while the lower part has the names of the next generation, Pudsey Jesson and his family. The last in the Pudsey Jesson line was William Jesson Pearson, who died near Lisbon in the Peninsular War in 1910 aged just 26. His memorial plaque is now on the wall in the north-west corner of the church (behind the kitchen serving area).

Another branch of the Pudsey family, which is descended from the original two Harman marriages, was headed by great-grandson Thomas, who is noted in burial records as being buried in 1691 in the Pudsey vault (Fig. 71), where his wife Elizabeth is also buried. (Evans, 1987, pp. 28–31).

SIR WILLIAM WILSON

William Wilson was a local stonemason and architect who is reputed to have studied under Sir Christopher Wren. Certainly he was well-known in the Midlands and designed many of the larger homes and halls, some of which survive to this day. In 1681 he supervised the renovation of Nottingham Castle and, as county architect for Warwickshire, he was responsible for the restoration of St Mary's, Warwick after the devastating fire of 1694. He also built Peddimore Hall. In terms of Wilson's reputation, William Kirkpatrick Riland Bedford records that 'most of the old Sutton houses bear traces of his design, which probably influenced later builders'. (Riland Bedford, 1891, p. 33) It is alleged that he designed the rectory of 1701.

Jane Pudsey engaged Wilson to design the monument to her husband, which would also commemorate her in due course (Fig. 71). It is not clear whether both the busts which are on the monument (of Henry and Jane) were prepared while she was alive or not. This would not have been unusual at that period, and she would have been expecting to be buried in the family vault in due course and for all her family in time to be similarly buried and also commemorated on or around the monument.

Jane and William fell in love and were married. In the 1680s, William designed Moat House for them to live in. It is a house on the Lichfield Road which is now part of the land of the grammar school and is no longer moated.

Jane secured a knighthood from Charles II for William. According to a record of the time (*The Warwickshire Worthies*), when the King asked what estate William had, the honest response was that his lady had £800 per annum and he had £3. (Colvile, 1870, p. 830). Colvile reports that following Jane's death, Wilson happily returned to work as a stonemason, and the Ffolliotts were happy to let him work from one of their outbuildings.

Fig. 72: *The Moat House designed by Sir William Wilson (SCL)*

Jane died in 1697 and William expressed the wish that he might be buried there in due course. The Jessons at Langley were much less open to supporting Wilson and are noted as being particularly outraged at this suggestion from a 'mere' stonemason. William's reply is recorded thus:

> I will be buried on the outside the church directly opposite the vault where my wife lies and there will be only a single stone wall betwixt us: and as I am a stonemason, there will be no kind of labour or difficulty in cutting my road thro' the wall to my old bed-fellow. (Ibid., pp. 830–831)

When Wilson died in 1710 he was indeed buried in the churchyard adjacent to the outer north wall of the church. The heartwarming ending to this story is that many years later, in 1874, the clergy vestry was added on that outer side of the Vesey chapel and William's grave was now within the church. A new memorial was erected by a grateful succeeding generation of stonemasons, which is now in the clergy vestry on the south side. This describes Wilson as 'a person of great ingenuity, singular integrity, unaffected piety and very fruitful in good works – the only issue he left behind him'.

Clearly the author of *The Warwickshire Worthies* (Colvile) supported the majority view of Wilson's likeable and hard-working character in suggesting that the Jesson family 'had nothing to brag of but the being descended from a glover of Coventry who was knighted' (Ibid.), whereas Sir William Wilson was a man of talent who had risen to become an eminent architect and master mason.

As Wilson had no children, he left Moat House to his nephew, John Barnes. There is a memorial to John's son, also called John, who died at the age of 18 in 1730, in the south aisle, just in front of the entrance to the choir vestry. The very moving epitaph by his parents to their only child speaks of 'The only living off-spring of his parents – their only hope. Alas. Their harrowing anxiety.'

As this young man did not survive, Moat House then passed to his father's nephew, William Lunn, and it was sold by Lunn to Joseph Duncumb, whose memorial in Holy Trinity is opposite that of John Barnes. Duncumb was warden of Sutton in 1760–1, a Capital Burgess (magistrate) and a Commissioner of the Peace for Warwickshire. Duncumb's daughter Elizabeth is also commemorated on the memorial. She inherited Moat House and married a lawyer by the name of Mr Shirley Farmer Steele Perkins, who himself became warden in 1804. The shield on the memorial stone reflects all the families on the Steele Perkins side together with Duncumb in the centre denoting Elizabeth as sole heiress. (Evans, 1987, p. 45)

SACHEVERELL

George Sacheverell's story is recorded in Chapter 3, which includes the developments of the eighteenth century, as it relates mostly to the vault and memorial he had had built in the church.

He was related to Henry Sacheverell, a renowned 'High Church' preacher, whose story is told as one of the changes and controversies in Chapter 14, as Henry was not actually a parishioner but preached a controversial sermon in the church.

The story of New Hall, the home of the Sacheverell and Chadwick families from 1590 to 1897, is briefly recounted in Chapter 6.

LUTTRELL

A noteworthy, and in some instances notorious, member of the congregation at Holy Trinity in the eighteenth century was Simon Luttrell. Roger Lea describes him as 'an ambitious politician in need of an English country house' (Lea, Bad Lady Betty/Luttrell Family, HS 157, 10 June 2011) and he bought Four Oaks Hall in 1746 following the death of Elizabeth Ffolliott (widow of Henry, the 3rd Baron Ffolliott and née Pudsey) in 1744.

Simon lived there with his wife and eight children. He was 'a Member of Parliament from 1755, and spent most of his time at court, where his rakish behaviour earned him the title "King of Hell".' (Ibid.).

He was at court and was created Baron Irnham of Luttrellstown in 1768 and Earl of Carhampton in 1785. These names are all now represented in roads in the Four Oaks area of Sutton Coldfield, but they relate to other places associated with the Luttrell family, whose branches extend from Lincolnshire and the village of Irnham (formerly Gerneham), through the West Midlands to Somerset (Dunster and its Castle), and on to Dublin – Luttrellstown.

Margaret Gardner brought together the story of the Luttrell family history in three articles in the parish magazine, which were included in the collection of articles called 'Around the Church' (Gardner, 2000, pp. 23–5).

Two of his daughters achieved notoriety in very different ways too. Ann was apparently very beautiful, and, when widowed at the young age of 24, attracted the attention of the Duke of Cumberland, brother to King George III. The couple were married in 1771, causing a scandal, as the King only heard of it after the event, with his brother informing him of the deed by letter from France. Ann, as Duchess of Cumberland, became a society hostess and was apparently a favourite of Queen Charlotte.

By contrast, Ann's older sister Elizabeth, who had often been a companion to Ann, lived the high life with parties back at Four Oaks Hall. Lea describes her downfall as follows: 'Gambling brought about Elizabeth's downfall in 1797, when she only escaped prison by paying fifty pounds to get married to a baker; she then went abroad to escape the disgrace.' (Ibid.)

She died in 1799 at the age of 62. Apparently, a play was written about one of the house parties called *Bad Lady Betty*. Elizabeth is in a painting with her sister and the Duke of Cumberland by Thomas Gainsborough (painted 1783–5 and now part of the Royal Collection at Hampton Court).

More about Four Oaks Hall itself is in Chapter 6.

As befitted his understanding of his status, Simon Luttrell saw the need to have a gallery constructed at Holy Trinity for the exclusive use of his family. The timing worked well for him with the new pewing and galleries to north and south in the work of 1760. The resulting new Four Oaks gallery (the smaller west end one was pulled down) was apparently magnificent in appearance and it was erected in a central position in the west arch (i.e. the opening to the tower), which would have commanded the best view of the nave and chancel areas, especially for Simon himself whose seat was in the centre. The choir gallery would have been behind this one, and it is probable that the light was blocked to those in the new box pews underneath. (Evans, 1987, p. 13) Gardner quotes an anecdote that has been handed down: 'it is said, he would arrive late to divine service, causing the entire proceedings to be held up whilst he and his family processed into their places in the aforesaid gallery'. (Gardner, 2000, p. 23)

HARTOPP

Sir Edmund Cradock Hartopp (1749–1833) is notable in Sutton Coldfield as the owner of the Four Oaks estate, which he enlarged in 1827 through the addition of Ladywood from Sutton Park, enclosing this in exchange for land between Powells Pool and the park, and also some land near the entrance so that the approach to the park from the town would be easier.

The baronetcy is actually for Freathby in Leicestershire. Sir Edmund was succeeded by his surviving second son, also Edmund (1789–1849). When this Edmund died childless, he was succeeded by his younger brother (Edmund Senior's third son), Sir William Edmund Cradock Hartopp (born in 1797).

William was warden of Sutton Coldfield in 1835 (before he inherited the Baronetcy). 'Sir EC Hartopp' (William's father) is listed in 1823, with 'GHWF Hartopp' listed the same year in the entry above. (Riland Bedford, 1891, p. 85).

Lady Hartopp is listed in fundraising bazaar programmes (see Chapter 6) and was also a benefactor to the church. A particular gift in 1856 is recorded in *Aris's Birmingham Gazette* of 24 March:

> Lady Hartopp of Four Oaks Park, with her usual liberality and good feeling, has given a rich pile carpet for the floor of the Communion, and an elegant crimson velvet cushion for the pulpit of the Parish Church of Sutton Coldfield. This handsome present was received (in the absence of the Revd WKR Bedford, the Rector, now ill in London, but who, we are glad to find, is rapidly recovering) by the Revd James Packwood, the Curate, and the Churchwardens, Mr Richard Sadler and Mr William Smith, at the Vestry on Thursday last, and used for the first time yesterday (Easter Sunday) in accordance with her Ladyship's request.

Roger Lea paints the Hartopp family in a different light:

> 'Verily there are snobs of every degree' – so wrote Richard Holbeche in 1892. He was remembering the 1860s, when the Hartopp family of Four Oaks Hall always arrived late at church and made a great display of going to their seats with 'ridiculous dignity' … Sir William had succeeded his brother Sir Edmund Cradock Hartopp, to whom the poet H. H. Horton dedicated his pastoral poem *Sutton Park,* published in 1850. According to the poet, their father, old Sir Edmund, was remembered with affection:

> How goodness beamed around his aged face,

'His looks adorned the venerable place'
Nor did his features all his worth belie,
Though high his rank, his virtues stood as high.
No doubt the high-ranking Hartopps welcomed such flattery.
(Lea, Hartopps, HS 46, 20 March 2009)

It seems that the Hartopps followed the example of the Luttrells in arriving late for worship.

Sir William died in October 1864 and his widow, Jane (née Keane), erected a brass memorial to his memory. This is now in the Vesey chapel (in the south-west corner of the chapel below the Hacket memorial) and is in the form of a large cross in brass. However, according to a press report of 1865, the memorial had just been placed 'against the chancel wall' and near to the east window. The report goes on to lament this positioning in a dark corner where the window overshadows it, and it is partly obscured by 'a monument at right angles to it'. It also expresses the hope that the church will find a better place but cannot see how, 'the outer walls of the north and south aisles being encumbered with inconvenient and unsightly galleries'. The final comment that the church should not miss out on the progress made in other areas of the town is a prescient one, as, in fact, the woodwork from Worcester Cathedral was bought at this point and the major addition of the north aisle and gallery in 1879 swept away other galleries. It is not known if the Hartopp memorial was moved at this point or in the Vesey chapel redecoration of 1929, but the former seems more likely, as the alterations to accommodate the newly acquired woodwork would have initiated major changes in the chancel.

The press cutting gives a useful description of the memorial, made by Messrs Hardman and Co, and the inscriptions. (*Aris's Birmingham Gazette*, 20 May 1865)

On William's death, their son John inherited the Four Oaks estate, but did not live there. He let the hall and then sold the land (see Chapter 6). He lived in Kingswood, Surrey, ultimately going bankrupt. The baronetcy passed down various members of the family, only becoming extinct in 2000 (see Wikipedia for a full history).

HOLBECHE

This large family is one of the best known of those associated with Holy Trinity and perhaps from the perspective of the twentieth and twenty-first centuries we feel their daily life was more like our own than that of the grand families who lived in the big halls.

Three members of the family wrote about the town and the church, observing the behaviours of their neighbours. These were generally reminiscence-based, so there is a different flavour to them from a traditional daily diary. The three were Sarah (1803–82), her sister Helen (1821–95) and their nephew Richard (1850–1914).

The family association starts with Thomas Holbeche (d. 1848), who married Sarah (d. 1841). They had fourteen children in all, of whom Sarah was the oldest, and Vincent the oldest son (and heir). The second youngest was Helen, and she and Sarah were the two 'diarists' of this generation.

Thomas established the family firm of solicitors in the early 1800s, and this would be continued by his son Vincent and grandson Thomas Vincent. A very useful online family history site for the Addenbrooke family includes the following information about Thomas:

> Admitted as a Solicitor of the High Court of the Chancery, at Westminster, May 19 1795; member of Sutton Coldfield Corporation 1796–1807; Warden of Sutton Coldfield in 1798; Retired from firm of Holbeche, Son and Willoughby, Solicitors, Sutton Coldfield 1841; J. P. 1841; Chairman of Aston Board of Guardians 1841. Inherited Worcs. property from his first cousin Thomas Vincent Holbeche in 1833.

Sarah Holbeche was born in 1803 at Ivy House, now number 20 High Street. In her diary she noted that in 1804, 'My father and mother with their one child moved to what is now Mrs. Sadler's House (now 36 High Street).' She went on to list the siblings that followed: Mary, Vincent, Thomas, Elizabeth, Francis, Jane, Aemilian, Martin and John.

Four more followed, presumably at the next address. Amazingly for the time, all but one (Martin, 1814–15) of these fourteen children survived to adulthood. Thomas Holbeche rented 36 High Street from Mr Guest, who, according to Sarah, 'sold the house over my father's head' in 1817, leaving the Holbeches homeless. The Rector of Sutton came to the rescue, offering to sell the house he owned in Sutton – now numbers 1, 3 and 5 Coleshill Street. She wrote: 'My father bought it in 1817, it was the property of our old Rector Revd John Riland who offered it to my father, sympathising with him. £1700 the purchase money.' (Lea, The Holbeche Swan, HS 396, 22 January 2016)

Vincent qualified as a solicitor and joined the family firm. He lived at 22/24 High Street, then Park House in the park and finally in the family home in Coleshill Street, where he is recorded in the censuses of 1841–1861.

Vincent married Emma Addenbrooke (c. 1845) and they had seven children (of whom Gertrude and Arthur were twins). The third of these was Richard

(1850–1914), whose diary speaks particularly of the congregation at Holy Trinity in the 1860s.

Vincent and his brother-in-law Henry Addenbrooke, also a solicitor, formed what was to be the highly prominent and successful legal partnership of Holbeche and Addenbrooke in Sutton Coldfield. Thomas Holbeche had been appointed deputy steward to the Warden and Society of Sutton before 1835, and Holbeche and Addenbrooke were jointly deputy stewards from about 1851. As such they were at the centre of local events for many years. Vincent died in 1867. (Information from Addenbrooke family website).

The oldest two children of Vincent and Emma were Thomas Vincent (1846–1904) and Edward Addenbrooke (Ted) (1847–87) who were educated at Rugby and Marlborough respectively.

Thomas Vincent became Sutton Coldfield's first town clerk. Janet Jordan has written about this (see References). A wooden lectern at Holy Trinity was also given in his memory, with his name inscribed, shown front right of Fig. 73.

Fig. 73: *Chancel c.2008 showing Holbeche lectern (KJ)*

In later years, six of the sisters of the older generation (not Mary) all lived at 58 High Street in Sutton Coldfield. This building was opposite what is now the Royal Hotel and had to be demolished in 1869 when the railway came to Sutton Coldfield. Roger Lea's 'History Spot' article (Lea, High Street 2, HS 477, 25 August 2017) gives the full story of this and includes a photograph of the Holbeche sisters' house. Sarah also gave a stained glass window commemorating one of the Rectors of Holy Trinity, Dr Williamson (see Chapter 9).

Helen's memoir in 1884 described life 'three score years ago'. Richard was a lieutenant colonel in the army, and on his return to Sutton from service in India felt compelled to record his memories. His writing in 1893 covers the 1860s, and two of its twenty-six pages refer to the church. It is very helpful in adding to stories about the parishioners of the time as well as the look of the church.

Janet Jordan of the Sutton Coldfield Local History Research Group has transcribed the manuscripts of both Helen and Richard, and these are available on the group's website.

BRACKEN

Agnes Ann Bracken (1800–77) is mainly remembered as one of the historians of Sutton Coldfield, alongside her sister, whose initial is L, possibly Louise. Richard Holbeche notes in his account of the 1860s that 'The Miss Brackens sat under us'. This would have been in a box pew in the nave area on the south side of Holy Trinity. Agnes was also an artist and her local views survive in a collection in Sutton Coldfield Library.

COLMORE

The Colmores settled in Birmingham in the fifteenth century. Norman Evans gives further detail of this prominent Birmingham family as follows:

> Charles Colmore was the fifth child of Thomas Colmore, who resided at Ashfurlong Hall and was Warden of Sutton in 1864-66. The Colmore family settled in Birmingham at the close of the 15th century and gave their name to Colmore Row. Charles was a solicitor in Waterloo Street and had two older brothers, Thomas Milnes Colmore who became the stipendiary magistrate for Birmingham, and the Revd WH Colmore who became Vicar of Moseley. (Evans, 1987, p. 46)

Thomas was warden of the town in 1864–66, dying in 1870, and the window in the south chapel (now the choir vestry) is dedicated to Quintus Charles Colmore (1851–1904) (see Chapter 9).

CHAVASSE

Charles Edward Chavasse was a churchwarden for several years and a wine merchant by trade. He was unusual in being the son of Dr Thomas Chavasse, who did not follow the family tradition of becoming either a doctor or a Bishop. The stained glass window on the south side of the south-west corner of the church is dedicated to him (see Chapter 9).

Norman Evans wrote: 'The Chavasses are well-known in the Midlands: Francis James Chavasse became Bishop of Liverpool, and his son was made Bishop of Rochester. The last of the Sutton doctors retired from his practice in 1948.' (Evans, 1987, p. 56)

WEBSTER

The Webster family owned Penns Mill at Walmley (now the site of the Penns Hall Hotel). One member of the family, Baron Dickinson Webster (1818–60), was particularly successful in the family business and pioneered the production of wire, which would go on to be used after his death for the first Atlantic cable (1865–66). The horizontal railing around the tomb in the churchyard is twisted to resemble a cable. There is also a memorial stone inside the church on the west end wall of the north aisle (behind the kitchen). Revd W. K. Riland Bedford noted, 'Messrs Webster were not only spinning the wire that was to bridge the Atlantic, in an electric cable, but entertaining their friends, the Darwins, Merivales, Robert Lowe and George Dawson.' (Riland Bedford, 1889, p. 158).

Roger Lea's book *The Sutton Coldfield Blue Plaque Trail* gives a fully illustrated account of Baron Dickinson Webster and other famous residents of the town who are commemorated by a plaque erected by the Sutton Coldfield Civic Society on their former home.

14

CHANGES AND CONTROVERSIES

This chapter views the 700 years of spiritual life at Holy Trinity in terms of changes in religious persuasion and affiliation which led to controversy. Some further causes of tension are also described, which arose as the result of divergent political or religious views.

An unexpected source provides a useful summary of worship in mediaeval times. Prof John Davies, then head of the Department of Theology of Birmingham University, wrote in a report about the church in 1985 as follows:

> To the parishioners of Sutton Coldfield in the 14th century, the communion service was essentially the offering of the priest, he himself being ordained and this being understood as setting him rigidly apart from everyone else. The action was not in the midst of the congregation but in another room i.e. the chancel and what was required from the laity was not participation but attendance and attendance without communicating. [the term 'communicating' here means receiving the bread (and wine) of communion] (Davies, 1985, section 2.4)

CHANGES IN LITURGY

Norman Evans presents in his book a chart showing changes in religious persuasion from the pre-Reformation period through the reign of Henry VIII and succeeding monarchs until the time of George II. This chart (Evans, 1987, p. 140) is reproduced at Fig. 74 as it clearly lays out these changes that led to the establishment of the Church of England.

Evans also summarises the physical changes at Holy Trinity that were made as a result of changes in the liturgy, also from pre-Reformation times, but through to the restoration of the monarchy (Ibid., p. 144). This is tabulated below.

Pre-Reformation	Altar against the east wall; probably of stone. Rood screen. Roman Catholic setting, images and paintings, etc.
Edward VI	Stone altar replaced by wooden altar in the chancel. All Catholic artefacts removed and vestments destroyed. First Book of Common Prayer in English used. Rood screen removed.
Mary	Altar placed against the east wall. Roman Catholic services.
Elizabeth	All traces of Catholicism removed. Wooden altar placed against east wall, parishioners kneeling before it for communion. No altar rail. Burials in chancel recorded. Second Common Prayer Book.
James I	Wooden altar placed in the centre of the chancel. Parishioners knelt all around it for communion.
Charles I	Wooden altar placed against the east wall and elevated on steps, with an altar rail on three sides of it.
Commonwealth	Puritan period. Wooden altar in chancel. Everything plain and simple. Walls whitewashed. No music. Vestments and surplices destroyed. Pastor dressed in black.
Charles II	Wooden altar placed against the east wall and protected by a straight single altar rail. Chancel floor unobstructed, burials recorded here throughout the seventeenth century.

Table 9: *Summary of liturgical settings in Holy Trinity: sixteenth and seventeenth centuries*
Note: the floor level of the chancel was not raised until 1875.

From a modern perspective one can only guess how this affected worship year by year, though it is probable that the people expected to defer to the priest in these matters and would go along with changes that were imposed in this way. For those ultimately wishing to pursue the 'true' Roman Catholic faith as they would see it, life would become very difficult, and the many injustices to those of the Catholic faith have been noted elsewhere. By the eighteenth century, times were changing across the country, and the Catholic Relief Acts of 1778 and 1791 lifted most of the penalties to which Catholics had previously been subject.

Roger Lea notes that 'mass was being celebrated in a private house in Sutton in the 1820s, and the Catholic Emancipation Act of 1829 gave Catholics the right to vote'. (Lea, Mendham Catholic, HS 444, 9 December 2016)

Lea also notes in the same article that the Baptist chapel not far from Holy Trinity was converted into a Roman Catholic church in 1834. This apparently led the curate, Joseph Mendham, to write an 'Address to the Inhabitants of Sutton Coldfield on the Introduction of Popery into that Parish'.

COMMONWEALTH –
BIRTHS, MARRIAGES AND DEATHS

Norman Evans did a good deal of research for his history of the church examining the registers of baptisms, marriages and deaths. These are particularly revealing in relation to the period known as the Commonwealth under Oliver Cromwell as Lord Protector.

His list of christenings, marriages and burials is reproduced below as Table 10. Evans says of this period:

> although there is no record of militancy in Sutton, the outbreak of the war in 1642, the hasty departure two months later of the incumbent the Rev. Anthony Burgess when King Charles was known to be in the vicinity, and the destruction of Lichfield Cathedral in 1643 had its impact on Holy Trinity. (Evans, 1987, p. 161)

At Lichfield Cathedral, the Bishop was confined to his castle at Eccleshall, where he died in 1644. The new appointee appears not to have taken up his post. This and other facts would account for a dip in the number of events in 1642. The noteworthy change at this time is in the officiant at all these events. It is not known who officiated at christenings or burials at this point, but 'the established Church was annulled and all the former rituals in the Prayer book were abolished, magistrates being empowered to conduct marriages privately' (Ibid., p. 165).

Evans describes the magistrates thus empowered, who carried out the marriages recorded in the table below. These were:

- Waldive Willington at his home in Hurley Hall, two miles east of Kingsbury.
- Thomas Willoughby at his house in Sutton – now known as Vesey House in High Street opposite Midland Drive. Willoughby was buried in the chancel at Holy Trinity (see Chapter 8).
- William Lethunt at his house in Birmingham. This location is not known but believed actually to be in Sutton as all the couples whom he married were from the town.

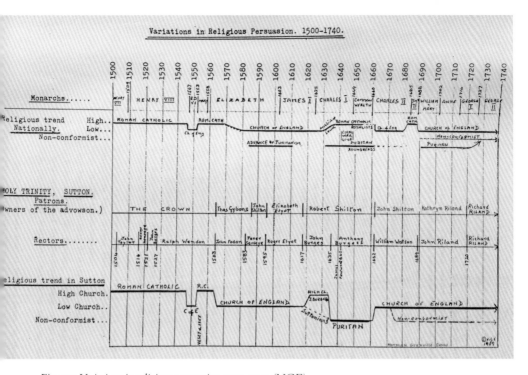

Fig. 74: *Variations in religious persuasion 1500–1740 (NGE)*

- Richard Batman, an alderman from Tamworth who conducted most of the weddings of Suttonians in 1656.

Further facts of interest about this period concern, firstly, a couple coming before Willoughby whose banns had not been read in church (as they should still have been) but at the Market Cross of Sutton Coldfield. This stood at the junction of High Street and Coleshill Street and was thought to have been derelict and removed when Bishop Vesey built the Moot Hall in 1530, but was clearly still extant in 1655.

Secondly, a Sutton couple who came before Lethunt comprised a groom named Evan Thomas and his bride, Elizabeth Harman. Their marriage on 9 September 1656 was actually conducted by Lethunt (a layman) in Holy Trinity. Evans surmises that the bride may have been descended from Vesey's family, and also notes that a Thomas Vesey was warden at this point. Both these factors might have encouraged her to insist on a wedding in Holy Trinity (Ibid., p. 166).

Thirdly, Richard Batman also conducted a wedding in a church, though on this occasion it was St Editha's in Tamworth.

Another record of note is the marriage during this time of George Pudsey's daughter Susannah in 1656 at her home, Langley Hall. The last wedding before a magistrate in Sutton was 12 November 1657 (Lethunt), as Anthony Burgess had returned and recommenced services in Holy Trinity a fortnight before.

One positive outcome of the regulations at this time was fuller records including occupations of the bridegroom, which may be a boon to family historians.

Year (More Vetere)	Totals Christenings	Totals Marriages	Totals Burials	including		Rector	Events
				Child	old*		
1635	27	8	19	5		Anthony Burgess D.D.	
1636	34	9	35	7	1	"	
1637	39	6	25	8		"	
1638	32	11	28	3		"	
1639	34	10	26	2	1	"	
1640	37	10	23	7	5	"	
1641	29	1	23	7	4	"	
1642	16	5	35	10	7	"	Civil War, 22 Aug Burgess fled in Oct. James Fleetwood presented. Lichfield Cathedral destroyed. Sutton records cease.
1643	17	–	8	2	1		
1644							
1645	1	1					
1646	18	4	9	2			Register re-commences.
1647	34	4	25	10	2	Anthony	
1648	31	8	8	1		Burgess	
1649	32	3	2			"	King Charles executed. Commonwealth Established Church was abolished.

1650	33	6	11	2		"	
1651	32	–	8			"	
1652	27	–	19	1	7		Burgess's sermons first printed.
1653	25	–	20	2	3		
1654	45	16	32	5	1		Marriages were before magistrates from Sept 1654 onwards.
1655	39	17	31	4			
1656	45	14	21	4	1		
1657	38	8	42	6			Last 'civil' wedding
1658	30	7	56	4			
1659	15	4	37	6	1		
1660	40	2	25	9			Charles II crowned
1661	30	1	23	7			
1662	24	–	24	7	2		Anthony Burgess retired – objecting to new 1662 Prayer Book. William Watson inducted

Table 10: *Registers of baptisms, marriages and deaths at Holy Trinity 1635–62 (Evans, 1987, p. 163)*

* *Evans' use of the terms 'child' and 'old' here is taken to mean the number of burials classed as children or old people, though no indication of age range for either is given.*

CONTENTIOUS PREACHERS

Henry Sacheverell was a Church of England clergyman, the third son of Joshua Sacheverell and his wife, Susannah Smith, and was baptised at St Peter's parsonage in Marlborough on 8 February 1674.

He was a staunch and notably vitriolic supporter of the Jacobite cause. George I ascended the British throne after the deaths in 1714 of his mother and his second cousin, Anne, who had been Queen of Great Britain from 1702–1714. George was Anne's closest living Protestant relative under the Act of Settlement 1701.

The Jacobites were trying to depose George and replace him with James Francis Edward Stuart, who was Anne's Catholic half-brother.

Sacheverell's first major sermon to cause him trouble was at St Paul's Cathedral on 5 November 1709. As a result of this he and his associates printed vast quantities of copies of his sermon, estimated in total at 100,000 copies, which were probably seen by most of the electorate of the country at the time (estimated at 250,000 people). He was popular with the political right of the time, who secured a sweeping victory following this sermon being both preached and read. Sacheverell was accused of treason but received only a suspended sentence for three years.

Once free of the sentence, he embarked on a preaching journey through the Midlands. An entry in Wikipedia notes that he stayed with various friends while on this tour, commenting: 'He spent ten days with Lord Craven at Coombe Abbey, then went to New Hall Manor owned by his kinsman George Sacheverell.'

This is supported by another comment which states that he was not proud of his immediate family connections to dissenting preachers but that 'he was more proud of distant relatives who were Midlands landed gentry that had supported the Royalist cause during the Civil War.' This references a work by Geoffrey Holmes recounting the trial of Sacheverell. (Holmes, 1973, pp. 4–5).

Writing in a book about Samuel Johnson's life (Clark and Hill, 2002), Paul Monod says:

> One week before George I was crowned, Henry Sacheverell delivered a furious Tory sermon at Sutton Coldfield, only nine miles from Lichfield ... Sacheverell was later obliged to deny in a public letter that his sermon had anything to do with the violent anti-Hanoverian riots that followed coronation day at Birmingham, Nuneaton, Shrewsbury, Worcester and Hereford. The riots had ominous Jacobite undertones. 'Wee will pull downe this King and sette up a King of our own', cried one rioter, while others shouted, 'Damn King George, Sacheverell for ever.' (Clark and Hill, 2002, pp. 16–17).

Monod explains further how in the summer of 1715 the meeting houses of dissenters were destroyed across the Midlands in an attempt to sway opponents to support the Jacobite cause.

The sermon at Holy Trinity was on Sunday 20 October 1714, and the congregation was apparently augmented by 'some two hundred Birmingham Jacobites'. (Riland Bedford, 1891, p. 34)

According to Riland Bedford, after the riots, the government dropped its support of Sacheverell, and he 'like many a popular idol, before and since, was altogether forgotten when the generation of his admirers had given way to a new one'. (Ibid.) He went on to serve a parish in Holborn and died in 1724.

FURTHER PREACHERS

The Revd R. B. Riland, Rector in 1772, wrote 'two sermons have been preached every Lord's day in this church ever since I have been incumbent thereof'. The Revd Francis Blick was his curate and continued in the role when John Riland became Rector in 1790. Mr Blick preached a sermon (from the present pulpit) in 1791 which infuriated the Rector – the sermon seemed to imply that men should be guided by their consciences as well as by the scriptures. His comments were seen as open to the interpretation that they were aimed at particular individual gentlemen. The sermon was published and sold over 1,600 copies, but, in spite of widespread support, Mr Blick had to resign.

His replacement, Revd Joseph Mendham, was in tune with John Riland's views and the pair both preached from an anti-Catholic standpoint. Mendham preached a particularly forceful sermon on Sunday 27 February 1820, on the occasion of the death of King George III. This was also published. After six pages of compliments about the monarchy, Mendham turned to a description of the qualities of George III as a defender of the Protestant religion, and the remaining seven pages are a diatribe against Catholics and against any relaxation of the restrictions under which Catholics suffered: 'We owe it … to the true fortitude of our late Sovereign that the subjects and zealots of a foreign, a corrupt, an arrogant, and a sanguinary church, have not become part of the legislation of a Protestant country.' (Lea, Mendham Catholic, HS 444, 9 December 2016)

Lea concludes his article on Mendham as follows:

> Mendham retired as curate and concentrated on his studies. He was 'possessed of a rare attainment in scholarship' and continued to publish books and articles until his death in 1856. He formed a very fine library now housed at Canterbury Cathedral Library and the University of Kent – 106 of the most valuable books were sold at Sotheby's in 2013 for £1,180,875. (Ibid.)

The sermons preached by John Burgess and Anthony Burgess are described in Chapter 11. However, in relation to changes of the Prayer Book of 1662, Norman Evans recounts important changes of doctrine from the time of Elizabeth I and how this particularly affected Holy Trinity. One of the key differences articulated between Roman Catholics and Anglicans was 'transubstantiation', the belief that the bread and wine taken at the mass/holy communion actually become the body and blood of Christ rather than being symbols of that body and blood. Queen Elizabeth sanctioned in the Prayer Book two phrases still in use today and said by the priest as these elements are given to the congregation: '"The body/blood of Christ" (to appease the Catholics) and "Eat this/drink this in remembrance" (to appease the Protestants)' (Evans, 1987, p. 143)

The Queen also proceeded to enact that magistrates (or the warden in the case of Sutton Coldfield) must ensure that the services in the Prayer Book were followed precisely and that people attend church regularly. Absence on a Sunday would result in a fine of one shilling (approximately £5.26 in today's terms). (Ibid., p. 144)

The warden and each of the twenty-four members of the society in Sutton Coldfield had to swear allegiance to the throne, sign a declaration that he did not believe in transubstantiation and also provide proof that he had received the Lord's Supper (holy communion) in the parish church. This was done on joining the society and again from time to time. The first Roman Catholic admitted to the society after the Catholic Emancipation Act of 1829 was in 1832.

Roger Lea has written further about the development of the 1834 Holy Trinity Chapel in History Spot 445. Janet Jordan has also written the history of *The Roman Catholic Church in Walmley: updated for our Diamond Jubilee year 2018,* which begins with a useful summary of the early years of faith and worship in Sutton Coldfield.

CONCLUSION

The history ends with a chapter about controversies, which may appear surprising. However, the UK in the twenty-first century is a very different place from that of previous centuries, and some appalling acts and attitudes of injustice and intolerance that were carried out in the name of Christianity need to be acknowledged and in some measure to be atoned for. Sadly, such acts and attitudes continue, and acknowledging history may be a way of enlightening those who misunderstand others.

Along with many other faith communities of all kinds, across the world, those of Sutton Coldfield have reached out to one another in recent years to try to build on common ground and provide solidarity in the face of negative attitudes to religion, whichever faith might be tested. In terms of Christian denominations working together there are councils of churches in most towns, and organisations like Christian Aid work across a range of churches.

In terms of groups meeting from different faiths, the formation in the twenty-first century of a group of Muslim and Christian women in the town, called Sutton Sisters, is but one example of this positive and united response to religious tension here in Sutton Coldfield.

The story of Holy Trinity is a long one and still not fully revealed. The following pages will hopefully be useful for reference. They are a timeline of key events, a glossary, further reading and an index.

In 1865 a newspaper article said the following: 'It is to be hoped that the present state of the church will not long continue as a kind of holdback to the progress Sutton Coldfield has made in other respects during the last three or four years.' (*Aris's Birmingham Gazette*, 20 May 1865)

The last major extension of the church happened soon after that comment was made. The members of Holy Trinity recognise that they are both beneficiaries and custodians of a rich heritage. While there is still much to do and no work of this kind is ever completed, in the twenty-first century the congregation has fulfilled a modernisation programme which aims to ensure that the church is both well looked after and available to the whole community, and that it retains its partnership with the town, offering a place for worship, reflection and fellowship on the hill.

Fig. 75: *Holy Trinity by candlelight 2018 (BHD)*

TIMELINE OF EVENTS RELATING TO HOLY TRINITY AND CONTEMPORARY EVENTS

Year	Event relating to Holy Trinity	Contemporary events in Sutton Coldfield or the wider world
1086		Domesday Book – there is an entry for the manor of Sutton Coldfield but not for a church.
1250	Archaeological evidence points to a first building being constructed in the second half of the thirteenth century. The footings (brickwork) of the east end wall are the only visible evidence of this stonework from the outside (Coleshill Street).	
1250	Simon de Daventry is named as the first incumbent on the Rectors' Board in the church entrance.	
1291	Church recorded in the Vatican records of taxation (Pope Nicholas).	
1451	The earliest suggested date for John Vesey's birth (from the tomb inscription). Other sources have 1462 or 1465.	
1452	John Arundel made a Bishop (incumbent of Holy Trinity from 1431 to 1433).	
1471	Richard Neville, Earl of Warwick and patron of Sutton Coldfield, dies – advowson passes to Crown.	Battle of Barnet – where the Earl died. Followed by the Battle of Tewkesbury.
1450–1500	Tower built and a single bell hung (sanctus bell) The first north aisle (now Vesey aisle) and the south aisle are added to the nave. The stone archway of the former south door is moved to new south wall.	
1519	John Vesey becomes Bishop of Exeter.	
1523	Joan Harman (John Vesey's mother) and his brother Hugo Harman die. Vesey returns to Sutton Coldfield.	
1525		Canwell Priory dissolved, part of the dissolution of the monasteries under Henry VIII.
1527		School founded by Bishop Vesey (now Bishop Vesey Grammar School).

1528		Bishop Vesey secures a royal charter from Henry VIII for the manor of Sutton Coldfield led by a warden and society of 24 men. Also for Sutton Park to be given to the people of the town.

1530–33   Bishop Vesey builds chapels either side of the chancel (now the Vesey chapel and choir vestry) and gives an organ to the church. Bells installed from Canwell Priory.

1541   Bishop Vesey Grammar School – first stone building on land which is now included in the south-west part of the churchyard.

1549	Holy Trinity has a Tudor royal coat of arms installed.	Edward VI orders all Roman Catholic decorations to be removed from churches.

1554   Bishop Vesey dies on 23 October at Moor Hall and is buried in the north-west corner of the church, in an area since renamed the Vesey chapel.

1559   The advowson (patronage or living) of the church is sold by Queen Elizabeth I on 3 December to Glascock and Blunt, who on the same day sell it to John Gibbons, LLD.

1560   The advowson of the church is again sold on, this time by John Gibbons to Thomas Gibbons of New Hall.

1586   The advowson is sold on by Thomas Gibbons of New Hall to John Shilton.

1606   Brass memorials on the north side of the east end of the chancel record the death of Rector Roger Elyot's wife, Barbara, at the age of 24.

1609   A silver communion cup, cover and paten are given to the church by Roger Elyot in memory of Barbara.

1621   Josias Bull, gentleman, is buried in a vault in the chancel. His brass memorial is on the wall of the chancel (south side).

1626   A silver chalice and cover are given to the church by Cornelius Burgess, DD, the husband of Abigail, the youngest daughter of the Rector Dr John Burges, following her death on 19 March 1626. These are in Birmingham Museum and Art Gallery.

| 1642 | Anthony Burgess flees in the face of royalist supporters being in the vicinity. James Fleetwood, DD, is presented to Sutton Rectory by the Crown (King Charles I) but not inducted. He is commemorated in the Vesey chapel 'Bishops' east window. | Civil War. |

1649 — Execution of King Charles I.

1654 — Magistrates officiate at marriages in private houses, not in church.

1657 Burgess returns. Marriages resume in church. — Last 'civil' wedding.

1656 Sir William Dugdale publishes his *Antiquities of Warwickshire*, which references the church extensively. Dugdale notes at this point that the brasses on the gravestones on the floor of the Vesey chapel are missing.

1660 The royal coat of arms of Charles II and three boards displaying the Creed, Commandments and Lord's Prayer are placed above the archway at the east end of the nave. — Charles II crowned.

1662 Revd Anthony Burgess resigns as Rector in disagreement over the new Prayer Book. — The Prayer Book is issued by Elizabeth I

William Watson becomes Rector.

1671 Thomas Dawnay Esq. is buried in the churchyard to the north of the sundial.

1677 Henry Pudsey is buried in the family vault he had created in the Vesey chapel.

1689 John Riland, MA, the first Rector of the family whose members would continue in this role over a 200-year period (Rilands and Riland-Bedfords), is presented to the rectory by John Shilton.

1690 A silver flagon and two patens for use in Holy Communion are given to the church by Henry Walter, a native of Sutton Coldfield and three times High Steward of the County of Clare. These are currently in Birmingham Museum and Art Gallery.

1697 Jane Wilson, wife of Sir William Wilson and widow of Henry Pudsey, is buried in the Pudsey family vault in the Vesey chapel.

1701 The Queen Anne Rectory is built for John Riland in what is now known as Rectory Park, opposite what is now Bedford Road.

1704   The studded oak door is added to the south porch archway. Thomas Abell and Thomas Martin are named as churchwardens.

1706   John Riland acquires the advowson of the church as well as being Rector. This enables him to appoint his successor and for the living to remain in the family for over 200 years.

1708   Henry, Lord Ffolliott, who had built Four Oaks Hall, has a private gallery constructed across the north-west end of the nave for himself and his wife. (His wife Elizabeth was the elder daughter of Henry and Jane Pudsey).

1709   George Sacheverell Esq. of New Hall obtains a faculty to construct a vault in the south-west corner of the church.

1710   Sir William Wilson, the stonemason who married Jane, widow of Henry Pudsey, is buried in the churchyard adjoining the Pudsey vault (the memorial is now in the clergy vestry, built subsequently).

1715   George Sacheverell Esq. is buried in the vault he had had constructed in 1709.

1716   Henry Ffolliott, 3rd Baron Ffolliott, dies, though is not mentioned as having been buried in the church or churchyard.

1725   Sir William Jesson of Langley Hall is buried in a vault in the Vesey chapel. The Jesson and Pudsey families are joined by marriage.

1720   Rector John Riland (I) dies and is buried in a vault in the chancel. His son, Revd Richard Riland MA, becomes incumbent, serving until 1757.

1727   Bishop Vesey Grammar School's current building on Lichfield Road, which now forms the main entrance to the school, is built.

1730   A new edition of Sir William Dugdale's famous book, *The Antiquities of Warwickshire*, which references Holy Trinity, is published, with corrections and additional prints, by Revd William Thomas, a Rector of Exhall near Alcester.

1742   Elizabeth Ffolliott (née Pudsey), wife of Henry, the third baron Ffolliott, is buried in the Pudsey vault in the Vesey chapel.

1745   The roof requires extensive repairs. This is paid for by the Warden and Society of Sutton Coldfield with money obtained from the sale of oak trees in Sutton Park.

1746   A well-known parishioner, Simon Luttrell, buys Four Oaks Hall from the widow of Henry, Lord Ffolliott, following her death in 1742.

1748   The effigy of Bishop Vesey on the tomb is restored, raised and placed in a niche in the adjoining north wall, with railings round to protect it.

1754   Thomas Bonell, gentleman, a solicitor and author of a history of Sutton Coldfield, applies for a faculty to build a gallery for himself and his family over the south aisle.

1758   The Corporation allocates £100 for new pewing in the church.

1758   A clock is erected in the tower by John Height of Pershore.

1759   A faculty is granted for a new window in the north wall (opposite the south porch). However, this was in the wall before the addition of the north aisle, so is no longer in place.

1760   Following an attempt to install new pews in 1759, the foundations of the nave are found to be faulty. Major work is carried out by William Hiorn of Warwick, including the present pulpit in the church and new box pews.

1760   Simon Luttrell, now Baron Irnham, has a large gallery built into the west end arch (in front of the tower) for his family.

1762   Thomas Bonell writes his *History of Sutton Coldfield by an impartial hand*.

1762   Complaints are made by some parishioners in the Spiritual Court in Lichfield about the occupation and position of some of the new box pews.

1779   Robert Lawley of Canwell Hall erects a small gallery at the north side of the enlarged west end Four Oaks Hall gallery.

1784   A new ring of five bells is hung at a cost of £100.

1790   The Revd Richard Bisse Riland, Rector for 32 years, dies and is succeeded by his brother Revd John Riland, MA.

1794   Six new bells are hung, replacing the five which had
        been added in 1784.

1802   Sarah Holbeche is born. She goes on in her 150-page
        diary to tell the story of her large family and their
        life in Sutton, living close to the church and being an
        important part of it.

1806   The two outer (wooden) doors are hung in the south
        porch (still in place today).

1810   John Hacket Esq. of Moor Hall dies. (He was the great-
        great-grandson of John Hacket, the former Bishop
        of Lichfield, who is commemorated in the 'Bishops"
        window in the east end of the Vesey chapel).

1810   William Jesson Pearson dies, the last in the male line
        of the Pudsey/Jesson families.

1817   The Archdeacon of Lichfield reports on the condition
        and inadequacy of the burial ground at Holy Trinity.

1817   Mary Ashford dies in suspicious circumstances at
        Penns on 27 May 1817. She is buried in Holy Trinity
        churchyard near the south porch.

1822   Revd John Riland (II) is buried in a vault in the
        Chancel, aged 85, and Rector for just three years.
        He is succeeded by the Revd William Bedford MA,
        the grandson of the Revd Richard Bisse Riland
        (died 1790).

1825   Town school opens at the foot of what is now Trinity
        Hill (the buildings are now Sutton Baptist Church).

1826   William Kirkpatrick Riland Bedford is born, the
        penultimate Rector of Holy Trinity from this family,
        and possibly the most influential.

1828   Following the establishment of town school in 1825,
        galleries are built on the north and south walls to
        separate the children from the adults when they
        attend Sunday service.

1828   The yew tree in the churchyard near the south-east
        entrance is planted in April by the Rector, the Revd
        William Riland Bedford.

1829   Charles Chadwick Esq., of New Hall, and nephew of
        George Sacheverell, is buried in the Sacheverell vault.
        His sister Mary had been buried there in 1770 and his
        wife Frances in 1804. Both George and Charles died
        without issue.

1829 The pulpit tester (roof) is removed.

1832 The churchyard area is enlarged, taking in some of the land which was previously part of the first grammar school (at the top of what is now Trinity Hill).

1835 The Archdeaconry of Coventry (including Sutton Coldfield) is taken from the diocese of Lichfield and added to the diocese of Worcester.

1835 A chapel is built at Hill (Mere Green) to cater for the increasing population – a 'daughter' church to begin with, not a separate parish.

1836 Blind Lane is renamed Trinity Hill and widened and straightened with adjustments to the church boundary.

1838   Coronation of Queen Victoria.

1843 The Revd William Riland Bedford (who had been Rector for 21 years) dies, and his cousin the Revd Dr Richard Williamson DD becomes the incumbent.

1844 Rectory in Coleshill Street built.

     This building, on the other side of Trinity Hill, was used as the rectory until 2000.

1845   St John's Church, Walmley is built, making Walmley the first of the neighbouring areas of the expanding town of Sutton Coldfield to have a church erected as part of a separate parish.

1848 Thomas Holbeche dies, a solicitor and county magistrate who lived at 1–3 Coleshill Street and whose sister, Sarah, and grandson, Richard, both wrote memoirs about life in Sutton.

1850 Gas lighting – by fish-tail jets – was installed in the church.

1850 The Revd William Kirkpatrick Riland Bedford MA becomes Rector (son of Revd William Riland Bedford).

1852 The earliest recorded photographs of the church are taken by William M. Grundy.

1854 Fundraising bazaar in Sutton Park to raise funds to build a new church in Boldmere.

1856   The present font is installed, a gift from Mr Richard Sadler (a churchwarden) whose father had previously retrieved it from use as a horse-mounting block outside an inn in Shustoke.

1856   The Revd Joseph Mendham, curate for thirty-two years and a distinguished scholar, dies aged 87.

1857   St Michael's, Boldmere is consecrated by the Lord Bishop of Worcester on 29 September.

1859   The Revd William Kirkpatrick Riland Bedford becomes the first Master of the Warden Lodge, the first masonic hall in Sutton Coldfield.

1863   The current stained glass at the east end of the nave is installed in memory of William Riland Bedford (Rector, died 1843).

1863   A new organ, by Gray and Davidson, is installed in the south-east area of the church.

1863   The Queen Anne reredos (altarpiece) is removed to the new town hall in Mill Street (now the Masonic Hall).

1863   Whitewash is removed from the interior walls of the church (to reveal the sandstone brickwork). The only area currently whitewashed is the south side of the church.

1864   The church roof having been declared unsafe in 1863, the building is closed while a new roof is built – the level of the ridge of the roof being raised by 10ft. The new ceiling of the nave is left plain.

1864   Sir William E. Cradock Hartopp dies and his widow erects the brass memorial in the chancel (now in the south-west corner of the Vesey chapel).

1865   The first transatlantic cable is produced by a firm in Penns, Sutton, Messrs Webster (memorials in church and churchyard).

1868   The galleries erected in 1828 for the school children are removed. The doorways from the east end of church, either side of the chancel, are bricked up but remain visible from the outside. The girls' doorway is visible inside behind the Jesson memorial in the Vesey chapel.

1869 Revd James Packwood dies, curate at Holy Trinity for
      forty years and commemorated in the Vesey chapel
      east window.

1869 The windows in the south porch, which had been
      bricked up, are restored.

1869 A window on the west wall of the tower, depicting
      Faith, Hope and Charity, is installed to the memory of
      the Misses Blews of Maney.

1870 The stained glass is added to the east end window in
      the Vesey chapel, commemorating prominent Bishops.
      The benches for schoolgirls at the east end of the
      chapel are replaced by pews facing the chancel.

1870 Thomas Colmore Esq. of Ashfurlong Hall dies. He was
      a former magistrate, chairman of the Aston Board of
      Guardians and warden of Sutton from 1864 to 1866.

1874 The clergy vestry is built on to the north side of the
      Vesey chapel. The west door in the tower is replaced
      by a cast-iron tracery window so that the tower could
      be used as a vestry.

1875 Bishop Vesey's monument is opened, recorded and the
      tomb restored. The chancel floor is raised to its present
      level. Choir stalls and screens in the chancel are made
      from oak purchased from Worcester Cathedral. The
      pulpit is moved to the north side of the chancel.

1876 A new cemetery is built on Rectory Road,
      consecrated by the Bishop of Worcester on 4 May
      1880 (the first burial is Monday 1 November).

1878 A corrugated iron building for use as a church at Maney
      is consecrated in Church Road just above the smithy.

1878 Bishop Vesey's tithe barn
      in Sutton High Street is
      demolished to build the
      Midland Railway bridge.

1879 The current north aisle and north gallery are built,
      the ceiling of the old Vesey aisle being removed. New
      pews are installed, replacing the Georgian box pews.
      This was the last major extension of the church.

1884 Two more bells are hung in the tower.

1884 The clock in the tower is removed, both because it
      had become unreliable and because there was now a
      clock on the Town Hall.

1886		The Warden and Society is re-formed as Sutton Coldfield Corporation with a mayor at the head.

1889   The Revd William Kirkpatrick Riland Bedford publishes the history of his family's living, *Three hundred years of a family living: being a history of the Rilands of Sutton Coldfield.*

1890   The present communion table (altar) is given by the Rector, the Revd William Kirkpatrick Riland Bedford, in memory of his wife, (Maria) Amy. The altar is now on wheels, which allows it to be moved to a chosen position within the chancel.

1891   *The history of Sutton Coldfield* by the Revd W. K. Riland Bedford is published.

1891   George Bamford Preston, head of Sutton Town Boys' School for 33 years, dies and is buried in the churchyard.

1892   A misericord (a shallow seat set into a wall) dating from around 1490 is given to the church by Henry Charles Hill. A brass memorial to him is in the south aisle, although the misericord is no longer in the church.

1892   William Campbell Riland Bedford succeeds his father William Kirkpatrick as Rector, following the latter's retirement. He is the last in the line of this family to serve as Rector.

1893   Following the example of his aunts, Richard Holbeche writes an account of life and people in the town in the 1860s.

1898   The lych gate in Coleshill Street is constructed in William K. Riland Bedford's lifetime in recognition of his service to the town and the church. It is sited next to the family vault.

1900   An iron church is built in Whitehouse Common Road to replace a barn in Silvester Road (now Lindridge Road). It is the forerunner of St Chad's Church.

1901   A new pipe organ by Hope-Jones is added to the south gallery, powered by electricity.

         Plans are made for an extension to the east end of the church, but these are never executed.

1904   Quintus Charles Colmore (born 1851) dies. He is the
       dedicatee of the Colmore window in the choir vestry
       (former south chapel).

1905   The Diocese of Birmingham is created. Churches in
       Birmingham and surrounding areas including Sutton
       Coldfield are moved from Worcester Diocese to the
       new diocese.

1905   Holy Trinity is wired for electric lighting.

1905   The church of St Peter's,
       Maney, is consecrated as a
       separate parish by the Rt
       Revd Charles Gore, Bishop
       of Birmingham, on 28 June.

1905   William Kirkpatrick Riland Bedford, the most famous
       of the Riland Bedford family of Rectors, dies aged 79,
       and is buried in the family vault.

1908   All Saints Four Oaks is
       consecrated, another parish
       being created to meet the
       demands of an expanding
       population, taking its land
       from the parish of St James,
       Hill. All Saints is on the corner
       of Belwell Lane and Four
       Oaks Road.

1909   With the retirement of William Campbell Riland
       Bedford, the patronage of Holy Trinity is passed to
       the Bishop of the new Diocese of Birmingham, who
       appoints Charles W. Barnard as Rector.

1910   Bell-ringing tribute at Holy Trinity.   Death of Edward VII.

1911   Service at Holy Trinity.   Coronation of George V –
                                   town celebrations.

1914   The chancel ceiling is painted, the first of four painted
       ceilings at Holy Trinity created under the direction of
       architect Charles E Bateman.

1922   The death of William Campbell Riland Bedford,
       Rector from 1892 to 1909 and the last incumbent of
       the Riland Bedford family. He is buried in the family
       vault near the lych gate.

1926   William J Lyon becomes Rector, following the
       retirement of Charles William Barnard.

       The Scout Troop is formed at Holy Trinity.

1927   St Chad's Hollyfield Road is consecrated on 28 March 1927. It remained a daughter church of Holy Trinity until becoming a parish in its own right in 1959.

1928   A large-scale fundraising event – Bazaar in a Japanese Garden – is held at the town hall for restoration work subsequently carried out in 1929.

1928   The Sutton Coldfield Town Pageant commemorated the 400th anniversary of the granting of the town charter by Henry VIII in 1528. Bishop Vesey was played by Canon Frederick Stanley Golden, who was Vicar of St Peter's Maney from 1920–46.

1929   Restoration of the church including the exterior stonework of the Vesey chapel, the painting of three further ceilings (Vesey chapel, nave and tower) and the erection of the screen in memory of Rector Charles Barnard, which enclosed the Vesey chapel. The work was directed by Birmingham architect Charles Bateman.

1931   The Revd George L. Harvey MA becomes Rector, serving until 1945.

1935   The royal town holds celebrations for the Jubilee of George V, led by Alderman John Willmott, who also wrote a play.

1936   The rectory in Rectory Park is demolished.

1939   The Vesey Gardens are laid as a visible memorial to the Bishop for the town, a project led by Alderman Willmott.

1945   John Boggon is instituted as Rector, serving from 1945 to 1966.

1949   Holy Trinity is Grade I listed.

1950   The gravestones are moved from round the church and placed at the perimeter, overlooking Trinity Hill, where they now edge the car park.

1950   A new pipe organ by Hill, Norman and Beard is
        installed with pipes and pipework in the tower and
        console in the south-west corner just outside the then
        south chapel (now choir vestry), which housed an
        additional chamber organ.

1956   A window dedicated to Bishop Barnes (Bishop of
        Birmingham) is installed in the south chapel.

1956   The church choir, under the direction of Harold Gray,
        is affiliated to the Royal School of Church Music
        (RSCM), a support body founded in 1927.

1957   World Scout Jamboree is held
        in Sutton Park to celebrate
        fifty years of Scouting.

1959   The foundation stone of St
        Columba's Church, Banner's
        Gate, is laid by the mayor,
        Alderman Minnie Grounds JP.

1959   The early Georgian house built on the stone
        foundations of St Mary's Hall, at the corner of Trinity
        Hill and Coleshill Street, is demolished.

1960   A library in oak is built in the south-west corner
        chapel in memory of (William Edward) Douglas
        Clayton, a former churchwarden.

1964   Ralph Vale, a chorister at Holy Trinity for sixty-one
        years, dies aged 85. A memorial to him is in the
        stonework (south side) of the flight of stairs leading
        from the nave to the tower base.

1965   The stained glass window in the south chapel (now
        choir vestry) is given in memory of his wife by the
        Rector, Canon John Boggon.

1966   The Revd Canon Alaric Rose MA succeeds Canon
        John Boggon as Rector.

1968   *The history of Sutton Coldfield*
        by the Revd W. K. Riland
        Bedford is re-published by
        the Corporation of Sutton
        Coldfield.

1969   During repairs to the south aisle, the Sacheverell vault is
        opened and found to contain five coffins,
        all bearing names of Sacheverell and Chadwick
        families except one, probably that of George's wife, Mary.

1973   The eight bells are recast and rehung in an iron
        frame.

1974   Borough flag displayed.

        Following local government reorganisation, the
        Royal Borough of Sutton Coldfield flag is moved to
        permanent display in the church. It is currently on the
        south wall of the tower.

1974   As part of local government reorganisation, Sutton Coldfield moves from Warwickshire to Birmingham. A new county of the West Midlands is created comprising seven metropolitan authorities.

1983   The inner oak doors are fitted in the archway of the
        south porch in recognition of fifty years' ministry by
        the Rector, Alaric Rose.

1984   The Revd Edward (Ted) G. Longman MA is
        appointed Rector following the retirement of
        Canon Alaric Rose.

1985   Canon Alaric Rose, Rector from 1966 to 1984, dies
        on 27 December.

1986   The exterior stonework of the church undergoes
        major repair.

1987   The first interment of ashes following cremation takes
        place in a small garden of remembrance between the
        south porch and Coleshill Street.

1987   Norman G. Evans writes *An investigation of Holy Trinity
        Parish Church Sutton Coldfield.*

1987   Major repairs to church and roof are completed
        at a cost of £75,000. Traces of a chimney stack, on
        the south side of the tower at the head of the spiral
        stairway, are removed.

1990   The wooden board with the words of the Ten
        Commandments, Lord's Prayer and Creed in gold
        on a turquoise background, is made by Brian Dixon,
        churchwarden, and Robert Alloway, chorister, and
        erected on the corner surrounding the font at the
        west end of the nave. Following re-ordering in 2016, it
        now stands in the south-west corner of the church.

1992   Students from Sutton College (now Birmingham Metropolitan College, Sutton Campus) create four mosaic panels in the Vesey chapel under the east window.

1995   A service is held to mark the laying of the Trinity Centre foundation stone and a 'time capsule' of memorabilia is buried underneath.

1996   The long awaited two-storey facility on the church site, known as the Trinity Centre, is formally opened.

1997   The Revd Dan Connolly becomes Rector at new year 1997, serving until December 1998.

1998   The large 120-year-old plane tree on the corner of the churchyard at the top of Trinity Hill is made safe, and the crumbling wall repaired at a total cost of £60,000 borne by Birmingham City Council.

2000   A large-scale flower festival is held in church with community groups of all kinds contributing displays, to celebrate the 700th anniversary of the church (approximately).

2000   On 18 February 2000 the Revd James Langstaff MA was inducted as Rector. He served until 2004, leaving to become Bishop of Lynn, the first incumbent to go on to be consecrated Bishop since John Arundel left in 1433 and became Bishop of Chichester in 1452.

2001   A new post is filled by Cheryl Slusser to provide a town chaplaincy service. Sadly, this post was not renewed at the end of Cheryl's tenure.

2006   The Revd John Routh MA is inducted in January 2006, having previously served as vicar of the neighbouring parish of St Chad's, Hollyfield Road.

2008   The rectory in Coleshill Street, which was used from the nineteenth century until 1998, is renamed Bishop's Lodge and changes its use after some uncertainty as to its future, becoming the home of the Bishop of Aston.

2011   A weekend at the end of September turns unexpectedly warm for a fundraising flower festival, with arrangements reflecting the theme of Creation.

2013   The Friends of Holy Trinity is established to organise
       concerts and other events in aid of the church fabric
       fund to help keep the building in good repair.
       A Christmas Tree festival is held for the first time.

2016   A major re-ordering (refurbishment) of the church   A new town council is set up
       interior is undertaken to create a new entrance and   for Sutton Coldfield.
       a flexible and accessible space for worship and other
       activities.

2016   A service of dedication is held at 10 a.m. on Sunday
       2 October 2016 as the formal reopening of the newly
       reordered church. The president at Holy Communion
       is the Lord Bishop of Birmingham, Revd David
       Urquhart. A commemorative plaque is placed in the
       new church 'Vesey entrance'.

2016   A Heritage Lottery Fund grant is awarded in
       December for 'Holy Trinity Parish Church: heritage at
       the heart of Sutton Coldfield' (2017 to 2019).

2017   The church wins two trophies in the Sutton Coldfield
       Civic Society Design Awards of 2017, one for Best
       Restoration Project and the other for Outstanding
       Project of the year.

2017   A new website for Holy Trinity is created as part of the
       HLF grant, offering information about every aspect of
       church life including a substantial 'Heritage' section.

2018   The pipe organ of 1950 is removed from the tower
       and a new digital instrument installed. Work begun
       in 2016 is completed, exposing both the stained glass
       west window and painted ceiling in the tower which
       had been hidden since 1950.

2018   In December a new church guidebook is published as
       part of the culmination of the heritage project.

2020   This book is published by The History Press as part of
       the legacy of the heritage project.

GLOSSARY

Term	Definition or description
Advowson	In ecclesiastical law, the advowson is the right to recommend a member of the Anglican clergy for a vacant benefice, or to make such an appointment. This is now termed patronage and is usually held by the Bishop of the local diocese, known as the patron. Another term for this is the 'living'.
Chamfer	In woodwork this describes a symmetrical sloping surface at an edge or corner.
Clerestory	The upper part of the nave, containing a series of windows.
Curate	A member of the clergy serving in a parish under a vicar or Rector. Often a newly ordained deacon who serves a three-year curacy, during which time he or she will usually be ordained priest at the end of the first year.
Dado rail	A decorative waist-high moulding around the wall of a room, which also protects the wall from damage. At Holy Trinity this is in wood.
Dissenter	See Non-conformist.
Glebe land	The worked land area from which workers had to give tithes (qv).
Grotesque	A style of decorative art characterised by fanciful or fantastic human and animal forms often interwoven with foliage or similar figures that may distort the natural into absurdity, ugliness, or caricature. Definition by Merriam-Webster. At Holy Trinity there are grotesques on the tower and also the font.
Incumbent	See Rector.
Light	In stained glass each separate area/panel of a window is called a light.
Liturgy	The agreed wording of services taking place in a church where this follows a set pattern, especially in the Roman Catholic church and the Church of England.
Living	See advowson.
Non-conformist	Also called **Dissenter,** or **Free Churchman,** any English Protestant who does not conform to the doctrines or practices of the established Church of England. Nowadays applied as a generic term for other Christian denominations such as Baptists or Presbyterians.

Ogee	Usually of a window where the frame at the top joins the two halves, which look like mirrored elongated 's' shapes ('z' and 's') rather than a simple curved join. The inner frames of the east end window at Holy Trinity are ogees while the outer frame is a simple arch shape. See en.wikipedia.org/wiki/Ogee.
Ordination	The specific process by a Bishop to make priests or deacons.
Patronage	See Advowson.
Rector	The priest assigned to a parish by the patron. Sometimes titled a vicar or 'priest in charge' and any of these is known as the incumbent (post-holder). In earlier centuries the Rector specifically received tithes from the people in his parish.
Reredos	A large altarpiece, or screen or decoration placed behind the altar.
Sanctus bell	Sanctus is Latin for 'holy' and is the word from which we derive a number of words in current usage, notably 'saint'. There is a part of the liturgy (qv) of the service of Holy Communion known as the 'Sanctus' as the words in English begin 'Holy, holy, holy …' Just before this point in the service a bell might be rung, and at the start of the service, to remind the congregation to be particularly prayerful and attentive at this point.
Stringing	Refers to a thin line of protruding brickwork visible on an outer wall. In the case of Holy Trinity, mediaeval stringing marks the height of the earlier south wall of the church between the porch and the point where the south chapel begins.
Tithe	Originating in the bible (Deuteronomy), a system of taxation whereby individuals and later businesses paid one tenth of their income to the landowner, often the Rector of the parish.
Vicar	A term now interchangeable with Rector (qv). In early days 'vicars general' deputised for Bishops and 'vicars choral' were appointed by cathedral canons to take their place in the cathedral choir.

REFERENCES
AND FURTHER
READING

This is a list of sources consulted and further reading about the church and town of Sutton Coldfield. References are made in the text according to the Harvard system whereby the text gives in brackets the author by surname only (unless there are two authors with the same surname, in which case the first name will also be given) and then date of publication and relevant page numbers.

Reference is made in the text following direct quotations and also to sections which might relate to the work of a particular writer. For this reason the list below is by surname, first name and date, followed by the title, publisher and any further bibliographic information that might be useful for readers following up on particular sources. Any additional notes by the editor are in square brackets.

Normally the convention is followed that hyphenated names start with the name before the hyphen and those using two surnames with the actual surname. The exception to this rule is the filing of William Kirkpatrick Riland Bedford's works under 'Riland Bedford' as members of that family are usually thought of as being 'Riland' or 'Riland Bedford' rather than simply Bedford.

Anonymous or unattributable texts are filed alphabetically within the sequence by title. They will be referenced accordingly in the text. Any undated work is abbreviated to n.d. to signify 'no date'.

Press cuttings are not listed here but referenced in full where they appear in the text. Similarly, the 'History Spot' series of articles by Roger Lea, which were published in the *Sutton Coldfield Observer* between 2009 and 2017, are cited in the text using the following format: (Lea, Title, HS xx, full date). All of these are available and easily searchable on the website of the Sutton Coldfield Local History Research Group here: sclhrg.org.uk/history-spot.html

BOOKS AND JOURNAL ARTICLES

Ballard, Phillada (ed.) (2009) Birmingham's Victorian and Edwardian architects. Oblong Creative Ltd for the West Midlands Branch of the Victorian Society. [Brief mentions of Holy Trinity and one illustration in chapters on Yeoville Thomason and Charles Bateman. The chapter on Bidlake does not mention his work at Holy Trinity.]

Bates, Sue (1987) Sutton Coldfield: a pictorial history. Phillimore

Baxter, Marian (1994) Sutton Coldfield. Tempus

Baxter, Marian (2013) Sutton Park. History Press. Images of England Series [First edn 2006]

Baxter, Marian and Field, John (2002) Then and now: Sutton Coldfield. Tempus

Bayliss, Jon (1991) 'Richard and Gabriel Royley of Burton-upon-Trent, Tombmakers', Church Monuments (The Journal of the Church Monuments Society) vol VI, pp. 21–41.

Bird, W. Hobart (1940) Old Warwickshire churches. Ed. J Burrow. p. 104

Bonell, Thomas (1762) History of Sutton Coldfield by an impartial hand.

Bracken, Agnes (1860) History of the forest and chase of Sutton Coldfield. Simpkin, Marshall & Co. p. 76ff

Cartwright, T. H. and Ellison, Thos (1911) Coronation of King George V June 1911: programme of festivities held at Sutton Coldfield, 22 and 23 June 1911. D McMichael, Printer, Swan Passage, Worcester Street, Birmingham. [Includes Souvenir. 22 June 1911. Short history of the Royal Town of Sutton Coldfield by T. H. Cartwright. 33pp. The book has no page numbers.]

Charters… (1935) Charters granted by Henry VIII, Charles II and Victoria. Press of The Birmingham Printers. [Charters translated into English. Authorised by Arthur E Terry (Mayor) and R. A. Reay-Nadin (Town Clerk)]

Chatwin, Philip B and Harcourt Edgar G (1942) The Bishop Vesey houses and other old buildings in Sutton Coldfield. Charles Batey OUP

Chibi, Andrew Allan (2003) Henry VIII's Bishops: diplomats, administrators, scholars and shepherds. James Clarke and Sons. Antique Collector's Guide. [quoted by Roger Lea, qv]

Colvile, Frederick Leigh (1870) The worthies of Warwickshire who lived between 1500 and 1800. Henry Cooke and Son. [Available at: https://archive.org/stream/worthiesofwarwic00colv/worthiesofwarwic00colv_djvu.txt]

Cooper, Tim (1999) The last generation of English Catholic clergy: parish priests in the Diocese of Coventry and Lichfield in the early sixteenth century. Boydell Press, Suffolk.

Courtney, William Prideaux (n.d.) 'Veysey, John'. Dictionary of National Biography, 1885-1900, Volume 58. Available at: https://en.wikisource.org/wiki/Veysey,_John_(DNB00) [downloaded 28/5/19]

Coutts, Cathy (2019) Holy Trinity Church, Sutton Coldfield: archaeological observations during re-ordering works in 2016. Archaeology Warwickshire Report No 1981

Duffy, Eamon (2009) Fires of Faith: Catholic England under Mary Tudor. Yale University Press [p. 6 and p. 20 relate to woodwork now in Holy Trinity]

Dugdale, William (1656) The antiquities of Warwickshire. Thomas Warren. [pp. 666–671. Available at: archive.org/details/antiquitiesofwaroodugd/page/n5]

Dugdale, William (1730) The antiquities of Warwickshire. 2nd edn with additions by William Thomas. Thomas Warren. [pp. 909–919. An interesting history of the work is at: worcestercollegelibrary.wordpress.com/2016/11/30/ex-libris-james-campbell-william-dugdales-antiquities-of-warwickshire]

Evans, Norman Granville (1987) An investigation of Holy Trinity Parish Church Sutton Coldfield. [Typescript. 206pp. The appendices (pp. 117–205) were finalised in 1992, as confirmed by a note at the end.]

Evans, Norman Granville and Gardner, Margaret (1987) Holy Trinity Sutton Coldfield. [Church guidebook, reprinted with additional material and new foreword and image, and additional information about the Trinity Centre on p. 25; 1996]

Ferguson, Sheila (1983) Village and Town Life. David and Charles

Field, John C. and James, Peter W. (1965) Sutton Park: a history and guide. West Midlands Press

Fryer, Geoffrey R. D. (1997) John Vesey and his world: a biography of Bishop Vesey of Sutton Coldfield. GRD Fryer [publ]

Gardner, Margaret (2000) Around the church. Holy Trinity Parish Church, Sutton Coldfield [32pp booklet ed. Stella Thebridge. A collection of Gardner's earlier writings in the church magazine.]

Hodder, Michael (1988) 'The development of some aspects of settlement and land use in Sutton Chase'. PhD Thesis

Hodder, Michael (1989) 'The prehistoric and Roman periods in Sutton Coldfield' in Lea (1989) qv, pp. 67–76

Hodder, Michael (2004) Birmingham: the hidden history. Tempus

Hodder, Michael (2013) The archaeology of Sutton Park. The History Press

Holbeche, Helen (1885) Threescore years ago. [unpublished. Transcript by Janet Jordan. Available at: sclhrg.org.uk]

Holbeche, Richard (1893) Diary. [unpublished. Transcript by Janet Jordan. Available at: sclhrg.org.uk]

Holbeche, Sarah (1884) Diary. [unpublished. Transcript by Janet Jordan. Available at: sclhrg.org.uk]

Holland, William Richard (1923) Some records of the Holland family. Philip Allan [includes ref to John Taylor (Rector)]

Ince, Laurence (2012) A History of the Holbeche Family of Warwickshire and the Holbech Family of Farnborough. Brewin Books.

Jones, Douglas V. (1984) The Royal Town of Sutton Coldfield: a commemorative history. 3rd rev edn. Westwood Press.

Jones, Graham (1995), Four Oaks Hall. [A 4-page leaflet with chronology and maps]

Jordan, Janet (2001) 'Sarah Holbeche: a Victorian lady who lived in Sutton Coldfield'. A Talk (with illustrations) given at Sutton Coldfield Library on Wednesday, 27 June 2001. Available at: https://sclhrg.org.uk/]

Jordan, Janet (2014) Tall tales from the top of Trinity Hill. Sutton Coldfield Local History Research Group

Jordan, Janet (2019) The box pew rumpus of 1762. Unpublished. Compiled for Holy Trinity's Heritage Open Day 2019

Kendall, Margaret (1989) From Church Hill to Vesey Gardens. Sutton Coldfield Local History Research Group

Kingman, M. J. (1978) 'Markets and marketing in Tudor England', Warwickshire History. IV (1). pp. 16–27.

Lea, Roger (ed.) (1989) Scenes from Sutton's past. Westwood Press

Lea, Roger (2000) The Sutton Coldfield Blue Plaque Trail. Sutton Coldfield Civic Society

Lea, Roger (2003) The Story of Sutton Coldfield. The History Press

Lethbridge, John P. (2007) Foul deeds and suspicious deaths in Warwickshire. Wharncliffe [Chapter 7 – 'The man who was tried twice …' (Ashford case law changes)]

MacCulloch, Diarmaid (1998), 'Worcester: a Cathedral City in the Reformation', in The Reformation in English Towns (eds P. Collinson and J. Craig) Basingstoke and London: Macmillan

McEvoy, Bernard (1878) Wandering among the aisles: a series of articles on the churches and chapels in the neighbourhood of Sutton Coldfield and Erdington. WT Parsons, Birmingham and at Sutton Coldfield [Reprinted from 'Sutton Coldfield and Erdington News'. Section on HT – pp. 34–40]

MacFarlane, Andrew (1989) 'Holy Trinity Parish Church Sutton Coldfield'. [in Lea, Scenes from Sutton's Past (qv) pp. 55–66. Excellent summary of the history including early Rectors]

Mee, Arthur (1947) The King's England: Warwickshire. Hodder and Stoughton. pp. 248–53

Midgley, W. (1904) A short history of the town and chase of Sutton Coldfield with two maps and many pictures. Midland Counties Herald

Moss, Hilda (1973) A royal town and its park: a history for junior citizens. Birmingham Public Libraries [ill. Sue Beeson. Originally pubd SC Corporation. Reprinted 1977, 1984]

NADFAS Sutton Coldfield Branch (2000) Unpublished report for church use only. [(National Association of Decorative and Fine Arts Societies) An inventory with images of internal features of the church including stonework, furniture, textiles, paintings and stained glass. A new survey is expected to be undertaken in due course to update the record.]

Old Veseyan Vol 3 No 4.

Oliver, Revd George DD (1861) Lives of the Bishops of Exeter, and a history of the cathedral. William Roberts [Publ: William Roberts, Broadgate, Exeter. Ref to co-eval account of John Vesey's death – pp. 124-5]

Osborne, H. W. S. (2017) An armchair and the pipe of peace. Bannister [Ed. Geoffrey Howell, Osborne's grandson. Fascinating reminiscences of aspects of HT life in the early twentieth century, especially in chapter 5]

Osbourne, Kerry (1990) A history of Bishop Vesey's Grammar School: the first 375 years (1527-1902). Sadler House, Sutton Coldfield

Osbourne, Kerry (2000) A history of Bishop Vesey's Grammar School: the twentieth century. Sadler House, Sutton Coldfield

Osbourne, Kerry (2007) The street names of Sutton Coldfield. Sadler House, Sutton Coldfield

Pevsner, Nikolaus and Wedgwood, Alexandra (1966) Warwickshire. Penguin (The Buildings of England) [pp. 424–9. A new edition of this work in relation to the Sutton Coldfield area is in preparation by Andy Foster. This will include a thorough appraisal of Holy Trinity.]

Pritchard, Ethel (1985) Unpublished list of the monumental inscriptions of Holy Trinity, on behalf of the Birmingham and Midland Society for Genealogy and Heraldry.

Quennell, Marjorie and Quennell, C. H. B. (1918), A History of Everyday Things in England. Vol. 1: 1066–1499. pp. 71, 181, 180, 230.

Reed, Alison (2005) Sutton Coldfield: a history and celebration. The Francis Frith Collection

Riall, Nicholas (2019) 'Exiled to Holy Trinity Parish Church, Sutton Coldfield, Warwickshire: the refugee Marian choir stalls from Worcester Cathedral.' The Antiquaries Journal, 2019, pp. 1–38. doi:10.1017/S0003581519000012X

Riland Bedford, Revd William Kirkpatrick (n.d.) The Luttrells of Four Oaks: an episode of North Warwickshire history. The Vesey Club

Riland Bedford, Revd William Kirkpatrick (1887) Vesey Papers

Riland Bedford, Revd William Kirkpatrick (1887) Sermon on the Jubilee

Riland Bedford, Revd William Kirkpatrick (1889) Three hundred years of a family living, being a history of the Rilands of Sutton Coldfield. Birmingham: Cornish Brothers.

Riland Bedford, Revd William Kirkpatrick (1891) History of Sutton Coldfield [also reprint, 1968, by Sutton Coldfield Corporation. Saxton (Printers)]

Riland Bedford, Revd William Kirkpatrick (1893) The Vesey buildings at Sutton Coldfield. A paper read before the members and friends of the Vesey Club, Sutton Coldfield, 26 October 1893, and printed at their request.

Riland Bedford, Revd William Kirkpatrick (c1900) Peeps into the Curious Past: Reminiscences of an Aston Magistrate.

Riland Bedford, Revd William Kirkpatrick (1901) The Manor of Sutton, Feudal and Municipal. Dedicated by Permission to the Vesey Club. Printed at the Boy's Home, Regent's Road, N.W.

Riland Bedford, Revd William Kirkpatrick (?1904) The Real Vesey. Two papers by the Revd W. K. R. Bedford MA, late Rector of Sutton Coldfield. Price one shilling. Martin Billing, Son & Co, Livery Street, Birmingham. Read before the members and friends of the Vesey Club, Sutton Coldfield and printed at their request.

Roud, Steve (2008). The English Year: a month by month guide to the nation's customs and festivals from May Day to Mischief Night. Penguin

Salzman, L. F. (ed) (1947) Victoria County Histories: Warwickshire, v4, Hemlingford Hundred. pp. 241–245 [Available at: https://www.history.ac.uk/research/victoria-county-history/county-histories-progress/warwickshire]

Sidwell, G and Durant, W. J. (1900) The popular guide to Sutton and Park. Printed by Buckley and West, Church St, Birmingham. [3rd edn. [(1st: 1890; 2nd: 1893)]

Slater, Terry (1981). A history of Warwickshire. Phillimore. (Darwen County Histories) pp. 53–57.

Smith, Christine (2002) Sutton Coldfield under the Earls of Warwick. Acorn

Strange, Edward F (1904) The cathedral church of Worcester: a description of the fabric and a brief history of the episcopal See. George Bell and Sons.

Sutton Coldfield news cuttings (volumes compiled in Sutton Coldfield Library) 1929–1942; 1970–1973.

Sutton Park: national nature reserve. Birmingham City Council and English Nature. [no author or date but post 1998]

The story of New Hall, Sutton Coldfield (n.d.) [four-page leaflet, no author or date, c1990. Includes timeline of history of the hall and a history of the mill]

Thebridge, Stella (2017) An informal and personal history of music at Holy Trinity Parish Church to 2017. Holy Trinity Parish Church, Sutton Coldfield

Thebridge, Stella (2018) Holy Trinity Parish Church, Sutton Coldfield: a guide for visitors. Holy Trinity Parish Church, Sutton Coldfield. Printed by Bluflame [Editorial collaboration: Kristina Routh]

Thompson, A Hamilton (1947) The English clergy and their organization in the later

Middle Ages: the Ford Lectures for 1933. Oxford University Press [Reprinted 1966]

Tracy, Charles (2011) Holy Trinity, Sutton Coldfield, Warwickshire: a significance assessment of the carved woodwork. [Unpublished report for Holy Trinity Church]

Trinity Monday news cuttings (volumes compiled in Sutton Coldfield Library)

Twamley, Zachariah (1855) History of Sutton Coldfield. A translation and index by Janet Jordan, 2009. [Available at: https://sclhrg.org.uk/images/stories/transcriptions/Website-Translation-and-Index-of-Twamleys-History-of-Sutton-Coldfield.pdf]

Williamson, Revd Dr Richard (1850) Address on the opening of the first library in Sutton Coldfield. MS in Sutton Coldfield Library.

WEBSITES

Currency convertor
That of the National Archives was used to give an idea of the value of money from earlier centuries. It is not possible to be sure how accurate this is for every commodity, however. Available at: www.nationalarchives.gov.uk/currency-converter

Grade I listing. British listed buildings. Entry for Holy Trinity, 1949. Available at: britishlistedbuildings.co.uk/101319961-church-of-the-holy-trinity-sutton-coldfield#.Xc8PrFf7TIU

Vesey Pageant, 1928
Angela Bartie, Linda Fleming, Mark Freeman, Tom Hulme, Alex Hutton, Paul Readman, 'Sutton Coldfield Pageant, The Redress of the Past'. Available at: www.historicalpageants.ac.uk/pageants/1385

INDEX

Whole chapter headings and their main topics are not indexed, nor the individuals surnamed Riland or Riland Bedford, except where these are mentioned in other parts of the book than chapter 12.

Generally, different features are indexed according to their place in the church, e.g. chancel, nave, tower. These are cross-referenced.

R followed by a name refers to information in the references where this is not in the main text.

T followed by a date refers to information in the timeline where this is not in the main text.

graveyard – *see* churchyard
Grove, Percival Allen 146

Hacket, John 160
Handy family 154
Harman family 45-6, 126, 141-2, 235
  see also Vesey
Hartopp family 114, 174, 196, 226-7
Harvey, George 194
Haynes family 154
Heneage, George (aka John) 188
Heritage Project (2017-19) 13, 104, 117
Hilary, Robert 185-6
Hill, Henry Charles 146
Hiorn, William 67
Holbeche family 114, 227-30
  Helen 228, 230
  Robert 228-9, 230
  Sarah 82, 161, 228
Holbeche window – *see* Vesey Chapel
  Holbeche window
Honeyborne family 142

Jesson family 220ff

Kersey weaving 49

Langley Hall 220
Langstaff, James 103, 160, 187, 194
library (church) *see* Choir Vestry
library (Sutton Coldfield) 118-9
lightning strike (1907) 113-4
liturgy *see* worship
Longman, Ted 99, 194
Lowe family 155
Lucas family 155
Luttrell family 70, 175, 203, 224-5
  see also Four Oaks Hall

Lyon, William 193

Maddy, Watkin 155
Manor House 29-30, 33, 48
market for Sutton Coldfield 108ff
Mary Boggon window – *see* choir vestry
memorials 139ff *see also* area of church *or* individual family names
Mendham, Joseph 142-3, 196, 239
Mendham, Robert 143
Moat House 64, 222-3
Moor Hall 54-8, 125-6
Moot Hall 47, 113, 156
mosaics 98

nave 32, 36, 39, 66-7
  ceiling 134-5
  East window – *see* Chancel East window
New Hall 74, 125
Noel, Laurence 52-3
north gallery (1879) 83, 175
north wall window 163

organs
  (1530) 50, 53
  (1863) 80, T1863
  (1901) 91-2
  (1950) 94-5, T2018
Osborne, Harold WS 93
Oughton family 143, 196
Oulton family 153

Packwood, James 174, 196
pageant (1928) 58, 128-9
parish (1770s) 70-1
parish records 150, 234ff